Building in a New Spain

Building in a New Spain

Contemporary Spanish Architecture

Edited by

Pauline Saliga
Martha Thorne

Essays by

Kenneth Frampton
Antón Capitel
Victor Pérez Escolano
Ignasi de Solà-Morales

GG

Editorial Gustavo Gili, S.A.
Barcelona

The Art Institute of Chicago

Building in a New Spain: Contemporary Spanish Architecture was published on the occasion of the exhibition of the same title, organized by The Art Institute of Chicago in cooperation with the Ministry of Public Works and Transportation, Madrid.
The exhibition was shown at the Gallery of the Ministry of Public Works and Transportation in Madrid from April 23 to May 26, 1992 and at The Art Institute of Chicago from October 24, 1992 to January 3, 1993.

Exhibition Advisory Committee
Gabriel Ruiz Cabrero
Antón Capitel
Victor Pérez Escolano
Ignasi de Solà-Morales
Fernando Villanueva

Co-Curators
Pauline Saliga
Martha Thorne

Exhibition Designers
Gabriel Ruiz Cabrero
Antonio Riviere

SPAIN '92 FOUNDATION

This book and the exhibition were made possible by grants from:
Dirección General para la Vivienda y Arquitectura, Ministerio de Obras Públicas y Transportes
The Design Arts Program of the National Endowment for the Arts, a federal agency
The Seymour H. Persky Fund for Architecture at The Art Institute of Chicago
Empresa Nacional de Electricidad, S.A. [Endesa]
The U.S.-Spanish Joint Committee for Cultural and Educational Cooperation
United Airlines
The Graham Foundation for Advanced Studies in the Fine Arts

This book is a publication of the Ernest R. Graham Study Center for Architectural Drawings at The Art Institute of Chicago.
Travel assistance was provided by United Airlines, the official airline of the exhibition.
This is an official project of the Spain '92 Foundation.

Copyright © 1992 by The Art Institute of Chicago, Michigan Avenue at Adams Street, Chicago, Illinois 60603.

The English edition of this book was copublished by The Art Institute of Chicago and Editorial Gustavo Gili, S. A.,
Rosellón 87-89, 08029 Barcelona, Spain.
ISBN 0-86559-098-2 (softcover)
ISBN 84-252-1577-3 (hardcover)
Depósito Legal: M-18.093-1992.
Library of Congress Catalog Card Number: 92-53939
All rights reserved. No part of this publication may be reproduced or transmitted in any form or by any means, including photocopy, recording, or any other information storage and retrieval system, without prior permission in writing from the publisher.

Edited and produced by
The Art Institute of Chicago
Associate Director of Publications:
Robert V. Sharp
Special Projects Editor:
Carol Jentsch

Designed by:
Linda Bozarth, Venice Studios, S. A., Madrid
The typeface used in this book is "Frutiger," designed by Adrian Frutiger in 1975-76. The paper is "Ideal"; 135 grams per square meter for the interior and 300 grams for the cover, produced by Tomás Redondo, S.A., in Spain.

Printed in Spain by:
Epes Industrias Gráficas, Madrid

Translations:
Essays by Antón Capitel, Victor Pérez Escolano, and Ignasi de Solà-Morales were translated from Spanish by Kathryn J. Deiss, Evanston, Illinois.

To Fernando Villanueva Sandino

Contents

11	**Foreword** James N. Wood	101	**Part II: Contemporary Spanish Architecture** Martha Thorne
13	**Acknowledgments** Pauline Saliga and Martha Thorne	102	Bank of Spain, Gerona
		108	Museum of Navarra, Pamplona
15	**Introduction** Pauline Saliga and Martha Thorne	114	Public Library of Aragon, Zaragoza
		120	Housing for the Olympic Village, Barcelona
		126	Olympic Archery Ranges, Barcelona
	Part I: Building in a New Spain	132	Municipal Sports Stadium, Badalona
		138	Convention Center, Salamanca
19	**Homage to Iberia: An Assessment** Kenneth Frampton	144	Ministry of Agriculture Headquarters, Castile - La Mancha, Toledo
47	**Contemporary Spanish Architecture: From the Foundation of a New Modernism to the Appearance of Eclecticism** Antón Capitel	150	Navigation Pavilion, 1992 World's Fair, Seville
		156	Santa Justa Train Station, Seville
		162	International Airport, Seville
		168	Restoration and Adaptation of the Ronda Promenade and Bastions, Palma de Mallorca
67	**The Architecture of Democratic Spain** Victor Pérez Escolano	175	**Architects' Biographies** Maurice Blanks
91	**The Prodigious Decade** Ignasi de Solà-Morales	183	**Selected Bibliography**

Foreword

The year 1992 marks the quincentennial of the first European contact with the Americas. This occasion has provided cultural institutions such as The Art Institute of Chicago and the Ministry of Public Works and Transportation (MOPT) Gallery in Madrid with the opportunity to plan celebratory exhibitions and programs to commemorate the anniversary. One such ambitious project is the exhibition "Building in a New Spain: Contemporary Spanish Architecture." This exhibition, which is accompanied by joint Spanish and English catalogues, examines a select group of the most remarkable buildings that have recently been constructed in Spain. These projects are largely the result of the renaissance of building activity that has dominated Spain ever since the country embraced a new democratic form of government in 1975.

The Department of Architecture at the Art Institute and MOPT Gallery have a history of collaborating on celebratory exhibitions. In 1987 the Art Institute sent the exhibition "The Unknown Mies van der Rohe and His Disciples of Modernism" to the Ministry Gallery to commemorate the centennial of the birth of Ludwig Mies van der Rohe, the father of European and American modernism. That exhibition exchange was appropriate because in both Madrid and Chicago the power of the modernist aesthetic has dominated building design since the 1940s. The architects of both cities share an alliance in their appreciation of the modernist aesthetic, and this shared appreciation has brought the two institutions together once again, this time in 1992 to celebrate Spain's recent architecture.

We at the Art Institute are most grateful to the Ministry of Public Works and Transportation Gallery for co-sponsoring this exhibition. We also thank the Committee of Advisors that guided us in the selection of projects for inclusion in the exhibition, as well as the many sponsors who made the exhibition and catalogue a reality, in particular the Design Arts Program of the National Endowment for the Arts. Although the quincentennial celebrates Spain's past, we hope that this exhibition will present the strength of Spain's future.

James N. Wood
Director and President
The Art Institute of Chicago

Acknowledgments

The planning of this exhibition began five years ago, in 1987, when The Art Institute of Chicago sent one of its architecture exhibitions, "The Unknown Mies van der Rohe and His Disciples of Modernism," to the Ministry of Public Works and Urbanism (MOPU) Gallery in Madrid. The collaboration was so successful that the two institutions decided to work together on another project in the future. With the celebratory year of 1992 looming on the horizon, the participants decided to organize an exhibition focusing on contemporary Spanish architecture. In the ensuing years, Martha Thorne, an independent architectural curator working in Madrid and former curator at MOPU Gallery, and Pauline Saliga, Associate Curator of Architecture at the Art Institute, nurtured the exhibition and catalogue to completion. The co-curators acknowledge the following individuals and organizations that made possible this book and the exhibition it accompanied.

The exhibition "Building in a New Spain: Contemporary Spanish Architecture," and the catalogue of the same title were inaugurated in Madrid in April 1992. The project itself would not have been possible without the participation and support of the Art Institute's co-sponsor, the Ministry of Public Works and Transportation Gallery (as it is now known) in Madrid. As partners in the process of organizing this exhibition, the Art Institute assumed primary responsibility for overseeing the production of the exhibition catalogue, while MOPT Gallery oversaw preparation of the exhibition. We are very grateful to Blanca Sánchez Velasco, Curator at the Ministry of Public Works and Transportation Gallery, for her efforts to realize this exhibition. We are particularly indebted to Cristina Narbona, the Director General of Housing and Architecture and Sub-Director Manuel de la Dehesa, who provided substantial support for the exhibition through the Ministry of Public Works and Transportation. We also owe a great debt to the architects who are represented in this exhibition for lending their works and for their many efforts to provide the best photographs and material for the catalogue. We are very grateful to them and their collaborators for their enthusiasm and support, and for their willingness to meet with us repeatedly and devote both their time and that of their office staff to this project. We also want to acknowledge the public institutions that have generously agreed to lend architectural models to the exhibition.

Considerable planning preceded the organization of both the contemporary Spanish architecture exhibition and catalogue. In 1989 the Design Arts Program of the National Endowment for the Arts funded a two-day symposium at The Art Institute of Chicago, during which a select group of Spanish architects met with staff at the Art Institute to discuss the focus of the exhibition. We are indebted to NEA for funding this important planning conference, and to the members of our Advisory Committee for sharing their input and expertise to help us determine the unique characteristics of contemporary Spanish architecture. This Advisory Committee, which consisted of Antón Capitel, Victor Pérez Escolano, Ignasi de Solà-Morales, Gabriel Ruiz Cabrero, and the late Fernando Villanueva, later decided which twelve projects would be the focus of the exhibition. The first three of these advisors also wrote essays for this volume. Gabriel Ruíz Cabrero advised both MOPT Gallery and the Art Institute on the installation of the exhibition. This entire project was enriched by their expert advice, and we sincerely thank them for their involvement in it from beginning to end. It is with great sadness that we note the death of one of our advisors, the Seville architect Fernando Villanueva, who generously shared his time and expertise with us until one week before his death in February 1992. We dedicate this book to his memory.

Additional planning funds for this project were provided in 1989 by the U.S.-Spanish Joint Committee for Cultural and Educational Cooperation, which gave a grant to the Art Institute and MOPU Gallery so that the curators could begin the work of planning the exhibition. In the following year, the Design Arts Program of the National Endowment for the Arts and the Graham Foundation for Advanced Studies in the

Fine Arts provided implementation grants to the Art Institute to underwrite the production of the exhibition catalogue, its essays, photographs, design, and the like. We are very grateful to all three of these organizations for their early and substantial support of the project. Without their vote of confidence and seed monies, this exhibition and catalogue could not have been produced. Additional corporate support from the Spanish utility company, Empresa Nacional de Electricidad [Endesa], and travel support provided by United Airlines, the official airline of this exhibition, further ensured the success of our endeavor. Finally, support for the installation at the Art Institute was provided by the Seymour H. Persky Fund for Architecture at The Art Institute of Chicago.

In order to produce a publication such as this, we relied upon the assistance of many people, and we, therefore, owe a debt of gratitude to many individuals, including our distinguished essayists, who toiled to bring new insights to the impressive body of recent Spanish architecture and to make this subject understandable to audiences in the United States. We are also grateful to a number of photographers and photographic and historic archives—all of which are identified in the photographic credits at the end of this publication—as well as to Expo '92, the Olympic Committee, and the journal *D'A* for providing images for this catalogue. We thank Maurice Blanks for compiling and writing the architects' biographies, Luis Feduchi, Pilar González and Blanca Sánchez Velasco for skillfully translating the English text into Spanish, and Kathryn J. Deiss for translating Spanish text into English. We also wish to express our thanks to the Publications Department of MOPT for their work on the Spanish edition of this catalogue. Without the work of the Art Institute's editors, Robert V. Sharp, Associate Director of Publications, and Carol Jentsch, Special Projects Editor, none of the work on this book would have been brought to fruition. We are most grateful to them for their enthusiasm for the project, their willingness to learn about a completely foreign subject, and their persistence in providing fine editorial work under a difficult schedule. Finally, we wish to thank Lynda Bozarth and Nuria Novoa of Venice Studios in Madrid, for the elegant and intelligent design of this book. Additional organizational support was provided by Pilar de Diego in Martha Thorne's, office José L. Benito, Manuel Castillo, José M. Alvarez Enjuto and Teresa Ortín of the MOPT and, Arturo López Bachiller, and Linda Adelman in the Department of Architecture at the Art Institute.

Pauline Saliga
Martha Thorne
Co-Curators of "Building in a New Spain: Contemporary Spanish Architecture"

Introduction

During the past decade and a half, Spanish society—its culture, politics, and economics—has undergone a change as dramatic as the recent collapse of the Berlin Wall and the fall of Communism in Eastern Europe. Peaceful yet profound, the change in Spain has occurred since the death of dictator Generalísimo Francisco Franco in 1975, and it has been marked by the transformation of Spain into a social democracy with strong regional governments. The subsequent political changes jolted the country after forty years of isolation. Under its new democracy, Spain is now becoming a full economic partner in Europe, and the larger European community considers Spain a strong political and economic force. The major events of 1992—the Olympic Games in Barcelona, the World's Fair in Seville, and the designation of Madrid as the Cultural Capital of Europe for that year—have propelled the country forward, perhaps moving it ahead faster than would have been possible otherwise. More than fifteen years into the social democracy, however, some of the optimism and euphoria of the first years have given way to a more practical and mediated attitude. In many aspects of culture in particular, from art to theater, literature, and architecture, important early trends and experimental efforts have yielded to more institutionalized and conservative trends. On the other hand, some experimental efforts have been absorbed into the mainstream.

These changes, of course, have also had a dramatic impact on the field of architecture. Architectural commissions, which were tightly focused on the private sector during the last decades of the Franco regime, have dramatically shifted to the public realm. So much needed to be built: affordable housing and adequate neighborhood facilities, schools and universities, hospitals and health centers, government office buildings, airports and train stations, bridges and highways, libraries and museums, performing arts centers and sports facilities, urban spaces, and more. At the beginning of the transition to a democratic government, historic architecture became a metaphor for Spanish heritage, and the preservation and adaptive reuse of historic buildings became a regional and national priority, verging on an obsession. As a result of the needs for new and renovated structures, during the late 1970s, 1980s, and early 1990s, the regional and national governments of Spain became the greatest patrons of Spanish architecture in this century. It is difficult to describe the scale of construction and renovation that is transforming virtually every major city and numerous minor ones throughout Spain, most notably Barcelona and Seville. From the enormous kilometer-long transformation of the seafront of Palma de Mallorca (by José Antonio Martínez Lapeña and Elías Torres) to the construction of a new international airport in Seville (by Rafael Moneo), Spain is burgeoning with monumental new buildings and urban planning projects that are transforming it into one of the leading countries of 21st-century Europe.

In what state, then, is Spanish architecture today? This book, along with the exhibition it accompanies, attempts to answer that question in the essays that follow and in the presentation of twelve remarkable examples of recent Spanish architecture that suggest specific aspects of the state of the art. Although a selection of just twelve buildings can in no way represent all the architectural achievements of the country, each work has been chosen because it embodies qualities that are important or unique to Spanish architecture. Such qualities include the continued use of the canons of the modern movement as a source of inspiration, the careful attention to material and detail, the extensive use of brick and native materials, and the creation of structures that respect the existing historic architecture and environment. Finally, these projects all record the invention of designs that are intended to be constructed for use and pleasure; these are all commissions for specific sites, not simply theoretical exercises. In order to identify the characteristics that make Spanish architecture unique and to select projects of the highest quality, we relied on the expertise of an advisory committee of respected architects and historians who have an informed perspective on the history of Spanish architecture: Gabriel Ruíz Cabrero, Antón Capitel, Victor Pérez Escolano, Ignasi de Solà-Morales, and the late Fernando Villanueva. In many working sessions held in Chicago, Madrid, Seville, and Barcelona, this group of distinguished architects grappled with the question of what makes Spanish architecture distinctively Spanish, and which recent buildings best embody those characteristics or demonstrate Spain's contribution to architecture today. After four years of survey and debate, they identified the twelve buildings featured in this book and exhibition.

Their selection of buildings in no way seeks to classify Spanish architecture according to styles or trends. In Spain, many approaches toward architecture co-exist and enrich one another. As the following essays by Kenneth Frampton, Antón Capitel, Victor Pérez Escolano, and Ignasi de Solà-Morales indicate, many approaches to eclecticism, Italian rationalism, and Scandinavian modernism (with a rejection of postmodernism) have been key influences on the current architectural production of Spain. The buildings featured here, of course, do not represent all the examples of extraordinary architectural design that have been produced in recent years. Rather, we have opted for an in-depth view, concentrating on projects constructed between 1985 and 1992. A great many other buildings of outstanding quality have also been constructed since the mid-1970s, and while these could not be featured in this book, many are discussed and illustrated in the essays that follow.

If one were to try to identify the single most common feature of Spanish architecture, it would be the way that architects in Spain approach their designs. From conception to execution, the projects that involve Spanish architects are designed to be built. Theoretical projects and utopian competitions are not the norm in Spain. What is common are public commissions with very strict construction schedules and budgets. The ultimate goal of construction is evident in the design process itself and in the drawings produced. The majority of drawings that Spanish architects make (as can be seen in the works chosen for this exhibition) are black-and-white ones: preliminary sketches; developmental drawings that may record the evolution of a design; presentation drawings of plans, sections, and elevations; and actual working drawings, from which construction blueprints are made. Many times simple balsa wood or cardboard models are used for study purposes and are made in-house. Unlike architectural practices in other countries, such as Italy and the United States, architects in Spain have little time or need for elaborately colored renderings or professionally produced models. They do not need these "tools" to persuade commercial developers or investors since, in many cases, their clients are regional or federal government agencies.

All the projects featured in this publication and exhibition have been publicly commissioned. Some are for large-scale infrastructural projects, such as the Santa Justa train station in Seville (by Antonio Cruz and Antonio Ortiz). Others have been commissioned as a result of the confluence of unusual activities surrounding 1992, including the archery ranges for the Barcelona Olympics (by Enric Miralles and Carme Pinós) and the Navigation Pavilion for Seville's World's Fair, Expo '92 (by Guillermo Vázquez Consuegra). Spain's decision to update and upgrade major facilities, for 1992 and beyond, will continue the country's progress forward as an industrialized European nation.

The twelve works presented in the second part of this book, and in the exhibition, are by firms located in Madrid, Barcelona, and Seville. Although the advisory committee did not decide ahead of time to concentrate on these cities at the exclusion of cities in other regions of Spain, the result does reveal that the major centers of architecture, as of culture generally in Spain, are still Madrid, Barcelona, and Seville. These three cities continue to make their influence felt in other areas of Spain, not only through the strong architectural offices located there, but also through the influence of the architectural schools that are located there, as well as through the many architectural publications (*A & V, Quaderns d'Arquitectura i Urbanisme,* and *Arquitectura*) that are published in those cities.

Although the buildings featured in this book and exhibition represent a variety of typologies, almost all use traditional materials and construction methods. In his convention center in Salamanca, for example, Juan Navarro Baldeweg incorporates the natural golden-beige stone of Salamanca in order to complement, rather than compete with, the historic buildings of that city. Likewise, in project after project, from the new international airport in Seville (by Rafael Moneo) to the Ministry of Agriculture's regional offices in Toledo (by Manuel and Ignacio de las Casas and Jaime Lorenzo), architects try to blend their new architecture with the existing fabric of the city through design and careful selection of materials in order to respect the historic character of the cities in which they build. This trend indicates just how widespread this sensitivity toward tradition is among Spanish architects.

The year 1992 is, no doubt, an extraordinarily important one for Spain. To present only buildings designed for Expo '92 or the summer Olympics, however, would show a very limited view of the range of architectural activity in Spain. Although these events have triggered large investments in building, some of the finest examples of Spanish architecture today are found outside those realms. The collection of twelve buildings that we feature in the pages that follow have been compiled in an attempt to express an alternative view of Spanish architecture and to reveal the case that everyday Spanish architecture, supported by public institutions, is surprisingly innovative and of consistently high quality.

Pauline Saliga and Martha Thorne

Homage to Iberia: An Assessment

Kenneth Frampton

To the Spanish architects . . . the promised paradise of modern architecture was located beyond the horizons of the International Style. The obsession with progress and perfection as derived from the modern mentality was suppressed. Instead, there was a strong Spanish response to [Bruno] Zevi's opinions, which saw organic architecture as a mature and true modernity. Thus, the road towards the promised Eden changed its orientation. Organic criticism was decreed official, and Frank Lloyd Wright's and Aalto's work, as well as the development of modernity so clearly expressed in Le Corbusier's later work, rapidly connected with the sensitivity of Spanish architecture, the latter moving rapidly from enthroning the International Style to passionately pursuing the organic ideal. But this organic ideal, as can be seen in many international examples, embodied two different ways of understanding architecture. This ambiguity also underlay the work of the above mentioned masters and it implied a double alternative to the International Style.

The first of these alternatives was more closely aligned with certain anti-modern features. In Spain this was closely linked to the idea of tradition and the desire for a specifically Spanish culture. It was also derived from an interpretation of Aalto's career . . . . The second approach unequivocally championed Italian culture, be it Roman or Milanese, depending on whether the reference is to Barcelona or Madrid.

Antón Capitel[1]

The specific nature of the split running through contemporary Spanish culture has its origin in the unique character of the Spanish experience, colored, as it has been, by the opposing forces of retardation and modernization. These countervailing tendencies have enabled Spain to enjoy the stability of tradition while entering into an emergent modernity. It is hardly an accident that this ambiguous approach to modernity first came to the fore in Catalonia, a region that was in conflict with Madrid long before the tragic debacle of the Spanish Civil War. For where, in the second half of the nineteenth century, Madrid was land-based, agrarian, and patrician, Barcelona was sea-based, industrialized, and looking outwards towards Italy, France, the Orient, and the Americas. For the Catalonian avant-garde of the 1930s, modernization meant enlightened socialism in one form or another, and José Lluís Sert's identification with this position is evident not only from his association with GATEPAC (Grupo de Arquitectos y Técnicos Españoles para el Progreso de la Arquitectura Contemporánea), the Spanish wing of CIAM (Congrès Internationaux d'Architecture Moderne), but also from his authorship of the Spanish Pavilion erected by the Second Republic for the Paris Universal Exposition of 1937. In serving as a polemical setting for Picasso's *Guernica*, this building not only protested the first civilian casualties of aerial bombardment, but also drew attention to that particular combination of technology and abstraction that would make the destruction of a Basque town into a dress rehearsal for the *blitzkriegen* of the Second World War. And yet, paradoxical as it may seem in retrospect, the Franquista freezing of modern development in 1939 was not without its benefits, for it effectively postponed for twenty years the emergence of a consumerism in Spain, and it is still this delay that serves to separate Spain in terms of recent historical experience from the other countries of Western Europe.

Fig. 1. Josep Sostres. Casa Agusti, Sitges, Barcelona, 1953-55.

Building in a New Spain: Contemporary Spanish Architecture

The School of Barcelona

In the late 1940s Barcelona looked to Italy in more ways than one, first to Alberto Sartoris for his militant Mediterraneanism, which for him was inseparable from the ethical and spiritual core of the modern movement, and then to the combined postwar revisionist approach of Ernesto Rogers, Ignazio Gardella, and Franco Albini, without whom the mediated modernity of an architect like José Antonio Coderch could hardly have come into being. These Italian positions brought the leading Catalan architects of the late 1940s and 1950s, Josep Sostres and Coderch, to their respective points of departure; to wit, Sostres's masterly neo-plastic Casa Agustí (fig. 1), built at the coastal city of Sitges between 1953 and 1955, and Coderch's equally accomplished Barceloneta apartment building of 1951 (figs. 2 and 3). While these works crystallized the architects' mature styles, it is perhaps their earlier endeavors of the late 1940s that point explicitly to the vernacular origins of the Barcelona School. Thus, where Sostres began his career with the self-conscious regionalism of his Casa Elías (1948), Coderch would oscillate between his interpretation of the whitewashed vernacular of the Balearic Islands, as is evident in his Casa Ferrer-Vidal, Mallorca (1946), and the authoritarian symmetry of his Garriga-Nogués House, built at Sitges in 1947.

Coderch's transformation of the vernacular is of decisive importance in this early moment, for it will exercise a pervading influence not only on his own career but also on a more general topographic sensibility that will become the touchstone of contemporary Spanish architecture. I have in mind, not only the Casa Ferrer-Vidal, where multiple changes of level within the podium animate and inflect the axiality

Fig. 2. José Antonio Coderch. Apartment building, La Barceloneta, Barcelona, 1951.

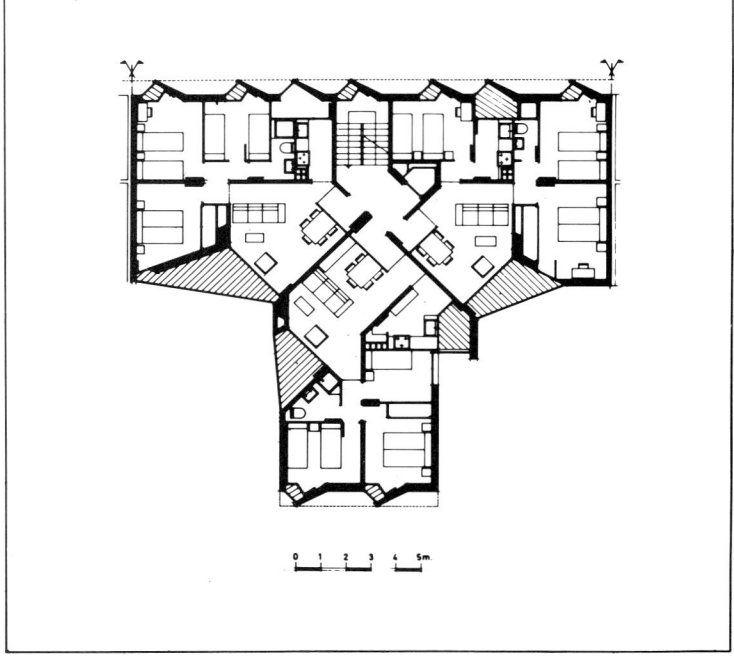

Fig. 3. José Antonio Coderch. Apartment building, La Barceloneta, Barcelona, 1951. Plan.

of the house, but also an unrealized development for Sitges known as Las Forcas (1945), in which individual house plans, walled in and terraced, recall the timeless, mud-brick, load-bearing building culture of North Africa. A similarly knowing, but unsophisticated, line leads from these pioneering works of the mid-1940s to Coderch's audacious Casa Ugalde (1951; fig. 4) and to the equally remarkable, but ill-fated, Torre-Valentina, a low-rise residential settlement designed for the Costa Brava in 1959, the rejection of which would bring about a psychological rupture in Coderch's early career. Close to Le Corbusier's canonical Roq et Rob project of 1949—a debt that with characteristic perversity Coderch would never acknowledge—Torre-Valentina is nonetheless a pioneering essay in low-rise, high-density, residential development. The project remains exemplary even today. That the client's rejection of the Torre-Valentina proposal left an enduring scar on Coderch is borne out by a 1978 interview.

We took such pains over the design for the Torre-Valentina. When the owners rejected it, I went through a great crisis. I dropped everything. I said that I had no work, the word got around and in 1960, I was left penniless. . . . They rejected my design saying that it looked like a Moroccan bazaar. . . . For the Torre-Valentina project, we had a drawing of the land on which we plotted all the pine trees with a diameter of over 5 inches. I think we put in somewhere between three and five thousand trees. When the model was done, the houses could not be seen from the sea, but since it had to be discussed at the board meeting, I had no choice but to take out two or three thousand pine trees, so that the promoters would have something to look at.[2]

The undeniable Italian influence on the syntactical and typological lines adopted by Sostres and Coderch came from two separate origins: from the pin-wheeling spatial type-form indirectly advocated by Bruno Zevi's re-interpretation of Dutch Neoplasticism, as set forth in his book *La Poetica della Architectura Neoplastica* (1953), and from the revisionist Italian palazzo format as this was perfected in Ignazio Gardella's Casa Borsalino apartments built in

Fig. 4. José Antonio Coderch. Casa Ugalde, Caldes d'Estrac, Barcelona, 1951.

Alessandria between 1951 and 1953. At the level of the individual family house, Coderch's Casa Catasus (1956) and Casa Ballvé, at Camprodón, Gerona (1957), would synthesize these two lines of influence, although as far as his large-scale work was concerned, it was Gardella rather than Theo van Doesburg who would carry the day—as we may judge from Coderch's Institut Francais, completed in Barcelona in 1972, and from Sostres's equally minimalist *El Noticiero* newspaper building of 1965. Through the influence of van Doesburg and Richard Neutra, Coderch was able to elaborate his complex reinterpretation of the Balearic vernacular, as is evident in a number of houses built between 1961 and 1971.

The enduring significance of Coderch resides in his precise formulation of a middle-class residential urban prototype that could be readily applied as a twentieth-century norm. Through his modest, but ethical, commitment to the craft of architecture as a *métier* removed from the allied fields of art and technology, Coderch, despite his disdain for the generic, became an advocate of the type-form. His ultimate masterwork, the Las Cocheras housing complex completed in

Building in a New Spain: Contemporary Spanish Architecture

the Parque Sarriá district of Barcelona in 1968, may be read as a general model applicable to large-scale urban development (fig. 5). Now, twenty years after its completion, it remains, in many respects, a model that has been unsurpassed. Coderch achieved an equally seminal version of virtually the same type in his Banco Urquijo apartments (1967). With such works Coderch attempted to resolve a number of contradictory requirements that are endemic to the design of high-rise apartments. In the first place, he provided sufficient terrace space for each apartment, thereby compensating for the fact that, unlike a house, it was detached from the ground; in the second, he was able to unify the resulting mass into a single urban block, served by a continuous street frontage and an inner court at grade and by a single parking garage in the podium. Both technically and syntactically this unified form depended upon the use of fair-faced brickwork throughout, the unity of the result depending upon the solidity of the revetment and the planting by which it was enriched. In addition, one has to acknowledge the remarkable organization of the domestic space itself; in particular, the chevron formation of the bedrooms as they radiate out from the living/dining core, and their diagonal inflection in depth, combined with a sensitive displacement of micro-space around certain transition points such as the entrance or the kitchen. As a result Las Cocheras surely stands out as one of the generic residential types of this century, and in this regard, it is of the same canonical caliber as Alvar Aalto's Hansaviertel apartments built in Berlin in 1956. That the urban, one might even say ecological, significance of Las Cocheras went beyond Aalto's Hansaviertel is borne out by Coderch's description of his 1976 entry for the Actur-Lacua residential competition in Vitoria, which was, in essence, a large-scale application of the Parque Sarriá prototype.

The planning significance of our solution is based on the . . . Parque Sarriá of Barcelona. Our solution consists of the use of articulated plans which make for terraced facades corresponding to the three types or modules employed. . . . Terracing effectively prevents the noise from the peripheral motor vehicle roads from reaching the interior of the homes.

. . . We believe that Richard Neutra was right when he said that plants and greenery are not only of fundamental importance in open areas but also in houses. That is why in addition to landscaping the streets and squares, we have designed flower boxes in the openings of the homes. In this design the streets have green platforms at different levels that isolate the ground floor homes. . . . The sidewalks are thus located in the center of the streets, set at different height than the windows and located at a certain distance from them. . . . As regards the parking of vehicles, we believe that the location of all relevant facilities on ground level would be inadmissible from the planning standpoint. Therefore the majority of the parking spaces are designed to lie under the central area of the pedestrian streets. These parking areas are reached by the vertical communication nuclei, with most supply services to the homes, as well as garbage collection being carried out through this system also. . . . We also consider corner windows to be very important, since they serve to enlarge rooms while allowing a diagonal view of the outside and selection of the most suitable orientation for obtaining sunlight.[3]

While one should guard against representing the architecture of Barcelona as being dominated by Coderch, I have stressed his contribution for two reasons: first, because his achievement seems never to have been adequately recognized, and second, because the best of his work typifies

Fig. 5. José Antonio Coderch. Las Cocheras, Sarriá, Barcelona, 1968.

certain attributes that can be found elsewhere in Catalonia during the period, above all perhaps in Raimon Duran i Reynals's little-known Avenida de la Victoria apartment block built in Barcelona in 1949. While Coderch seems to have been an ambivalent member of "Grup R," founded in collaboration with Sostres, Oriol Bohigas, and Antoni Moragas, he nonetheless subscribed to the "regional organic" position elaborated by Sostres in 1950, in which, after Zevi, Sostres argued that organic architecture was *concrete* rather than *abstract*, *relative* rather than *absolute*, and *realistic* and *sentimental* in its applications and associations rather than *idealized*.[4] The value of the organic for Sostres was ontological rather than epistemological, and it is this that gives his work its conviction. As he put it in 1950, the aim was "to conceive of a building as a general form not in the abstract sense but rather as a living organism that is evolved from the conditions of nature as though these constitute a law, an order, and also a unit of measure."[5]

While Bohigas was far more urbane in his affinities than either Sostres or Coderch, as is evident from his somewhat brutalist Carres de Pallars apartment block of 1960, Moragas proved his rationalist claim in his Hotel Park (1953) and his Avenida Sant Antoni M. Claret block (1958), both of which display an affinity for the finest postwar work of the Milanese architects Luigi Figini and Gino Pollini. The minimalism latent in the work of Coderch later resurfaced in the architecture of Helio Piñón and Albert Viaplana, as is evident from their Calle Galileo block, built in Barcelona in 1976. A similar restraint also appears in the more rationalist Thau School, completed outside Barcelona, at the same time, to the designs of Josep Maria Martorell, Oriol Bohigas, and David Mackay.

The School of Madrid: Fernández Alba, Sáenz de Oiza, and Moneo

As far as the Madrilene organic tradition is concerned, two works of seminal importance inaugurated the 1960s: Antonio Fernández Alba's El Rollo Convent, completed outside Salamanca in 1963 (figs. 6 and 7), and Francisco Javier Sáenz de Oiza's Torres Blancas apartment building, realized in Madrid in 1966 (fig. 8). Where the former is Aaltoesque in its inspiration, if not in its details, the latter is indebted to Frank Lloyd Wright, above all to his 1955 Price Tower in Bartlesville, Oklahoma. In as much as Wright's later sense of the organic implied the overt use of concrete cantilevered, tree-like construction, the cantilevered "flying saucer" form of Torres Blancas may be seen as an organic tour de force. More rhetorical, but less sensitively planned, than Coderch's contemporaneous Parque Sarriá

Fig. 6. Antonio Fernández Alba. El Rollo Convent, Salamanca, 1963.

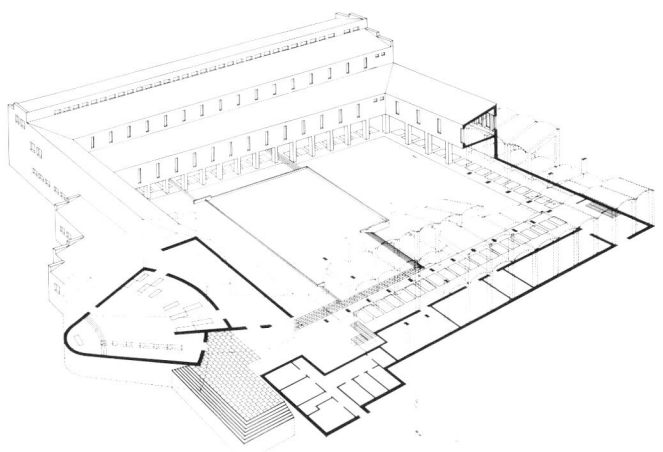

Fig. 7. Antonio Fernández Alba. El Rollo Convent, Salamanca, 1963. Axonometric drawing.

development, Torres Blancas rose on the outskirts of Madrid like the utopian silhouette of a Babylonic promise, and it remains so even today with luxuriant greenery cascading down the full height of a 24-story *béton brut* tower. In order to overcome what Sáenz de Oiza once characterized as the "stationary aeronautic" effect, each of the circular living spaces of which the tower is composed is surrounded by deep window boxes.

It is interesting to note, as Antón Capitel remarks, that the first esquisse for Torres Blancas started out as a variation on Le Corbusier's cellular perimeter blocks (*Immeuble-Villa*), although it was soon transformed into a Wrightian paradigm. Of its final form Capitel writes:

The Torres Blancas is important not only because of its spectacular qualities or its testimony to a particular historical moment. Rather, its importance lies in the peculiar eclecticism—or syncretism—and extreme ambiguousness which pervade its form. These qualities made it, in its day, both the greatest admirer of modernity and its major contester—depending on which type of modernity was invoked, an issue which was perfectly clear for professionals of the time. The characteristics of the modern Spanish adventure are superimposed and condensed in this one building, through its incorporation of aspects of different modernities which, under the guise of continuous and progressive development, vied for the hegemonic position of being a "true modern architecture." The design of the Torres Blancas reveals a desire to be loyal to the principles of function and technology, while simultaneously adhering to an organicist, expressionist, and sculptural architectural language.[6]

Throughout the eclectic trajectory of his architectural career, Sáenz de Oiza has repeatedly turned to Wright as the ultimate master and never more so than in his Banco Bilbao complex completed in Madrid in 1979 (fig. 9). While it may not be apparent on first encounter, the Banco Bilbao is a reinterpretation of Wright's 1944 S. C. Johnson and Son Research Tower in Racine, Wisconsin. It is a measure of Sáenz de Oiza's syncretic approach that this subtle reinterpretation should conceal its sources: for example, the tubular metal, window-cleaning *passerelle* running around the tower at each floor level may be seen as a transposition of the tubular clerestory glazing in the S. C. Johnson complex. Clad throughout in fixed glass and Cor-Ten steel, this cantilevered, reinforced concrete and steel construction is in fact a synthesis of a number of models. Mies van der Rohe's canonical Seagram Building of 1959 is obviously alluded to in the micro-detailing, while the subdivision of the tower into cantilevered concrete rafts every sixth floor, supporting four-story steel-framed structures in between, owes much to Amancio Williams's unbuilt high-rise office building projected for Buenos Aires in 1949.

While he was neither as prolific nor as consistent as Coderch, Antonio Fernández Alba introduced a Nordic line in Madrid with his El Rollo Convent of 1963, a building that while indebted to Aalto, was more formally arranged and fenestrated, so that it readily evokes not only the Iberian vernacular, with its mono-pitched roofs in Spanish tiles, but also a more formal concept of order as is evidenced by the grouped fenestration. At the same time the rather solemn orchestration of its blank perimeter walls recalled Gunnar Asplund's early functionalist manner or even perhaps the neoclassicism that informed Asplund's last project, the Woodland Cemetery (1935-40). In contrast to the fluidity that mixed rustic form with organic plastically in Aalto's Säynätsalo City Hall, El Rollo lay closer to the rationalized organicism of the British architects Leslie Martin and Patrick Hodgkinson, particularly as this is evident in their Gonville and Caius College, Cambridge, built at approximately the same time.

While Rafael Moneo was a protégé of Sáenz de Oiza and worked with him and J. D. Fullaondo on the detailing of Torres Blancas, he was nonetheless profoundly influenced by El Rollo, inasmuch as this work embodied an Olympian stillness that would elude Sáenz de Oiza no matter how spiritual his commissions might be. El Rollo may have affected Moneo's decision to experience the Nordic world firsthand after his three-year apprenticeship with Sáenz de Oiza. Thus, at the end of 1961 Moneo joined the office of Jørn Utzon in Copenhagen, there to contribute to an equally organic work, the Sydney Opera House, which was then being developed just prior to Utzon's departure for Australia.

Moneo's first building of consequence, the Bankinter Madrid of 1976 (fig. 10), designed with Ramón Bescós, may be seen in retrospect as a synthesis of a number of organic strands running through the Madrid School: on the one hand, the intersecting triangular configuration of the entry foyer clearly owes something to Wright, an affinity that is reinforced by its ornamental scheme; while, on the other, the chunky plasticity of the block, faced in brick tiles, owes much to Aalto and beyond that to Asplund and Nordic classicism. This last becomes even more of an influence in Moneo's Logroño town hall, completed in 1981, with its eurhythmic, atectonic stonework alluding not only to Asplund, but also to that other exponent of the "new tradition" in the 1930s, the German architect Heinrich Tessenow.

Fig. 8. Francisco Javier Sáenz de Oiza. Torres Blancas, Madrid, 1966.

Fig. 9. Francisco Javier Sáenz de Oiza. Banco Bilbao, Madrid, 1979.

Moneo's most exceptional achievement to date is unquestionably the Roman archaeological museum that he completed in Mérida in 1984 (figs. 11-13), a singular work that has since assured his unofficial status as *architect laureate* of his generation. This complex is remarkable at a number of levels, not least of which is the subtle stance that it assumes towards history, both real and imagined. Here the ruined world of the archaic is openly evoked by a building that is situated over the excavation site itself. Built of reinforced concrete and faced inside and out in brick tiles of Roman proportions, it straddles the antique foundations like a tectonic counterpoint, with its piers countermanding the remains of the original Roman city. The aura of the site is thus transformed into a Piranesian fantasy, while painstakingly reconstructed fragments drawn from here and elsewhere are prominently exhibited in the warehouse space above. From this point of view the building may be said to be suspended between the raw material of the mine and the representation of its refined ore.

Two ambiguous gestures impart a certain irony to this work. In the first place, a tunnel of seemingly indeterminate length serves to link its undercroft to two nearby Roman monuments, a theater and an amphitheater; in the second, the street facade, divided up by brick buttresses, corresponding to the concrete cross walls within, seems to allude to the missing medieval epoch that Mérida never experienced, since after its single hour of glory it fell into decline. As I have already implied, the whole structure, roofed with long monitor lights, has the aura of a warehouse or perhaps of an industrial building drawn from the turn of the century, somehow recalling the heroic factories of Peter Behrens and Hans Poelzig. At the same time an overriding archaic tone is provided by the the brick-faced concrete employed throughout, which simulates, quite directly, the former glory of Roman masonry.

Mérida has been a difficult act to follow not only because of its evident mastery but also due to the fact that succeeding works have been realized to Moneo's designs without his constant presence and attention; both the Atocha Station in Madrid (the first phase of which was completed in 1988) and the Previsión Española offices built in Seville in 1987, were completed during Moneo's five-year tenure as chairman of the Department of Architecture at the Graduate School of Design at Harvard University. Not

Fig. 10. Rafael Moneo and Ramón Bescós. Bankinter, Madrid, 1973-76.

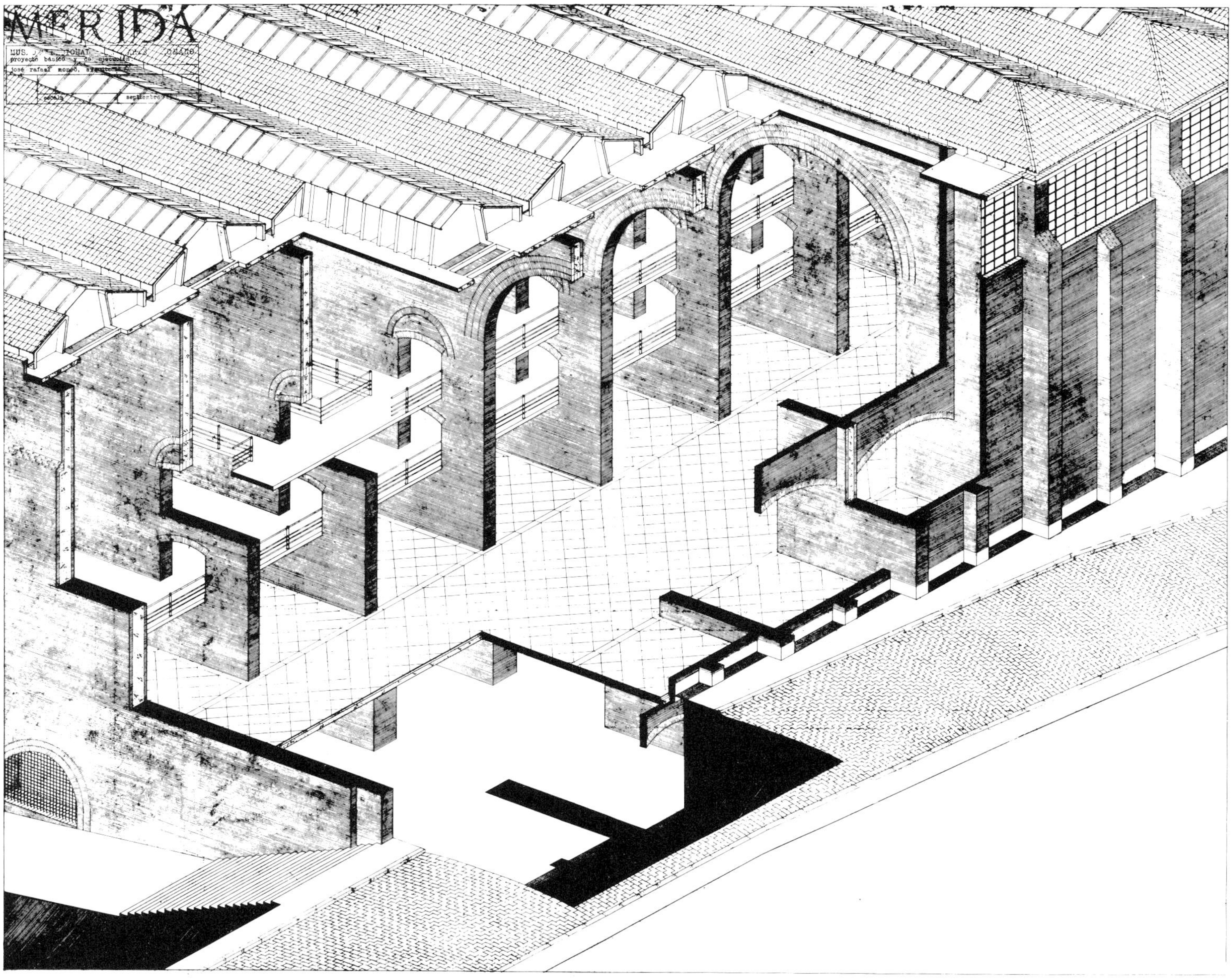

Fig. 11. Rafael Moneo. National Museum of Roman Art, Mérida, 1980-84. Axonometric drawing.

even this absence, however, can perhaps account for the decorative qualities of these works.

Moneo seems now to have regained his composure, notably in a remarkable design that he completed for the Kursaal complex in San Sebastián (fig. 14), which he won in a closed competition in 1990. This conference-cum-music center represents a categoric return to Utzon and the Sydney Opera House. Here, reminiscent of the *parti* of Sydney, Moneo's twin auditoria are inclined and rotated so as to align with the shifting axis of the promontory and the river, as they turn to face the sea. The full scope of this project is surely best conveyed by Moneo's own words:

Fig. 12. Rafael Moneo. National Museum of Roman Art, Mérida, 1980-84. Interior view.

Fig. 13. Rafael Moneo. National Museum of Roman Art, Mérida, 1980-84.

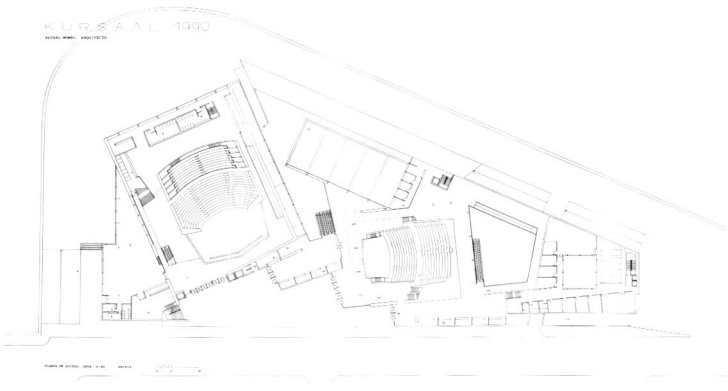

Fig. 14. Rafael Moneo. Kursaal Concert Buildings, San Sebastián, 1990. Plan.

Our proposal for the Auditorium and the Conference Hall, key pieces of the plan for the cultural complex, therefore understands these buildings as two gigantic rocks launched into the mouth of the Urumea: they do not belong to the city —they are part of the landscape. . . . Only the Auditorium and the Conference Hall are manifested as separate autonomous volumes. The exhibition halls, the meeting rooms and the associated services, the restaurants, etc. will be contained in the platform. . . we believe that (the system of glass block and steel frame construction will) ensure both stability and (appropriate) conditioning, yielding a luminous neutral interior space whose contact with the outside only occurs at the spectacular foyer windows overlooking the sea. . . .the glass block will convert the volume into a dense opaque mass, which will be reflective and changing during the day and transformed into a mysterious attractive source of light at night.[7]

A permanent faculty member of the Escuela Técnica Superior de Arquitectura in Madrid, Moneo now has a generation of followers who may be counted among his pupils. These include Gabriel Ruiz Cabrero and Enrique Perea, whose most important building to date is still their Colegio de Arquitectos, Seville (fig. 15), built between 1979 and 1982, and, Antonio Cruz and Antonio Ortiz, who following a small apartment building erected in the center of Seville in 1976 (see Capitel, figs. 9 and 10), have since gone on to realize a number of remarkable works, including their 1989 Carabanchel housing in Madrid (fig. 16), and even more recently the Santa Justa railway station built in Seville for the 1992 World's Fair (see photographs and project description in Part II).

Unlike Coderch's Parque Sarriá, the Carabanchel quarter returns to the rectilinear block form of European rationalism dating back to the types evolved by Otto Haesler in the 1920s, wherein each room is a standard orthogonal volume as opposed to the inflected character of Coderch's domestic space. Both housing schemes, however, may be said to maintain the unity of the urban block to a similar degree; Coderch through an elevated podium covering the entire

Fig. 15. Gabriel Ruiz Cabrero and Enrique Perea. Colegio de Arquitectos, Seville, 1979-82. Axonometric drawing.

Alejandro de la Sota and the Cult of Simplicity

There is perhaps no other architect in Spain who is at once so revered and yet remote as Alejandro de la Sota. Like the late Swedish master Sigurd Lewerentz to whom he may be appropriately compared, de la Sota has produced a body of work that is both known and unknown. His more monumental pieces have been fairly well published, but his architecture remains, at the same time, curiously unfamiliar due to its laconic, somewhat impenetrable character. It is not that his form is willfully esoteric or afunctional, for it is, in so many respects, only too accessible and serviceable. And yet like many other things that first appear to be simple, de la Sota's ultra simplicity is also extremely complex. Indeed somewhat like Brancusi's sculpture, it is both apparent and opaque; apparent because of its irrefutable presence as an artifact and opaque because of an intrinsically mysterious aspect that always suggests, as in Mies, the presence of some invisible principle, lying just beneath the surface. The scope of this sensibility has perhaps been best defined by José Llinás:

site, and Cruz and Ortiz through a perimeter masonry wall, which is relieved in places by wrought-iron paling. Despite its normative apartments, the double-fronted character of the Carabanchel slab breaks up after the first story into a stepped mass-form topped out with a thin cantilevering slab, reminiscent of Wright or of Gropius's neo-Wrightian Werkbund Exhibition building of 1914. This assimilation of the modern tradition, reinterpreted rather than reiterated, is manifest to an equal degree in the railway station, where Cruz and Ortiz, like Moneo, looked to northern Europe for their sources, to Poelzig and Aalto, for the fanlike, pleated vaults of the big train shed and the vast scale of the masonry walls that enclose its flanks (see photographs and project description in Part II).

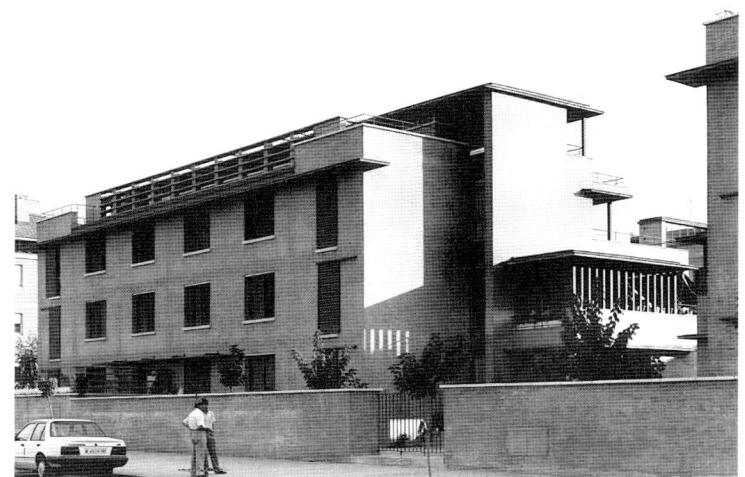

Fig. 16. Antonio Cruz and Antonio Ortiz. Housing development, Carabanchel, Madrid, 1989.

Possibly to satisfy the person or organization commissioning the architect, there is a kind of architecture based on exhibiting the instruments that have determined it. The architecture is an exhibition of economic power, technical media, historical knowledge and compositional patching. . . . But there is another way of making buildings, perhaps not so tied up with professional servitude. There is a conception of work that tries to neutralize these instruments and render them unrecognizable. This way, like some conjuring trick, the instruments remain invisible and one cannot appreciate the effort put into the execution of such a prodigious feat, nor imagine that there could have been any problems. Nothing here, nothing there. . . . Now you don't see it, now you do: a building! Or a piece of string becomes an umbrella. John Cage said he did not compose with musical notes but with noises. One could say of Alejandro de la Sota that he does not draw with compositional systems but with materials. As with Mies, this allows one to forget the architecture and concentrate on the form of the construction. However, Alejandro takes it a little further: he warps the materials. He turns a piece of string into an umbrella.[8]

Fig. 17. Alejandro de la Sota. TABSA aircraft factory, Barajas, Madrid, 1957.

This capacity for transforming the act of construction into a revelation of its material form is at once evident in de la Sota's first major work, the aircraft factory that he built near Madrid in 1957 (fig. 17). In this case, as in a number of other works, notably his Maravillas School Gymnasium, Madrid (1961; figs. 18 and 19), and his sports pavilion, Pontevedra (1966), the tectonic key depends upon a truss spanning over a large central volume that, in both the aircraft plant and the gymnasium, are catenary trusses designed in collaboration with the engineer Eusebio Rojas Marcos. In the case of the factory, the truss is turned upwards so as to support both the monitor lights over the assembly space and the gantry rails serving the work area; in the gymnasium the reverse is the case, that is to say, a horizontal upper chord supports a playground on the roof above, while a lecture hall and other teaching rooms are suspended within the depth of the inverted truss. The rest of the Maravillas assembly—the exposed steel framing, the strip clerestory glazing, the brick spandrel panels, and last but not least, the metal standards supporting the playground fence—all of these make up a kind of neo-Constructivist anti-architecture of which de la Sota would write:

The building was born in 1962 almost on its own. Taken up as we were with developmental difficulties, how to make the best of a bad site, and the economic problems. We had little time to worry about a specific architecture, which is why the building does not really have any architecture at all. Or perhaps that is an architecture in itself. . . . Once the volume of the gymnasium itself was correctly placed, the rest fitted in around it. . . . The external verandas give the big wall an urban scale. The finishing touch is the wall (fence) enclosing the yard, which matches the rest of the building and also acts as its facade.[9]

De la Sota's acknowledged masterwork and the building that would guarantee his preeminence was the Government Building in Tarragona, realized between 1954 and 1957 and recently restored by José Llinás (fig. 20). Strongly influenced by, but also distanced from, Giuseppe Terragni's Casa del Fascio, Como, of 1936, de la Sota's Government Building is a

Fig. 18. Alejandro de la Sota. Maravillas School Gymnasium, Madrid, 1961.

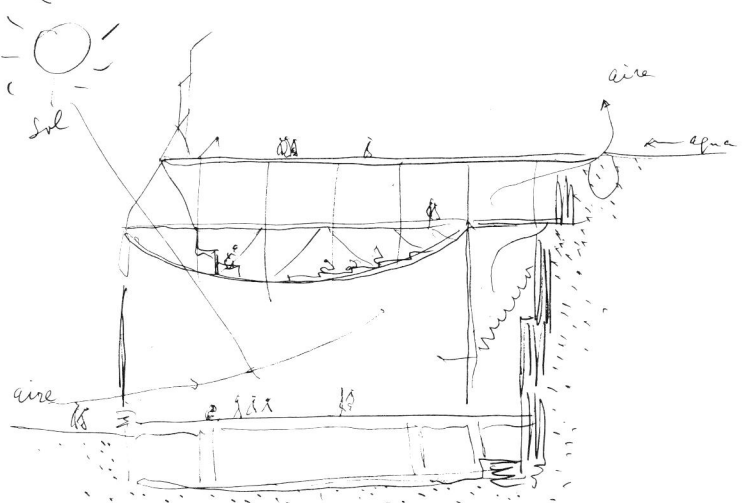

Fig. 19. Alejandro de la Sota. Maravillas School Gymnasium, Madrid, 1961. Sectional sketch.

frontal structure of a neo-Cubist character. Like the Casa del Fascio, the metaphysical aura emanating from the piece would depend upon minimalist detailing, ranging from flush-jointed masonry to subtle differences in surface modulation, which serve to distinguish in planar terms between the stone facing and the flush-glass fenestration. Beyond this, however, the two buildings could not be more different. Where the Casa del Fascio turned upon a multifaced, self-conscious reinterpretation of the palazzo prototype, complete with covered courtyard, the Government Building was centered about an asymmetrical axis, stressing the monumental frontage of its principal facade. Through this asymmetrical symmetry, both program and site were allowed to inflect the composition; to shift, as it were, the principal volumes and stairs from one alignment to the next as the building rose from floor to floor. Thus, where the ground and first floors variously serve representational and administrative purposes, the second to sixth floors provide for a hierarchy of residential accommodation ranging from the governor's suite on the second and third floors, to that of his entourage located on the floor above. Of the unification of the form through the application of a stone veneer de la Sota has written:

So in Tarragona. . . I used polished marble cladding on the outside, burnished marble on the floors and I remember I had the good fortune to make the porter's desk, a small parallelepiped desk out of stone, burnished on all faces except the top surface, which was polished (for filling in forms) showing the many marvels one can do with a single material. And for me, this instance is representative of all stone, even if it was just for the porter's desk. It was like the stone for the patio of Los Reyes in El Escorial, like the last stone.[10]

The flexibility of de la Sota's method is related to the fact that each building is formulated in a different material and hence in a different syntax, and that these tectonic choices are then orchestrated in such a way as to embody the type and engender the character of its spatial form. De la Sota's capacity to dance within the fetters of rational production is perhaps most evident in his application of modular metal

Fig. 20. Alejandro de la Sota. Government Building, Tarragona, 1954-57.

systems to rather large institutional structures, such as the classroom block that he built for the University of Seville in 1972 or the Post Office and Telecommunications Building that he realized more recently in León (figs. 21 and 22). Of this last project de la Sota has written:

Construction procedures are quite different nowadays and here we had to incorporate new possibilities in our thought processes before we even put pen to paper. Legacies from the past tend to be overvalued, so that fear and nostalgia are mixed together to create a way of thinking by which restoration is deemed more worthy than recreation. But this is not so. . . . The new Post Office and Telecommunications building in León is a "functional" building, made with state-of-the-art technology. Possibly this is all it is. The idea was to make a "cube that works" and that would be adaptable to future changes in the way it worked. This flexibility was to be achieved by the structural simplicity and by light and the spacious interior. Light and more light. Care is taken to provide the necessary magic touch to add the prestige that this peaceful parallelepiped merits as a public building. The endeavors to locate new materials in new buildings will continue forever. In León we used Robertson [steel] panels which are usually employed in Spain for supermarkets. Here, they were used for a quite singular and very important building and the result is perfectly acceptable. On the outside because they were painted the lion [León] color tone; on the inside because they were treated with great delicacy, humanizing them in order not to offend anyone's sensibilities.[11]

While few architects possess either the technical prowess or the intellectual assurance to follow de la Sota's rigorous, but playful, non-rhetorical approach, his influence, as a teacher and practitioner, has been extensive. And while one may identify a number of his pupils by name, much has rubbed off on many other Spanish architects since 1945, when de la Sota first began to practice and to teach. The depth of de la Sota's influence seems to derive from the authenticity with which he experienced the re-emergence of modern architecture in his own lifetime, going from the traditionalism of his Pareja-Dera House built in Guipúzcoa in 1945 to the rational constructivist phase of his career, which has culminated most recently in his self-effacing Spanish Embassy in Paris.

Rational Constructivism in Madrid and Barcelona, 1958-1990

Among the next generation who were to be associated with de la Sota, the most immediate successors were José Antonio Corrales and Ramón Vázquez Molezún, with whom he would successfully enter a competition for a children's vacation home in Miraflores de la Sierra in 1957. That Corrales and Molezún's Spanish Pavilion built for the Brussels Universal Exposition in the following year was influenced by de la Sota is borne out by the simple modular system from which it was assembled (fig. 23). It is significant that this structural system was *tectonic* and *topographic* at the same time: tectonic to the extent that the expressive form was inseparable from the basic structure, and topographic to the degree that the relative height of the hexagonal units from which it was assembled could be readily modified so as to vary the internal volume and accommodate the contours. The provision of a central tubular steel support and drain for each inverted hexagonal unit (cf. Joseph Paxton's Crystal Palace) facilitated the application of a equally modular system of horizontal fenestration wherein the uppermost glazing bars could be linked directly to the outer perimeter of the hexagons. The result was an exceptionally elegant structure—a limpid expression compounded of light, transparency, and continually unfolding space.

This de la Sota line would make itself manifest in a number of private houses erected in the late 1970s: in Corrales's own house built at Aravaca near Madrid in 1978; in the house that Llinás designed for Begur in 1980 (fig. 24); and lastly, in the house that Victor López Cotelo realized at Sota del Real, Madrid, in 1981. Each of these houses may be seen as reinterpreting the tectonic essence of de la Sota's Guzman

Fig. 21. Alejandro de la Sota. Post Office and Telecommunications Building, León, 1981. Interior view.

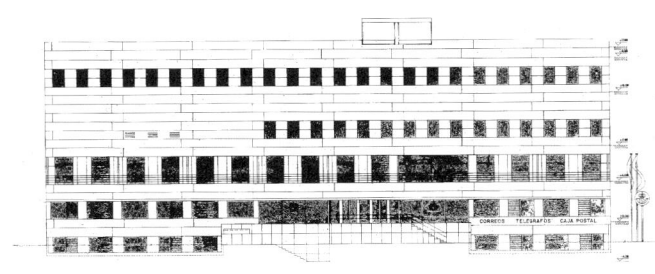

Fig. 22. Alejandro de la Sota. Post Office and Telecommunications Building, León, 1981. Elevation.

Fig. 23. José Antonio Corrales and Ramón Vázquez Molezún. Spanish Pavilion, Universal Exposition, Brussels, 1958.

House completed in Santo Domingo in 1972; that is to say, each house may be regarded as a further variation on the theme of low-slung roof planes with extending terraces, horizontal strip fenestration, and surface elaborations in tubular steel, combined with light, retractable canvas canopies. While the basic wall material will range from brick, to plaster, to metal paneling, each house will be layered into its site no matter how slight the fall of the land. With these houses one may sincerely speak of a school of modern architecture, as opposed to the forced individuality that so often masquerades today as originality.

Possibly no single practice has made a greater contribution to the evolution of what I would call "rational

Fig. 24. Josep Llinás. House at Begur, Gerona, 1980.

constructivism" in Spain than the partnership of Victor López Cotelo and Carlos Puente, particularly in their building for the pharmacology faculty at the University of Alcalá de Henares (1981-85) and in the public library that they realized in Zaragoza in 1989 (see photographs and project description in Part II). This latter project is exemplary not only for its evident contextualism, but also for the way in which it combines the tectonic rationalism of de la Sota with a more tactile expressivity, such as we find in the *funkis* manner of Gunnar Asplund or Arne Jacobsen.

Of the generation who are now in their forties, one of the most able followers of de la Sota is Llinás, who as we have seen assisted him in the restoration of the Government Building in Tarragona and who has since served as de la Sota's site architect for the Spanish Embassy in Paris. As a designer in his own right Llinás has a number of structural rationalist works to his credit, including a medical center in Ripollet (1982-84), a municipal library in Vilaseca (1986), and a college of civil engineering in Barcelona, completed in 1989. The medical center (Centro de Asistencia Primaria or CAP) at Ripollet was Llinás's first civic work at a median scale. Here, as in his Begur house, an apparently axial structure is asymmetrically inflected, not only in terms of its section, which responds to the idiosyncrasies of the site, but also with regard to the elevations where a subtle interplay between symmetry and asymmetry orchestrates the entire composition, setting up a counterpoint to the regularity of the horizontal windows and the cantilevered, feather-edged roof canopies of the ground and first floors (figs. 25 and 26; see also Capitel, fig. 11). Occupying a roughly triangular terrain and flanked by a highway, a river, and an access road, this building is oriented towards a parking structure and a future urban park. Ingeniously arranged so that it may be approached from either the upper or the lower parking levels, this health center steps down in three stages from a four-story slab to a single-story parking structure facing the park.

Evidently influenced by Italian rationalism and even to some extent by Wright, Llinás's CAP building is embedded in the

Fig. 25. Josep Llinás. Medical center (Centro de Asistencia Primaria or CAP), Ripollet, Barcelona 1982-84.

site, as though it were literally a *parterre*. This characteristic is reinforced by bands of shrubs that line the building on three sides, by green strips between the parking lanes, and finally by timber decking that serves to express the ambiguous nature of the upper parking level.

The contemporary Spanish penchant for structural expression goes well beyond the school of de la Sota, as we may judge from the large pergola or *umbráculo* erected in 1979 in a nature reserve near Madrid to the designs of Javier Vellés and María Luisa López Sardá (see Capitel, fig. 18) and two stadia by Esteve Bonell and Francesc Rius built in Barcelona for the 1992 Olympic Games. The ecological aim, structural order, and metaphorical significance of the *umbráculo* is best expressed in the architect's own words:

The idea behind this assignment was to site a building on the mountain which would encompass a series of services— bar, firewood sales, rest rooms, a swimming pool, lockers,

Building in a New Spain: Contemporary Spanish Architecture

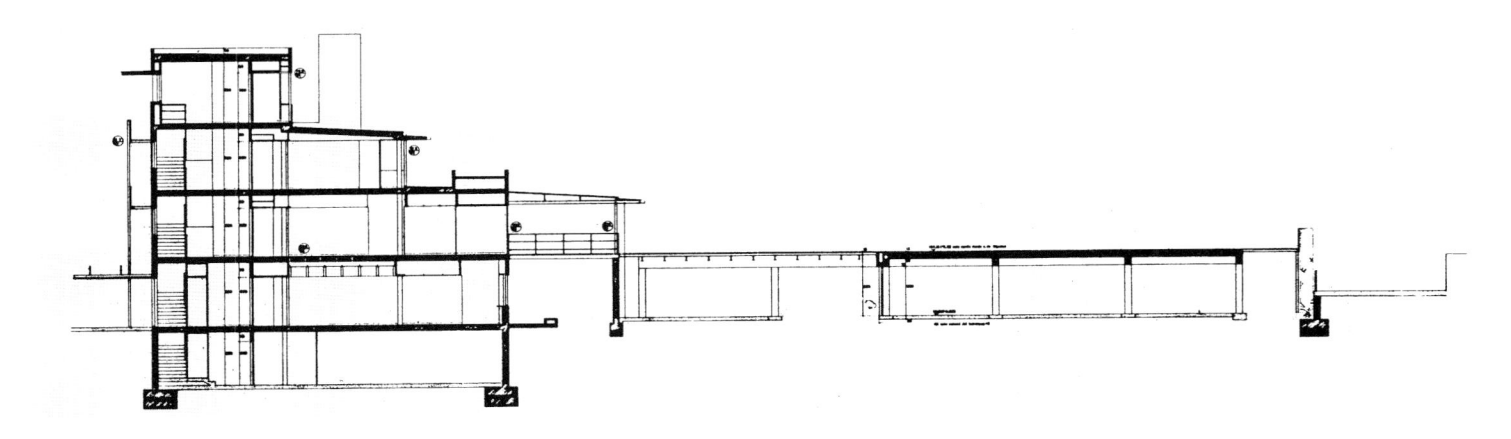

Fig. 26. Josep Llinás. Medical center (Centro de Asistencia Primaria or CAP), Ripollet, Barcelona, 1982-84. Section.

storage rooms, and offices—representing a center of interest, and concentrating in a specific place the greatest possible number of tourists, thus avoiding their dispersion and the uncontrolled use of the mountain. Located in a woods clearing, on the southern slope, the building is conceived as a great shade which recreates the light and shade atmosphere of pine-tree branches. Thus the plane resembles a musical artifact. Rietveld's chair knots [i.e., joints] were the key for organizing this elementary, light wooden construction, measured and articulated with archaic perfection and built with the very same mountain pines.[12]

Like Corrales and Molezún's Spanish Pavilion of 1958, this gridded structure is both *tectonically* articulated and *topographically* integrated, so much so that the architects seem more than justified in claiming an archaic, if not classical, precedent for their achievement. Like Gottfried Semper's primitive hut, this shade structure seems to be divided between the stereotomic earthwork of its base and the tectonic framework of its superstructure.

Aspiring to a tradition that lies closer to the vision of the French *grandes constructeurs* (Tony Garnier, Auguste Perret,

and Eugène Freyssinet), Esteve Bonell and Francesc Rius built a velodrome as a demonstration piece in the Vall d'Hebron district of Barcelona (fig. 27; see also Capitel, fig. 12). This tectonic tour de force, dating from 1984, that confronts us with a public building in which the monumental authority of the work derives from an interplay between the geometrical order of the form and the empirical specificity of the structure:

We planned a building . . . which, despite its dimension, would support itself on the terrain, would cause little disturbance, and would be as transparent as possible. A building having two scales, due to two [views], a distant one and a close one. On the other hand, we wanted a building with a clear image, with a unitary architectural definition, one that would be capable of organizing the immediate environment. . . . If we had to define the velodrome in a few words we would say that it possesses a certain classicism and at the same time an elaborated modernism. Classicism because of the way in which it sets itself on the landscape and because of the rotundity of its conception. Modernism because of its pragmatic and realistic appearance, because of its simplicity and the way in which construction is coherent with the materials used.[13]

Reminiscent of the opposition between ideal and empirical form in the work of Le Corbusier, the elliptical plan-form of the cycle track is enclosed here by a 4.5-meter-deep circular ring that accommodates a variety of services along its perimeter: portico, entry, toilets, bars, staircases, changing rooms, etc. The monumental stature of this work is guaranteed by its overall scale and proportion and by the hierarchical interplay between the concrete superstructure of the ring and the block-and-plaster infill of the 4.5-meter blades supporting the perimeter canopy. This roof constitutes a kind of vestigial cornice that, together with the diagonally inclined lighting masts in tubular steel, crowns the composition. Between the outer ring and the tiered seating that surrounds the banked cycle track lies the paved concourse that is at the disposal of spectators during intervals.

Since the realization of this facility, Bonell and Rius have gone on to achieve an equally exceptional basketball stadium at Badalona (see photographs and project description in Part II). Here again, one encounters a canonical work of a decidedly tectonic character. A light, stressed-skin metal roof, together with a spinal truss in tubular steel spanning the long axis of the arena, returns one to the elegant engineering achievements of the nineteenth century. One is reminded of the British engineer I. K. Brunel's Saltash Viaduct or of Gustave Eiffel's viaduct pylons in the Massif Central. And yet, as in the velodrome, the architects pay particular attention to the paving of the ground plane in polished local stone and to the overall emplacement of the piece within a somewhat restricted and irregular urban site, not to mention the hierarchical treatment of the structure as it rises from the concrete earthwork at its base to a thin, tubular skeleton loggia at its crown.

Atectonic Minimalism: Barcelona and Madrid, 1982-1990

Albert Viaplana and Helio Piñón have been practicing together since they graduated from the school of architecture in Barcelona in 1966. While their earliest works, such as their Can Bruixa apartments of 1976, were influenced by Italian rationalism, their most striking realizations to date have been largely topographic in nature; works in which the formation of the ground plane has been augmented by minimalist constructions in sheet and tubular steel. Three works in this genre, all built in Barcelona, exemplify the best of their production to date, the Parque del Besòs (1982), the Plaça dels Països Catalans before the Sants Station (1982-89), and last but not least, their Santa Monica Arts Center in the Ramblas, recently completed within the shell of an old convent.

The most ambitious of these works, the Sants Station plaza, amounts to the superimposition of a fictitious, dematerialized structure in an otherwise chaotic and desolate area facing the station (fig. 28; see also Solà-Morales, fig. 8). Every vector of this three-dimensional abstraction is initiated by shaping the ground plane, and this is henceforth transformed into a sequence of dynamic trajectories implied by diagonal paving and other vectors that are inscribed into the site. In this instance, a tectonic

Fig. 27. Esteve Bonell and Francesc Rius. Velodrome, Vall d'Hebron, Barcelona, 1984.

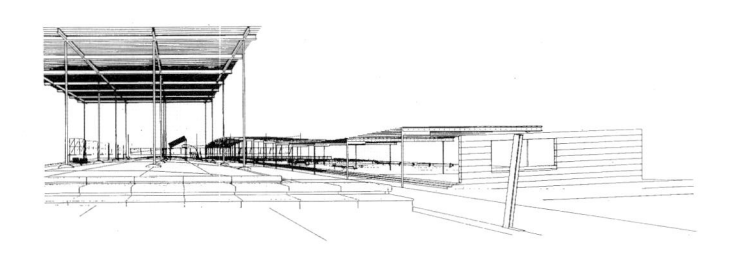

Building in a New Spain: Contemporary Spanish Architecture

Fig. 28. Albert Viaplana and Helio Piñón. Sants Station plaza (Plaça dels Països Catalans), Barcelona, 1982-89. Perspective drawing.

palimpsest gives rise to two large steel-framed volumes and to an amount of incidental furniture having a rhythmic or functional character, whether these are benches, fountains, light standards, or bollards. The bollards, in particular, seem to be uncannily reminiscent of airport furnishings or anti-tank emplacements. Certain metaphors are thus consciously evoked despite the sculptural severity of this abstraction. In this regard, the open cube suggests the silhouette of a civic structure, just as the undulating glazed pergola that flows out of the station would seem to compensate for the lack of a honorific shed in the station itself—a reference perhaps to the famous rail terminus of 1954 in Rome.

It is possible to see their recent Arts Center (see Pérez Escolano, fig. 29) as an equally "spectral" work in which, while the topography is still a decisive element, the mass-form of the existing building necessarily reasserts itself as a significant factor. The self-consciously diagonal paving of this section of the Ramblas becomes transformed into an open-boarded timber ramp leading up to the first floor of the convent. The ramp assumes the character of a warped ground plane that crashes into the side of the building like the deck of a beached ship. This association is carried over into the architectonic furnishings: I have in mind the steel-framed delicacy of the entrance canopy, or the frameless, plate-glass elegance of the *passerelle* that serves as a threshold to the main entrance.

Viaplana and Piñón have been closely followed in what one might call their "graffiti" style by their protégé Enric Miralles, who with Carme Pinós, entered into a similar genre of topographic creation, with a sculptural bravura that is altogether less severe than that of his mentors. Their somewhat paradoxical combination of minimalism with a fluid expressivity is already evident in the shade structure that they designed for a square in Parets in 1985 and a similar, tectonically anarchic impulse is evident in their archery center designed for the Barcelona Olympiad (see photographs and project description in Part II).

Minimalism of a very different kind distinguishes the work of the Madrid architect Alberto Campo Baeza, whose architecture has nothing of the topographic ambiguity that we find in the work of the Viaplana School. Instead, Campo Baeza's architecture is based as far as possible on Platonic forms, such as cubes, cylinders, and parallelepipeds, and on the revelation of these forms under light. In this respect his designs resemble the work of the Japanese architect Tadao Ando, particularly since, like Ando, Campo Baeza departs from the functional white architecture of the International Style to engage in a purification of its formal legacy. As with other late modern purists like Richard Meier, Campo Baeza's all-white architecture depends upon its susceptibility to light, and to this end he makes extensive use of glass block and large areas of plate glass. This minimalist palette, which

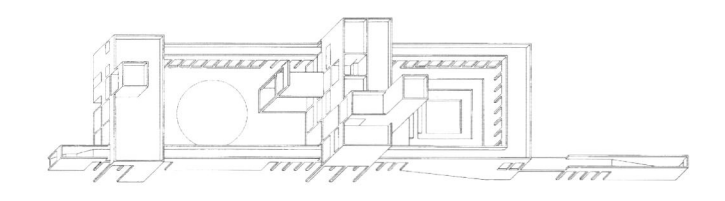

Fig. 29. Alberto Campo Baeza. Town hall, Fene, La Coruña, 1980. Axonometric drawing.

attains its most sensuous expression in the architect's private houses, for example, the Casa Turegano, completed at Pozuelo in 1987, becomes of necessity more typological in his public work such as the Town hall of Fene (1980; fig. 29) and the various schools that he built in the first half of the eighties (see Capitel, fig. 19).

The Basque Tradition: From Novecento to Rationalism, 1938-1988

It is an unfortunate outcome of separatism that the Basque region is often perceived as a country apart, and in consequence, one senses a certain critical neglect that is entirely absent in the case of Barcelona. This distance is all the more surprising given that the leading architects of both Madrid and Barcelona have always maintained close contact with San Sebastián and Bilbao. Coderch, Sáenz de Oiza, de la Sota, Fernández Alba, Campo Baeza, and Moneo have all worked in the Basque region at one time or another, while Basque architects have played prominent roles in the architectural culture of Madrid and Barcelona. As far as such exchange is concerned, there is even a longer link dating back to 1929 and the foundation of the Spanish wing of the CIAM in San Sebastián with the Catalans José Lluís Sert and García Mercadal joining the Basque architects José Manuel Aizpurua and Joaquin Labayen, to form GATEPAC. Aizpurua and Labayen would follow this polemical initiative with two remarkable rationalist works both built in San Sebastián in the late twenties and early thirties: the Club Naútico[14] and the Café Sacha.

While Basque rationalism was never entirely eclipsed during the Franquista period, Bilbao proved to be fertile ground for the Novecento, and it produced architecture that was strongly influenced by the northern Italian tendency of the same name led by Giovanni Muzio. The main Basque architects of this persuasion were Pedro Ispizua, Germán Aguirre, and Fernando Arzaden, although many other architects also worked in this idiom in the 1940s. The best local work in this Franquista manner is to be found in two canonical housing districts, the Torremadariago settlement, built in Irún in 1941 to the designs of Germán Aguirre and Emilio Amann, and the more extensive San Ignacio de Loyola development near Bilbao, realized in 1945 and designed by Aguirre, assisted by Hilario Imaz and Luis Lorenzo Blanc. The latter project may be seen as exemplary of the kind of perimeter block development for which Spanish architects have displayed an enthusiasm ever since, building some of the finest civic housing developments in Europe in this idiom.

The most important architects to emerge from the post-Franco era in Bilbao were Fernando Olabarria and Juan Daniel Fullaondo and the various architects with whom they collaborated from the early 1960s on, principally Alvaro Livano, with whom Fullaondo designed a number of ingeniously planned schools in fair-faced brick work. Fullaondo and Olabarria also participated in the evolution of a local version of the brutalist manner, realizing a number of brick-faced residential blocks during this period that were comparable in their plastic rigor to the early work of O. M. Ungers in Cologne. In 1967 Fullaondo began to edit his highly influential review *Nueva Forma*, published in Madrid. Over the next decade, as an influential professor at the Madrid school of architecture, Fullaondo would be active on a number of fronts at once, dividing his time between teaching, writing, and practicing in Bilbao.

Another Basque architect to emerge during this period is Luis Peña Ganchegui, who, after studying in Madrid, returned to his home town of Matriku in the mid-1960s to realize his canonical Casa Imanolena there in 1964. This colonnaded, pitched-roof house, structured about a top-lit patio, established the basic syntax of a neo-vernacular approach that Peña Ganchegui would further elaborate in a series of multistory dwellings built in Matriku in the sixties. Over the last two decades Peña Ganchegui's expression has varied widely, ranging from the Neo-Constructivism of a pharmaceutical factory erected in Irún and clad entirely in glass block (1974) to the neo-Jugendstil brick apartment building that he realized in Elorrio in 1987.

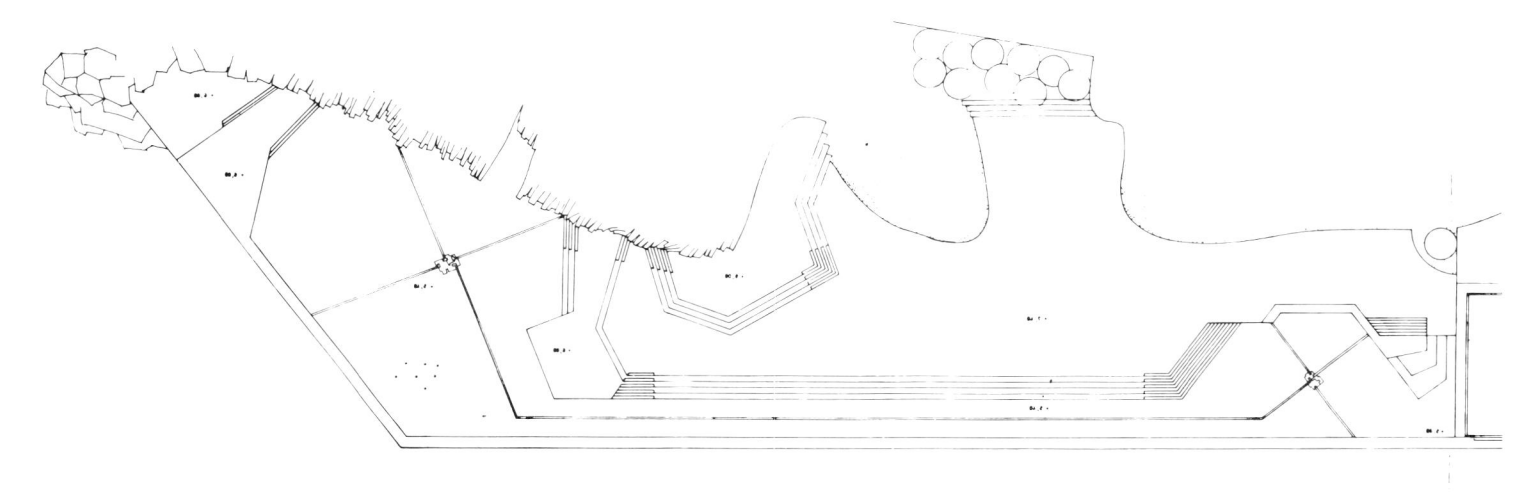

Fig. 30. Luis Peña Ganchegui and Eduardo Chillida. Plaza del Tenis, including *The Comb of the Wind (El Peine del Viento)*, San Sebastián, 1976. Plan.

Peña Ganchegui has been at his best as a landscape architect, notably in the Plaza del Trinidad realized in San Sebastián in 1976, in the ETA memorial fronton built into the wall of the Oyarzun cemetery in the following year, and last but not least in the highly topographic Plaza del Tenis (fig. 30; see also Pérez Escolano, fig. 13), finally realized outside San Sebastián in 1976 as an elaborate emplacement for Eduardo Chillida's sculpture *The Comb of the Wind (El Peine del Viento)*. Apertures in the granite surface of this sea-front promenade are the source of a fountain jet that is activated by wave movement penetrating into a disused sewer outlet beneath the plaza. Under certain light conditions this sporadic fountain spray creates a localized rainbow effect.

Throughout the 1970s and 1980s, the best of Basque architecture seemed to oscillate between two main lines of development. On the one hand there is the rational classicism introduced in the mid-1970s by the partnership of Miguel Garay and José Ignacio Linazasoro, in a school that they built near Irún and in an equally symmetrical factory and house realized to designs of Garay alone in 1976 and 1979, respectively. Over the next decade this line developed in two different directions: on the one hand, it veered towards classical pastiche; on the other, it turned back towards a form of rationalism that was always inseparable from the modern, such as we find in the stepped terraced form of a series of apartments realized in Basurto by Olabarria and Juan R. Villanueva in 1982 (fig. 31). More recently, an altogether lighter, more constructivist rationalism has emerged on the Basque scene in the work of Roberto Ercilla, as, for example, in a special school that he built in Lladró in 1986.

Fig. 31. Fernando Olabarria and Juan R. Villanueva. Apartment building at Basurto, Guipúzcoa, 1982.

Iberian Habitat: Housing and Urbanization

The Spanish achievement must be recognized first, for the remarkably high level of its general production, and second, for the high level of its civic culture as this is reflected in the caliber of its public housing and in the extent and quality of recent urban development and renewal. Apart from the Basque achievements in these areas, the post-Franco stance towards housing and urban development in Spain seems to have taken its first step in the low-cost Caño Roto housing district built in Madrid in 1961, to the designs of Antonio Vázquez de Castro and José Luis Iñiguez de Onzoño (fig. 32). The importance of this low- to medium-rise settlement resides in the delicacy of its detailing, the articulated nature of its open space and planting, and its ingenious play with Mediterranean courtyard-house typology. In many respects Caño Roto remains the best low-rise, high-density urban settlement that has been realized in Spain, although many versions of similar patterns have been built throughout the country in recent years.

As far as medium-rise infill housing is concerned, some of the best examples have been designed by the firm of Martorell, Bohigas, and Mackay; notably their Sabadell double slab of 1979 and their Eduardo Conde infill complex built in the Sarriá district of Barcelona in the same year (fig. 33). Although at different scales, both of these works are structured about top-lit internal access ways, and a similar generic type will crop up in high-rise housing prototypes built in Madrid over the same period, above all in the generic housing blocks of the new Palomeras district under construction on the outskirts of Madrid in the early 1980s. These generic double slabs, erected to the designs of Jerónimo Junquera and Estanislao Pérez Pita (fig. 34) and Manuel and Ignacio de las Casas (fig. 35; see also Capitel, fig. 7), were to posit variations on an unprecedented back-to-back typology, particularly the Casas brothers' block design, which was, in effect, a ten-story, back-to-back assembly of L-shaped courtyard houses. It is clear that this type lies in a line of development, extending from Le Corbusier's Immeuble-Villa blocks of 1922 to Alvar Aalto's Hansaviertel apartments built in Berlin in 1955.

Of equal stature are the perimeter-block prototypes that are part of the new Pino Montano district of Seville. Built into a twenty-block master plan designed by Cruz and Ortiz in 1980, the first stage of this development consists of four blocks, each 42 meters square, and four rectangular perimeter blocks, 42 by 84 meters. A whole team of young architects have collaborated on the design of these eight

Fig. 32. Antonio Vázquez de Castro and José Luis Iñiguez de Onzoño. Housing development, Caño Roto, Madrid, 1961.

blocks, including José Ramón Sierra and Ricardo Sierra, Antonio Hernández Ortiz, J. A. Sánchez Rodríguez, Raphael Ruiz Lucas, José Morales Alcalá, M. J. Muñoz, María Victoria Durán and Francisco Torres, and Antonio Barrionuevo. This achievement is remarkable not only at the block prototype level, but also for the fact that the whole quarter amounts to a city in miniature, comparable to the rationalistic block planning of the nineteenth century, the Ringstrasse of Vienna or the projected expansion (*Ensanche*) of Barcelona designed in 1859 by the engineer Ildefonso Cerdà. At the same time the general ergonomic approach and sensitive detailing in respect of the open space give the whole an exemplary character.

Barcelona Olympiad, 1979-1992

One of the most comprehensive pieces of urban renewal in Spain is that which has taken place in Barcelona over the last decade, namely, the progressive realization of a general plan for the refurbishment of the Catalan metropolis that was

Fig. 34. Jerónimo Junquera and Estanislao Pérez Pita. Housing development, Palomeras, Madrid, 1983.

first promulgated in 1976. Broadly conceived by Oriol Bohigas, who served as director of urban design for the municipality, the so-called *Plàns i Projectes per a Barcelona 1981/82* were put in hand throughout the 1980s. In terms of urban renewal this unprecedented undertaking amounts to the refurbishment of some eleven neighborhoods in the city; the creation of some ten parks (both new and restored); and the building of two new avenues and over thirty public spaces of various sizes, including the Moll de la Fusta, built to the designs of Manuel de Solà-Morales (fig. 36). This last project, erected over a trunk route running along the harbor waterfront, has been conceived as a new promenade complete with cafés, terraces, and palm trees lining its entire length.

Equally unprecedented as an urban type is the 140-meter-span Bach de Roda bridge, built in 1987 to the designs of the Catalan engineer Santiago Calatrava (fig. 37). Aside from the harmony of its profile as a bridge, for which it is indebted to

Fig. 33. Josep Maria Martorell, Oriol Bohigas, and David Mackay. Eduardo Conde apartments, Sarriá, Barcelona, 1975-79. Section.

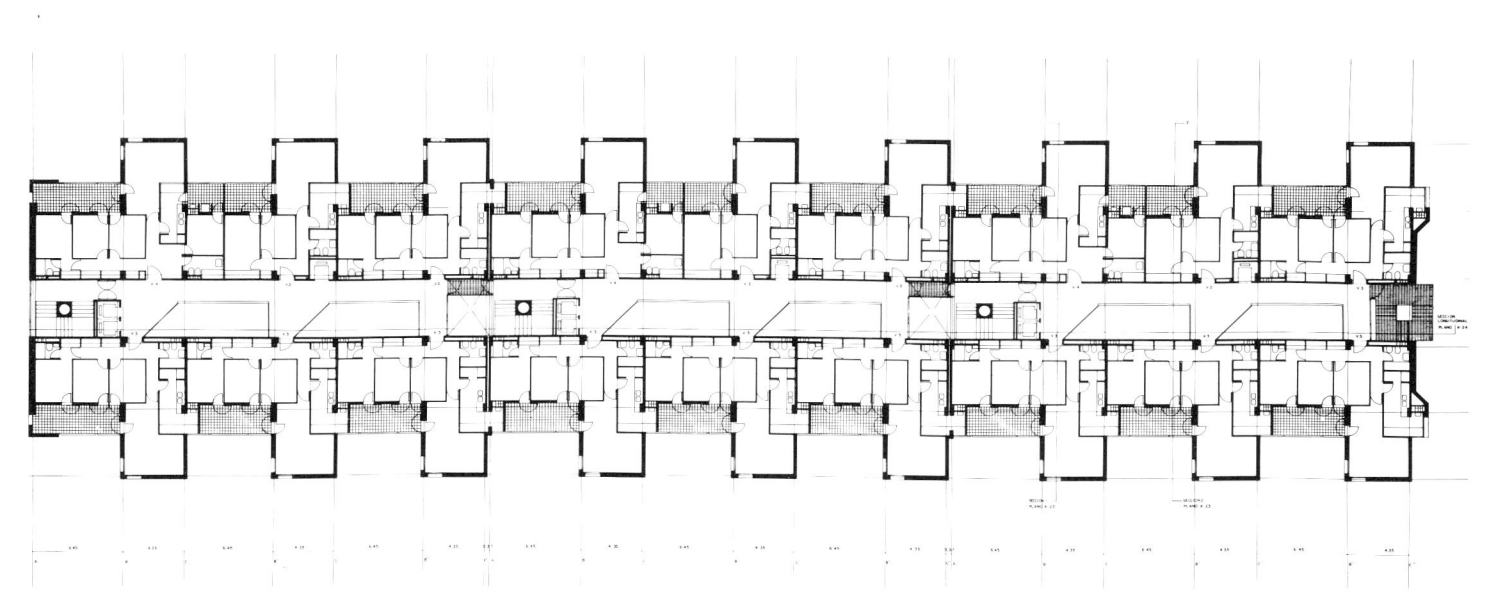

Fig. 35. Manuel and Ignacio de las Casas. Housing development, Palomeras, Madrid, 1980-84. Plan.

the pioneering works of Robert Maillart and Eugène Freyssinet, the most exceptional thing about this structure is its transformation of an engineering work into an instrument of urban design, evident in the way in which it activates the site at both a regional and a local scale. Besides bridging a nineteenth-century rail corridor cutting across Cerdà's gridded *Ensanche*, it also affords a pedestrian plaza cantilevering out on either side of its span. By virtue of this belvedere linked by stairs to public parks on either side of the tracks, the structure not only relates to the regional scale of the railroad but also to the intimate scale of the local urban grain on either side of the cutting. This work is reparatory in more ways than one. In the first place, it uses technical ingenuity to overcome the disjunctions created earlier by rail technology; in the second, it reduces the symbolic stature of the automobile by elevating the sidewalks above the roadbed, thereby enabling one to see over the traffic while slightly offsetting the worst effects of engine exhaust.

The policy of urban metastasis has been escalated by the choice of Barcelona as host for the 1992 Olympic Games, since this has had the effect of increasing the scope of the initial building program. Thus, aside from the strategy of refurbishing certain civic elements and of augmenting others with new facilities, Barcelona has had to commit itself to much larger undertakings, above all to the renewal and expansion of the existing sports facilities on the site of the 1929 International Exposition on Montjuïc overlooking the city and the construction of an entirely new residential quarter, accommodating some 10,000 people, that will serve as the Olympic Village during the games. Located in a former industrial quarter between the Ciutadella park and the Poble Nou district, this new settlement, known as Nova Icària (fig. 38), will reconnect the city to the sea, providing some 900 meters of beach between Barceloneta and the Bogatell storm-water outfall. Three infrastructural barriers had to be modified in order to realize this development: first, the removal of an east-west rail link running along the coast; second, the burial of a main line running inland from the Franca terminal; and third, the creation of a divided parkway running along the coast between Nova Icària and the sea. Designed by the firm of Martorell, Bohigas, and Mackay, in collaboration with the planner Albert Puigdomènech, this hybrid proposal may be seen as a synthesis of three basic

Fig. 36. Manuel de Solà-Morales. Renovation of the wharf area known as Moll de la Fusta, Barcelona, 1985-88.

Fig. 37. Santiago Calatrava. Bach de Roda-Felipe II Bridge, Barcelona, period 1984-87.

models: the utilitarian urbanism of Cerdà, of which it is a belated expansion; the picturesque topography of the English park tradition; and the grand manner of the Ecole des Beaux-Arts evident in the principal north/south axis that culminates in the two new 100-meter-high office towers facing the sea.

Conclusion

One cannot possibly do justice to Spanish architectural culture over the last twenty years in an article of limited length. One can only make up for the innumerable works omitted from this account by identifying those general processes and common principles that have helped to shape and sustain the high general level of contemporary Spanish architecture. Perhaps one has to start by acknowledging the relatively high societal and economic status that is still enjoyed by architects in Spain and by recognizing those national institutions that have contributed to architectural culture throughout the country. One has to take note of the duration and caliber of training to which Spanish architects are subject in their professional education; one that is longer and more technically focused than in many other countries. The average eight-year period taken to qualify in the field seems to be related to two other equally unusual conditions; first, the legal fact that no building may be erected in Spain without the signature of an architect, and second, the existence of a system of local professional organizations known as *colegios* that appear to operate like guilds, in exercising control over the more fundamental aspects of the building process. Each local *colegio* is responsible for representing every architect working in the region and in this regard almost every city of any size has its *colegio de arquitectos*. Since all plans submitted for building permission are as much subject to the scrutiny of the *colegio* as to that of the municipal licensing body, a certain minimal level of professional competence is assured, while various pernicious practices such as competitive fee-cutting are largely eliminated, as are the vagaries of unscrupulous clients who balk at paying for services in full. Since the *colegio* and not the individual architect collects the fees, and since it takes a percentage for this service, it possesses the power to obtain redress for any default in this regard. This combination of economic and regulatory power has also enabled the *colegios* to assume a degree of cultural leadership, in part through organizing lectures and exhibitions and in part through sponsoring critical magazines of the highest quality, such as *Quaderns* and *Arquitectura*, published by the architectural colleges of Barcelona and Madrid, respectively.

All of this points perhaps to the benefits of a retardation in Spanish economic and cultural development, and it serves to remind us once again that the consumer society did not arrive in Spain until the early 1970s, a decade and a half later than it appeared in most other European countries. Moreover, Spain entered into consumerism in a somewhat *retardataire* way, aspiring to progressive democratization while retaining centralized authoritarian control, and then, in order to meet the full flush of modernization, electing to devolve both power and revenue towards the periphery. This federalizing move has been consummated by shifting the full responsibility for maintaining and expanding the Spanish welfare state to the various provincial governments.

This partial sequence of events, combined with the endemic conservatism of Spanish institutions and the implicit resistance of the traditional trades and crafts, has meant that Spanish architects have had the fortune to encounter neo-capitalist modernization rather late and to do so in a retroactive manner, in which they have had the chance to become wise both before and after the event. Fortunately, history seems to have empowered them not only with the opportunity to build extensively, but also with a detached, one might even say critical, creativity that has enabled them to mediate a volatile reality in a manner that is simultaneously radical and conservative. While profoundly aware of all the pitfalls that unavoidably attend modernization in a postmodern age, Spanish architects have nonetheless retained a conviction as to the capacity of their craft to intervene effectively in the production of the environment.

For all its eclecticism, or despite its knowing recourse to the syntax of the modernist heritage, Spanish architecture remains grounded not only in respect of its literal anchorage in the ground, but also with regard to the expressivity of its material. In this respect, Spanish architects display an exceptional sensitivity towards both topographic and constructional form. Unlike contemporary practice elsewhere where the freestanding object is given inordinate importance and the site is often treated in a cursory manner, Spanish architects habitually inflect the contours of the situation in such a way as to reinforce and augment the expressive attributes of their three-dimensional form. One need only reflect on the wide range of work to which this principle has been applied to realize that this degree of care is omnipresent in Spain. It prevails throughout, irrespective of stylistic idiosyncrasies.

If the topographic is to be acknowledged as the first tell-tale indicator of Spanish practice, then the second key characteristic is surely the tectonic, that is to say, an evident poetic of construction that manifests itself over a wide range of building types and situations. Spanish architecture tends to be unphotogenic, and it is hardly an accident that it is impossible to do justice to Spanish building through perspectival representations. While contradictions of late modernity may be found everywhere, the fact remains that most of these works assert a palpable tectonic presence that is culturally resistant to the extent that it takes its distance from media consumption and from the cynical reductivism of the "decorated shed." Whatever the multiple readings and ambiguities that necessarily abound in this architecture, its tectonic core still holds, so to speak, against a global condition in which cultural form becomes progressively reduced to commodity.

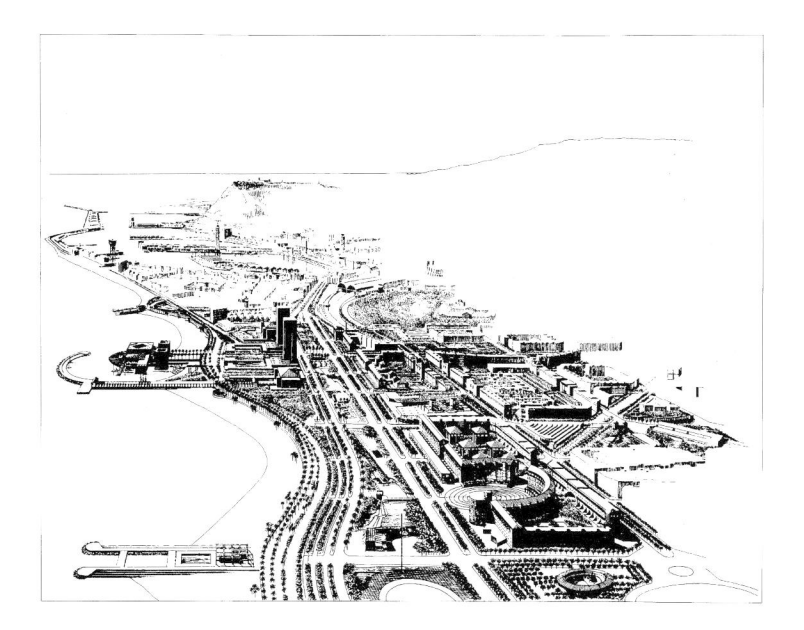

Fig. 38. Josep Maria Martorell, Oriol Bohigas, and David Mackay, with Albert Puigdomènech. Nova Icària, Barcelona, 1986-92. Bird´s-eye view of proposed development.

Notes

1. Antón Capitel, "The Modern Adventure of Spanish Architecture" in Antón Capitel and Ignacio Solà-Morales, *Contemporary Spanish Architecture: An Eclectic Panorama* (New York: Rizzoli, 1986), p. 16.

2. José Antonio Coderch, in an interview with Enric Sòria Badia in *Conversaciones con José Antonio Coderch de Sentmenat* (Barcelona: Editorial Blume, 1979), p. 144.

3. Coderch (note 2), p. 189-90.

4. See Helio Piñón, *Nacionalisme: Modernitat en l'Arquitectura Catalana Contemporánia* (Barcelona: Llibres a l'abast, Edicions 62, 1980), p. 23. Piñón quotes from an essay by J. M. Sostres, "El funcialismo y la nueva plastica," published in 1950 in the *Boletin de la Dirección General de Arquitectura* (Madrid).

5. Sostres (note 4).

6. Capitel (note 1), p. 17.

7. Rafael Moneo, quoted in *El Croquis* (April-June, 1990), pp. 13-23.

8. José Llinás, "Nothing here, nothing there," in *Alejandro de la Sota, Architect* (Madrid: Ediciones Pronaos, 1989), p. 11.

9. Alejandro de la Sota, quoted in *Alejandro de la Sota, Architect* (note 8), p. 74.

10 Ibid., p. 236.

11. Ibid., pp. 176-77.

12. Javier Vellés and Maria Luisa López Sardá, "Umbráculo," in Richard C. Levene, Fernando Márquez Cecilia, and Antonio Ruiz Barbarín, eds., *Arquitectura Española Contemporánea, 1975/1990* (Spanish Contemporary Architecture) (Madrid, El Croquis Editorial, 1989), vol. 2, pp. 408, 413.

13. Esteban Bonell and Francesc Rius, "Velodromo de Horta," in *Arquitectura Española Contemporánea* (note 12), pp. 438, 447.

14. It is interesting to note that this building was the only Spanish example to be included in the 1932 publication by Henry-Russell Hitchcock and Philip Johnson, *Modern Architecture: International Exhibition.*

Contemporary Spanish Architecture: From the Foundation of a New Modernism to the Appearance of Eclecticism

Antón Capitel

The Force of History

A grasp of contemporary Spanish architecture can be attained through an examination of its recent past, in which lie the keys that will open up an understanding of the intensity and the achievements of a culture that, until recently, has been unknown or greatly obscured. For a long time, contemporary Spanish architecture was unrecognized and overlooked by the Western world, even though it was a part of it and clearly depended upon it. But Spanish architecture is also the fruit of this isolation, an isolation that, paradoxically, contributes to its intelligibility.

This historical review must cover two principal periods. One corresponds to the consolidation of modern architecture in Spain during the 1950s and 1960s—these decades are the direct antecedents of contemporary architecture. During this period, the work of the teachers of the most significant present-day architects appeared, along with the earliest work of some of the students themselves. This period can be seen as entire, in spite of a powerful rupture of ideals and objectives between the two decades that compose it. The other principal period, which corresponds to the most important revision of modern architectural thought, began at the outset of the 1970s. This second period is the basis for the current situation, and it foreshadows it concretely and with notable continuity.

The first period, that of the foundation of modern Spanish architecture, influenced the present in two distinct, though contrary, ways that were, nevertheless, strongly interrelated, as the rest of this essay will describe. On the one hand, the development and triumph of modern Spanish architecture occurred in the years following the Spanish Civil War (1936-39). The catalyst was a national feeling of backwardness in the eyes of Europe and North America, which together constituted the proper or "correct" cultural world. The Spanish were anxious to join that world and to obliterate completely an extended historical rut that had been established by the dictatorial regime, which promoted historicism, the cultural cloak of Franquismo, as a nationalist talisman.

In this way, the most ambitious architects of the dictatorial period became the myth-makers of a modern architecture that they had not yet experienced. Meanwhile, in some foreign cultures, modern architecture had become the convention, and signs of revisionism had begun to appear. Modern architecture became for these Spanish architects, then, a genuine and incontestable "new good" that could overcome all evils, including non-architectural ones. In this mythification, to which neither the Catholic basis of Spanish sentiment nor the strong frustration experienced by the Franquista society were foreign, they were driven as much by the intensity of their work as by the pursuit of the mirage: modern architecture insinuated itself as the only pursuable good as well as an almost unattainable one. Thus, its identification was elusive and its achievement was progressive: each time they seemed to reach their destination, the road would again lengthen before them.

On the other hand, however, this mythification and the mysterious condition of modern architecture increased the difficulty of identifying its evolution, which was truly outside of Spain, in accord with the nature of architecture in progress. It was also difficult to see it in the compass of important revisionist ideas such as Italian neo-realism and the theory of pre-existing ambience, or in light of Scandinavian and North American organicism, for all of these ideas had special influence on Spanish architecture.

In the consciences and in the works of Spanish architects, the triumph of modern architecture—the triumph of the International Style—was celebrated, even though the Spanish version incorporated such important revisions as the organic and excluded the contradictions and mistakes created by it. Modern Spanish architecture of the 1960s turned into eclecticism without consciously realizing it or accepting it; that is, without ceasing to aspire to an ideal model, unique and exclusive, just as any movement professes. The attitude of the younger, succeeding generation might be described as the movement beyond the elusive ideal espoused by previous generations, eliminating as much the baggage of "truth" as the obsessive concern with "progress," but gradually accepting the unrecognized eclecticism that mattered in a more properly architectural respect. Ironically, the inheritance left by the modernists would be eclecticism—as much in attitude as in architectural practice—in which different issues were mixed, exactly as it would be in the peaceful coexistence of disparate trends. This would be one of the really important consequences that the new generation derived from the careers of their elders.

The search for the elusive modern ideal, the acceptance of modernism as an ideal in progress, and the subsequent revisions to the International Style, nevertheless, provoked in the Spanish architects of the 1950s and 1960s the creation of a dense and rich body of work. This was a complex adventure, long and difficult, but always of the highest order. The pursuit of modernism, continually surpassed and elaborated upon, presumed a collective effort of great breadth, and in the end it created a modern tradition that had not previously existed.

The Crisis of Modern Thought

At the beginning of the 1970s, however, the modernist architectural tradition underwent a profound crisis, parallel to the global cultural crisis. In Europe and America, a new and exalted interest in the creative application of technologies affected all the organic revisions; the bedazzling appearance of neo-vanguard movements such as Archigram occurred; the dream of design by computer was pursued; and the mythic belief in the methodologies represented by people like the American architect and writer Christopher Alexander, and very new interests, such as semiotics and structuralism, invaded the architectural discipline, displacing its content little by little. Architecture suffered such an identity crisis, that the discipline, according to Reyner Banham and others, had to lose the objectives and instruments that had once characterized it. The modernist adventure, which was one of cumulative effort, seemed to dilute itself. The younger generation then found itself standing before an empty horizon.

Although this younger generation of architects did not inherit a belief in the modern ideal, they did receive from their elders a faith in the value of architecture and the richness of their adventure. With these in hand, they reacted to the crisis within the discipline of architecture. At the beginning, their reaction was anti-modern—directly opposed to the idea of constant progress that modernism embodied and the very nature of its content: it no longer recognized function, technology, and society as basic values. On the contrary, its identification was with those very principles that modernism had discarded. Having been educated in the ambiguous cult of modernism, the younger generation explored, early on, the questions that the modernist mythification had denied them.

The younger generation found itself, then, in a very fertile environment for selecting new discourses. Although what they chose had not been generated in Spain, young Spanish architects interpreted these discourses in the context of their own preoccupations and within their own tradition. In this way, they at last overcame the traditional insularity that had characterized Spanish architecture to that point, and they were moving toward a vanguard position. Robert Venturi's answer to the modernist discourse, for example, had wide and diffuse repercussions in Spain, as did Aldo Rossi's contribution to the understanding of architecture as a discipline with its own nature and principles, legible in history. The latter was a highly important influence. The younger generation explored such issues as the autonomy of the discipline, the timelessness of the classical language, the meaning of authentic rationality, the continuity of history, the technical paper, the relation between work and ideology, and the construction of the city. They concerned themselves with questions that had not been answered during the turbulent years they were being schooled and that now seemed even more vital as many of them became professors themselves.

The Recovery of the Discipline

This change of thinking was produced, moreover, at a time when the geographic structure of Spanish architectural culture, long dominated by the traditional schools of architecture in the two great cities, Madrid and Barcelona, was being transformed. The change was articulated in the two great schools there, but its impact was also felt in other active centers, especially in the School of Architecture in Seville, but appearing also in other lesser areas such as the Basque country and Galicia. The recovery of the understanding of architecture as a discipline autonomous from actual projects and having its own principles generally became a common base for reflection in the schools, assuming specific nuances in each case.

In Barcelona, Rafael Moneo, educated in the School of Architecture of Madrid, but a professor at the School of Architecture in Barcelona in the 1970s, galvanized a group of young teachers with his mastery. Mentored by Moneo, a number of these young professors— Albert Viaplana and Helio Piñón, Elías Torres, Josep Llinás, Gabriel Mora, and a few others—are today the leaders of Catalan architecture. Moneo had experienced the final stage of the "modern adventure," but he had reacted with exceptional lucidity and agility during the "crisis of modern thought." As an elder brother to all, he conducted the so-called "disciplinary re-foundation" which began, in part, from the analysis of Aldo Rossi's philosophy. A working architect, as well as an exceptional teacher, Moneo became the symbol of a new era that might transcend the acute crisis of the modern tradition. If Moneo was inspired by foreign ideas, he used them according to his own point of view. (If one wishes to understand Spanish architecture, one should not forget the consequences of the country's will to understand its culture, traditional and contemporary. It is both a national and a local concern, a singular and a collective preoccupation with understanding itself.)

In Madrid, groups of young professors—among whom were Manuel de las Casas, J. M. López-Peláez, Gabriel Ruiz Cabrero, Javier Vellés, this author, and somewhat later, Juan Navarro Baldeweg—put together, little by little, a large and fragmented school following an orientation similar to that of Moneo's academy in Barcelona and based on the institutional authority of names of primary importance in the days of the "modern adventure": individuals like Antonio Fernández Alba or Francisco Javier Sáenz de Oiza. The inherent problems left at the end of the dictatorship and the beginnings of democracy in the late 1970s, together with the economic crises of those years, provoked a scholarly and critical school, active and libertarian, in which the vitality and instincts of the younger generation of professors, who were anxious to investigate and experiment with that which had been denied to them as students, generated an enormous and profound cultural growth in the teaching institutions. The discovery of and reflection on the totality of the architectural development of the twentieth century and of the history of architecture in general, as well as the recognition of architecture as an autonomous discipline, produced a built and scholarly body of work of important critical and theoretical depth locally and nationally. This notable achievement explains, in part, the awakened interest in contemporary Spanish architecture in the 1980s.

In Seville, Antonio Barrionuevo and Francisco Torres, Antonio Ortiz and Antonio Cruz, Guillermo Vázquez Consuegra, A. Trillo, and José Ramón Sierra, among others, came together in the school and in the city to reflect on emergent Rossian ideas, as well as to consider the culturally eclectic and professional orientation that Moneo had created in Barcelona. Madrid, Barcelona, and Seville in similar ways represented what was happening in Spain and they exemplified an architectonic philosophy of design and production that was built around the new interpretation of rationalism—that is, a version of the modern tradition that was especially esteemed as much in itself as in its method of incorporating the architect's contemporary concerns.

The Influence of "Tendenza"

In the Basque country and in Galicia, the new architectonic culture was not at first based in any school of architecture, but rather in the professional associations of architects. These centers represented more clearly, even schematically, the influence of Aldo Rossi and of the group that called itself "Tendenza" (including, among others, Giorgio Grassi, Massimo Scolari, and Manfredo Tafuri). Their influence fundamentally began after they were recognized at the XV Triennial of Milan in 1973. Another important group devolving from Rossi's thinking formed in Barcelona and expressed itself in the periodical *2C—The Construction of the City*.

Salvador Tarragó, director of the periodical *2C*, José Ignacio Linazasoro and Miguel Garay, organizers of the "Weeks of Architecture" at San Sebastián, and César Portela, a Gallegan architect who espoused the same ideas, synthesized an attitude that the rationalist tradition was the most important inheritance from the modern movement; at the same time they defended a contemporary classicism then in force, as well as the attention to the conscious relation between architecture and the city, and the value of a sense of place, or of tradition. It is this last context that gave body to an architecture of vernacular intent, in which the eclectic base of the principles of the Tendenza was reflected from the start, but manifested, however, in projects and concrete works, in the form of a pure adherence to the classical/rational line.

In the Spain of the 1970s, the ideas derived from Rossi's philosophy of architecture were the principal catalysts of the renewal of philosophy itself and, thus, of the principles held by the younger generation of architects who finished their schooling roughly between 1967 and 1973. To these must be added the singular and exceptional personality of Rafael Moneo (licensed in 1961) and, in Madrid, of Manuel de las Casas (licensed in 1964). Both of these architects represented, in their teaching and their professional works, the new way of understanding architecture that crystallized early on in the work of their younger colleagues. The architecture produced, however, was broader and more diverse. At the figurative extreme most opposed to the modern movement, the early work of the Basque architects José Ignacio Linazasoro and Miguel Garay, identified with the public school at Fuenterrabía (fig. 1), shows the impact of a contemporary classicism produced by voluntary reference to the work of Heinrich Tessenow, who had been rediscovered by the Italian architect Giorgio Grassi. The houses in the field of Galicia (fig. 2) by César Portela constitute a version of the classical/rational line, though favoring a neo-vernacular understanding of architecture. Both examples seem to transcend the modern movement, introducing a sophisticated treatment of an apparent (and non-existent) academic tradition.

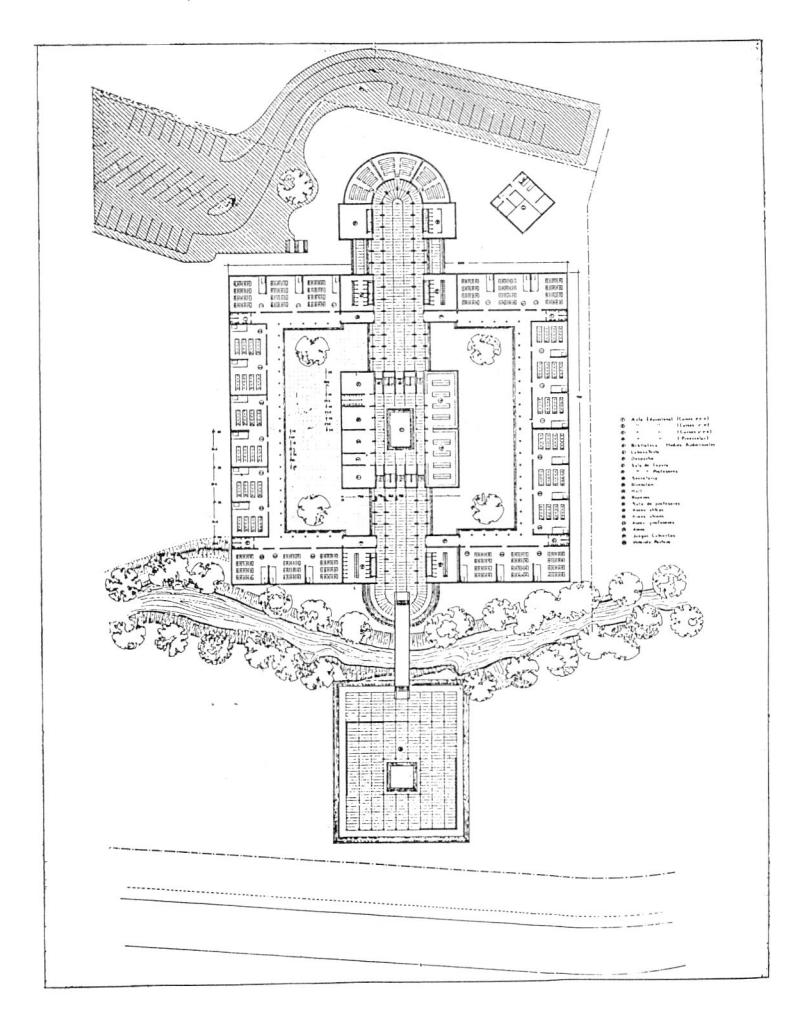

Fig. 1. José Ignacio Linazasoro and Miguel Garay. Public school, Fuenterrabía, Guipúzcoa, 1974-78. Plan.

Fig. 2. César Portela. Houses for gypsies, Campaño-Poio, Pontevedra, Galicia, 1971-75.

The Formation of Eclectic Rationalism

Although the capitals, some other centers, and the schools were distinct, as I have pointed out, in all their diversity they still shared similarities. Moneo's influence, as much in his teachings as in his evolution as an architect, extended one way or another to all locations, unifying broad but similar architectonic interests. Moneo and Bescós's Bankinter Building in Madrid (fig. 3) serves as a key to understanding the search for an architecture that broke with the immediate development of modernity. It demonstrated the rationalism that was believed to be the more vital and authentic part of modernism, and integrated it in its many different structural systems and its gestures, with diverse historical episodes of recent architectural history, both Spanish and foreign. The building alluded to Louis Sullivan and the Chicago School and to periods of Madrilene modernity before and after the Civil War in its use of the principles of "planar composition" as fulfillment of an urban expression of volume. But it also exemplified the ideas of Robert Venturi and, in a certain way, the poetic qualities of Alvar Aalto, taking an eclectic position that did not renounce either contemporaneity or pluralism. Nor did it renounce a relative continuity with the preceding "modern adventure."

The building became a complete emblem for the architects of the younger generation and for their students, an emblem that, like Moneo himself, tended to integrate the cultures of the different capitals, and an emblem of what would be the majority position of the new Spanish architecture for many years, that we can now define as "eclectic rationalism." Moneo himself would exhibit this quality in works such as the town hall of Logroño (fig. 4) or the National Museum of Roman Art in Mérida (fig. 5). Architects such as Manuel and Ignacio de las Casas in Madrid, Antonio Cruz and Antonio Ortiz in Seville, or Josep Llinás and Esteve Bonell in Barcelona were representative of this majority position, which produced a large number of notable buildings and projects. Brought together by their interest in the rationalist line of the modern movement, they shared in

Building in a New Spain: Contemporary Spanish Architecture

Fig. 3. Rafael Moneo and Ramón Bescós. Bankinter, Madrid, 1973-76. Elevation.

Fig. 4. Rafael Moneo. Town hall, Logroño, 1973-81. Interior of the vestibule.

a diffuse but nonetheless identifiable Spanish tradition of honest material construction, a fondness for pure composition, and the consequently simple, even schematic, form of expression. In the more immediate national tradition, the organicism practiced in the 1960s was rejected, unlike the rationalism of the 1950s, which invoked the memory of nationally renowned architects such as Francisco Cabrero or, even more so, Alejandro de la Sota. More remote architects such as Gunnar Asplund or Giuseppe Terragni were also sources of admiration, for they displayed the inspiration in history that Rossi had defended and advanced as an understanding of the discipline itself. A concern for the urban value of architecture was also born out of Rossi's philosophy, but this issue was applied to actual problems, and many times the architects returned to the very tradition that had already addressed these problems.

Perhaps the most significant works of the Casas brothers are their housing developments in Talavera de la Reina, Toledo (fig. 6), and in Palomeras, Madrid (fig. 7), because they represent both an important activity for architects within the capital—the construction of housing is oftentimes tied to the social politics of the state—and a certain austere and hard style, intensely synthetic and somewhat "metaphysical," which was identified with Madrid at that time (see fig. 8). The effort to demonstrate that the topic of collective housing is an important urban problem, including the idea of open building, appears in their works as much as in their typological investigations.

Of the works of Cruz and Ortiz, the housing development on the outskirts of Seville should be especially noted (fig. 9). There, the pursuit of modern architecture in its formal

Fig. 5. Rafael Moneo. National Museum of Roman Art, Mérida, 1980-84. Interior view.

Fig. 6. Manuel and Ignacio de las Casas. Housing development, Talavera de la Reina, Toledo, 1976-85.

Fig. 7. Manuel and Ignacio de las Casas. Housing development, Palomeras, Madrid, 1980-84.

components is compatible with the tradition and the logic of constructing around a patio (fig. 10). Like Moneo, of whom they are disciples, Cruz and Ortiz interpret rationalism broadly, and that broad definition permits them to operate in a stylistic arc that moves from loyalty to the "orthodox" rationalism of the 1920s to the "novecentismo" or moderate classicism of the pre-Civil War years. This intention should not be confused with a simple historicism, since it is an identification of architecture as a discipline capable of extracting from a selected past aspects appropriate for the project.

Josep Llinás's medical clinic (fig. 11), Esteve Bonell and Francesco Rius's velodrome in Barcelona (fig. 12), and Jaume Bach and Gabriel Mora's station in Bellaterra (fig. 13), all express clearly the "eclectic rationalism" of the young Catalan generation, always more inclined to the modern idiom and less to the "novecentista." This preference unified Moneo and many other architects of Madrid, Barcelona, and Seville in the practice of a common architecture that transcended geographies and local cultures, becoming, with all the variegations one would expect, "national." A great part of the Spanish architecture generated in this way appeared to constitute a certain school in force throughout the 1970s and 1980s, symbolized by the names and works already discussed, to such an extent that it tends to be confused with a particularly Spanish manner.

Fig. 8. Javier Frechilla, Carlos Herrero, José M. López-Peláez, Eduardo Sánchez and E. Rodríguez. Housing development, Palomeras, Madrid, 1982. Perspective drawing.

Fig. 9. Antonio Cruz and Antonio Ortiz. Patio of an apartment building, Seville, 1974-76. Preliminary perspective drawing.

Fig. 10. Antonio Cruz and Antonio Ortiz. Patio of an apartment building, Seville, 1974-76.

Fig. 11. Josep Llinás. Medical center (Centro de Asistencia Primaria or CAP), Ripollet, Barcelona, 1982-84.

The Influence of Venturi and the Leap to the Postmodern

To the enormous influence of Rossi's philosophy on his own direct disciples as well as on a broader majority position, which I have called "eclectic rationalism," we must add the important influence of Robert Venturi, which is reflected somewhat less in the works, at least directly, although it is present nevertheless. The thinking of both men had enormous importance for Spanish architects, as it replenished the very content of a discipline terribly devalued by the development of modernity, reduced to ideas of function, of technology, and of immediate social service. The recovery of architecture as a question of form and of composition, placing the idea of progress and the failures of the past in parentheses, and defending historical architecture as a source of wisdom, were discourses common to Rossi and Venturi. For Spanish architects they were important guides and supporters of their own sentiments, allowing them to eliminate some of the errors of their inheritance and to take advantage of the richness of their more recent tradition. Contemporary Spanish architecture resulted from this combination of issues, uniting its roots with the issues, including that which affects latent or apparently less represented previous trends. Venturi's influence, then, was complementary, and specifically important if we think of his insistence that architectonic languages are arbitrary conventions, or if we recall his belief in the density, complexity, and even permissiveness of the treatment of an image, and more generally, in the treatment of formal problems. This influence of richness and permissiveness can be detected in the works of Rafael Moneo or Manuel de las Casas. The profound introduction of Venturi's ideas, along with Rossi's philosophy, must be recognized in the collective culture of Spanish architecture. We can cite, nevertheless, some architects who early on responded to a more direct echo in the Venturian discourse. Among these, the most important is the team of Lluis Clotet and Oscar Tusquets, the youngest architects of the old "School of Barcelona" led by Oriol Bohigas. In the early years

Fig. 13. Jaume Bach and Gabriel Mora. Bellaterra Station, Barcelona, 1984.

of their careers they had an impact on the realism practiced by this group; influenced by Italian architecture, this represented in the 1960s the Catalan contribution to the development of the Spanish "modern adventure." But, after 1972, they would demonstrate a very radical attitude through a few small works, among which are the Belvedere Giorgina in Gerona (fig. 14) and the house on Pantelleria Island in Italy (fig. 15).

The Belvedere Giorgina—a work every bit as advanced as it was brilliant in the intellectual climate of the 1960s and 1970s—is a tiny, single-family dwelling in the country, a weekend refuge that confronts the difficulty of integration with the landscape and the appropriation of the image of a neoclassical "belvedere," the base of which contains the dwelling. This small and polemical work, loaded with

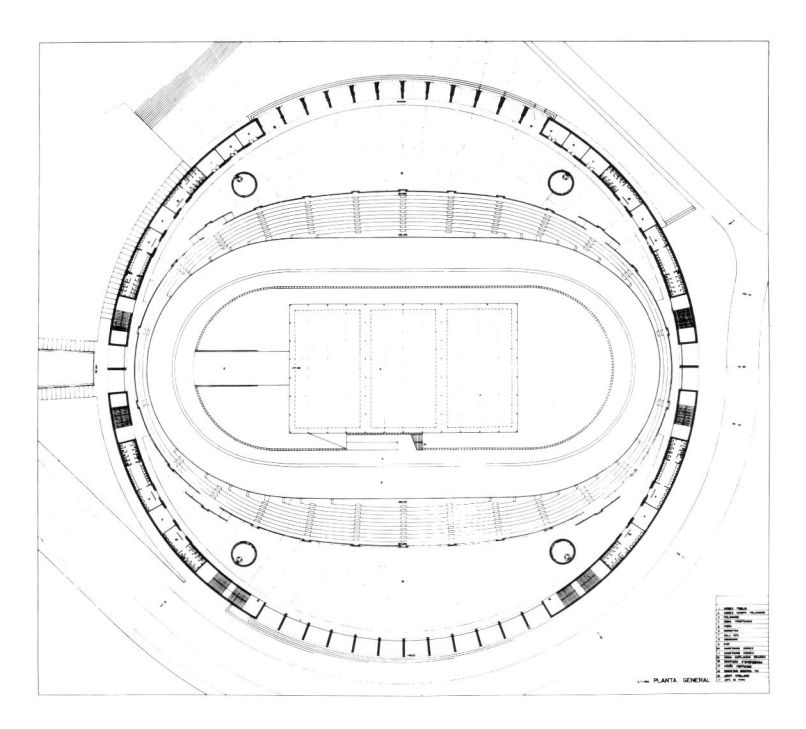

Fig. 12. Esteve Bonell and Francesc Rius. Velodrome, Vall d'Hebron, Barcelona, 1984. Plan.

conceptual ideas, signified immediately the sign of change in many things, as well as the attraction of the work of these architects. This was confirmed by the refuge in Pantelleria, also a very small house, this one facing the sea and similarly clothed in a columned image: the concrete pillars forming a pergola evoke, conceptually and figuratively, an Attic ruin. As designers of objects and personally sophisticated and attractive individuals, who, paradoxically, have been both influential and isolated, Clotet and Tusquets strengthened the scene we are sketching with their posture as lone gunmen. Their paths were later more diverse and separate: Oscar Tusquets was decidedly more inclined toward the kind of postmodern architecture exemplified by the Belvedere Giorgina; and Lluis Clotet followed more partisan paths closer to eclectic rationalism. Tusquet's restoration and expansion of the Palau de la Música Catalana in Barcelona, and Clotet's Bank of Spain in Gerona (done with Ignacio Paricio; see photographs and project description in Part II), show their more recent positions. It is inevitable at this point to refer to the work of Ricardo Bofill, without a doubt one of the most well known professionals outside of Spain and at the same time, one of the Spanish architects most foreign to Spanish culture. A member, in his day, of the School of Barcelona, following the leadership of Bohigas and the practice of realism, Bofill has developed a career in which he has explored the use of formal and figurative permissiveness, to the point of finally reaching the most extreme postmodern position on the national scene (see fig. 16). This was as much in relation to his indiscriminate use of historical languages as in his utilization of these languages; that is, the intention of architecture as pure scenography, a component quite foreign to the Spanish practice, which is generally tied to a certain linguistic asceticism and to the strong relation between form and construction material. His very different habits should explain the alienation between Bofill and the "intelligentsia" of Spanish architecture. The case of Bofill completes our panorama, demonstrating the plurality that would, in a very short time, complete a chapter that was born under the aegis of rational classicism and of the austere and intellectual "disciplinary recovery."

A Certain Modern Continuity

The reaction to the death rattle of organic modernity, Spanish and international, in the 1960s, expressed itself in the opposing paths of Rossianism or Venturianism; a willingness to compromise with history on a conceptual basis, as well as an attempt to do without a modern figurative legacy.

Several different influences shaped the basis for a way of thinking and of creating architecture in voluntary continuity with the original modernity; and these were the work of

Fig. 14. Lluis Clotet and Oscar Tusquets. Belvedere Giorgina, Gerona, 1971.

Alejandro de la Sota, the admiration awakened by a knowledge of the work of Terragni, and the brilliant contemporary example of a then-small North American group known as the "New York Five" (Peter Eisenman, John Hejduk, Michael Graves, Charles Gwathmey, and Richard Meier). This group directly opposed the practice of postmodernism (at least initially), and they were, in this way, similar to the eclectic rationalist group. By their existence, they give proof of the eclectic character of an architecture that was trying to find a new value for the discipline after the "late organic" excesses had diluted its content.

Attempting, at one extreme, to define the longevity of the rationalist tradition in a way that was dangerously close to the "aformal" utopia of Reyner Banham, and to trust in an architectural value of technology, the architecture of modern continuity became one of brilliant virtuosity, a sophisticated and attractive mannerism. Perhaps the best examples can be found in the works of Víctor López Cotelo and Carlos Puente (see, for example, the photographs and project description of the public library in Zaragoza in Part II), and to a lesser degree, Antonio Barrionuevo and Francisco Torres (see fig. 17) or Javier Vellés and María Luisa López Sardá (see fig. 18). At the other extreme, the

Fig. 15. Lluis Clotet and Oscar Tusquets. House on the Island of Pantelleria, Italy, 1973.

Fig. 16. Ricardo Bofill. Housing development, Montpellier, France, 1979-85. Detail.

continuity of the modern tradition derived from a plastic and compositional exploitation of the rational language it inherited. This exercise had a pure form, a mannerism of a distinct nature, but a mannerism nevertheless. A clarifying example may be seen in the work of Alberto Campo Baeza (see fig. 19).

This completed sketch shows the evolution of Spanish architecture from the early 1970s through most of the 1980s and the diverse situations that should be understood as resulting from a group that interrelated intensely—so intensely that it would be difficult to distinguish exactly the borders that separate some from others. Indeed, some of them seemed at times to leap back and forth across borders.

Neo-modernists and Figurativists

This explanation would not be complete, however, without highlighting the existence of a very important evolution that has arisen from the "re-foundation of the discipline" that gave origin to the aforementioned diversity. I refer to the most recent triumph of a group of people responsible for particular contemporary trends—those who have campaigned for the survival of the modern tradition, accepting its rupture with history and opposed to forcing a continuity; rather they wish to exploit its yet-untapped potential.

They started from the same examination of the discipline, just as their predecessors, having a similar point of departure as those architects we've seen group themselves around the symbol of eclectic rationalism. Yet, though their point of departure was similar, this group has been different in profile from the start; it includes Albert Viaplana and Helio Piñón, Elías Torres and José Antonio Martínez Lapeña, and Juan Navarro Baldeweg. Their collective position corresponds more to the international situation than to a specifically Spanish one. That is, they assumed a position in which eclectic rationalism barely existed as a compromise between tradition and modernity (as occurred especially in Spain) and which manifested itself as the point of departure between an alliance with the "postmodern" historicist scenographies or with the espousal, such as by this new group, of the new development of the modern tradition. To the names of the architects mentioned above I should add Enric Miralles, Javier Bellosillo, and the engineer-architect Santiago Calatrava.

Fig. 17. Antonio Barrionuevo and Francisco Torres. Sáenz House, Seville, 1976.

In general, these architects are affected by strong doses of conceptualism, by certain interpretations of the "minimal," and by the development of a modern language devoid of the ideas and connotations of the old vanguard. Some of their works also exhibit intentions that are reminiscent of organicism.

It could be said that, with all of these varieties, Spanish architecture offers an eclectic panorama of trends during the past fifteen or twenty years. These trends (buried in the interior of a culture that, though now noticeably more internationalized, always had a very strong sense of its own identity) refer to and succeed each other, influence each other, differ with or directly oppose each other. If these groups actually interrelated directly with what on the international scene came to be called "deconstruction," we cannot neglect, in the explanation of these "neo-modern" works, the significance of their voluntary opposition to the most sacred or experimental courses of the national architectural culture. That culture, if a clear distinction had been made between its richness and its ability to overcome the great cultural rut that the crisis of modern ideas signified, would have come to substitute the properly modern tradition with an eclectic, "novecentista" tradition.

It was a movement that was accused of compromise between tradition and modernity, of having too much affection for historicism, albeit "soft," and of seeming to anchor itself in the admiration of ideal architectures, such as those of the first third of the century, for instance, which reconciled classicism and the modern language.

If, however, the most attractive appearances of the neo-modern architectures belonged to the second period of the era we are analyzing here, e.g., from the beginning of the 1980s, then the most important personalities of these groups announced the future in the singularity of their earliest works.

Albert Viaplana and Helio Piñón began their careers in Barcelona with some "Venturian" experiences, e.g., the Jiménez de Parga house (with Gabriel Mora), in which an extreme degree of complexity and formal abstraction stands out. An apartment building in Barcelona (1977), of original character, but modest and disciplined, insinuates a no less

Fig. 18. Javier Vellés and María Luisa López Sardá. Umbráculo (pergola), Cercedilla, Madrid, 1976-79.

Fig. 19. Alberto Campo Baeza. School, Madrid, 1985. Interior view.

abstract and conceptualist path, which they developed in numerous competitions. Some of these projects were for parks or open spaces, and the implicit liberty of such opportunities allowed them a wide degree of formal experimentation, now taken to a "minimal" conceptualist level and to the elaboration of a vocabulary of unconventional formal elements. The plaza of the Sants Station in Barcelona (fig. 20) has been, in this respect, their most significant work.

José Antonio Martínez Lapeña and Elías Torres, also from Barcelona, began their careers in eclectic rationalism with a certain continuity with the assumptions of realism of the group surrounding Oriol Bohigas in the 1960s. Their posture evolved more and more toward a modern, neo-organic, and figurativist one, alert to the important value of the most superficial, to the formal liberty and to the imagination and the elimination of conventions. Their work can reflect the various influences of Alvar Aalto, the more organic and permissive José Antonio Coderch, the architect Josep Jujol (the disciple of Gaudí), the Portuguese Alvaro Siza Vieira, and the American Frank Gehry. The works in which they best expressed their creative form are the small stores, the free restoration of a chapel in Ibiza (1982-85; fig. 21), or in the small park of Villa Cecilia (Barcelona, 1986).

Juan Navarro Baldeweg of Madrid presents a completely singular profile. He is an investigator of form (see fig. 22), a conceptual artist and "minimalist," linked through a four-year stay at MIT with North American art—and actually a painter of high quality. He became known after two of his projects won competitions sponsored by *Japan Architect* magazine. One project was his House for an Intersection (1976), and the other was the House for Schinkel (1979); in both, the architecture was heavily weighted with ideas.

In these houses can be discovered the pretexts for his large-scale, more involved constructions such as the Hydraulics Museum (fig. 23) at the watermills in Murcia (1983-88) and in the Municipal Center for Social Services at the Puerta de Toledo (Madrid, 1985-88). His career as architect has been developing into one of the most brilliant and esteemed on the national scene, but his position, past and present, is not as radical as that of the architects previously discussed. His work shows a closeness to mainstream Modernism, including eclectic rationalism. His admiration for the works of Asplund, Aalto, and Siza Vieira should also be noted.

Diversity and Development of Spanish Architecture

Contemporary Spanish architecture has thus run, through the last two decades, a long and difficult course. On this

Fig. 20. Albert Viaplana and Helio Piñón. Sants Station plaza (Plaça dels Països Catalans), Barcelona, 1982-89.

Fig. 21. José Antonio Martínez Lapeña and Elías Torres. Restoration of a chapel, L'Hospitalet, Ibiza, 1982-85. Interior view.

course it negated in part (and, in part, continued) that which its elders had begun during the two preceding decades, having in common with them an enthusiastic and even passionate eclecticism that can be considered traditional, but without ever pursuing a true modernism. In addition, they had a passionate confidence in the values of architecture.

From the primitive idea of the recovery of the discipline to the most recent realization of the neo-modern trend, a complete panorama has developed, complete in the sense that we can offer a diagram (fig. 24) that may explain graphically the interrelationships within contemporary Spanish architecture.

The majority trend, eclectic rationalism, represents the compromise between tradition and modernism, a trend broad also in the sense of embracing a wide spectrum of neighboring tendencies at the borders. This majority movement is represented by the works of Rafael Moneo; the Catalans Bonell, Llinás, and Bach and Mora; the Sevillians Cruz and Ortiz, Vázquez Consuegra, and Barrionuevo and Torres; and of the Madrilenes, such figures as the Casas brothers, Estanislao Pérez Pita and Jerónimo Junquera, and Javier Frechilla and J. M. López-Peláez.

We can then situate "traditionalism," if by that we mean the architecture that, like the previous trend, manifested itself according to modern inheritance and a greater affinity for the recovery of classicism and historical principles. Here we might have Linazasoro, Portela, Manuel Iñiguez and Alberto Ustarroz, and those who radically interpreted the ideas of Aldo Rossi.

Postmodernism, understood in the international, specifically North American, sense will be represented by some works of Tusquets or Bofill—that is, those who have used history, not for its principles but as scenography, as language.

If we look to still another style related to eclectic rationalism, we can situate the "Modern tradition"

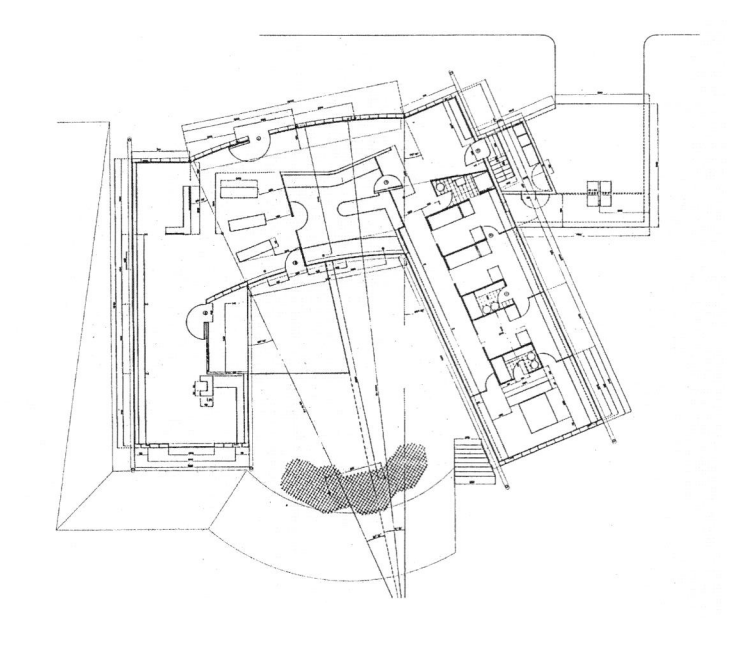

Fig. 22. Juan Navarro Baldeweg. House of Rain, Santander, 1979. Plan.

Fig. 23 Juan Navarro Baldeweg. Hydraulics Museum, Murcia, 1983-88. Interior.

directly opposite the postmodern, and give as examples the works of López Cotelo and Puente, Campo Baeza and Jordi Garcés and Enric Sòria. "Neo-modernism," which I have defined by works such as those of Navarro Baldeweg or of Piñón and Viaplana, would lie directly opposite traditionalism. Finally, in opposition to eclectic rationalism, we can note what I have called "figurativism" or 'neo-organicism," as expressed by the works of Torres and Martínez Lapeña, Calatrava, or Javier Bellosillo.

This schematic picture, if we take into account an eclecticism that embraces all the possibilities that its name implies, permits us an understanding of Spanish architecture as a unique and interrelated culture. Some of the bases, the constants, let us say, of this culture stand out. Among these is a constructive preoccupation or, if one likes, an intense relation between construction and form which characterizes practically all the tendencies of Spanish architecture, which is itself always conceived to be realized and never to be spent on a "paper architecture," no matter how ambitious and subtle the formal objective. These characteristics, the strong relation with the construction and the pre-meditated realism, are traditional characteristics and are complementary but different.

Another widespread habit regarding the use of forms and languages, intensely intended but spare of expression, can also be observed. It is affected by a voluntary economy of formal means, including tendencies to the "minimalist." This particular tradition is, as well, an equally strong descendant of modernism.

The now-apparent eclectic condition is another of its principal characteristics, along with the strong relationship between its trends, schools, and individuals that influence and answer each other, configuring an independent unity, complete and unique, within Western culture. Perhaps this can indirectly explain the unitarian Spanish sociology as it can be directly explained by the strong interdependence of working professionals whose relationships continue to be intense in the schools and through publications.

Nevertheless, it may be that this is also a merely traditional characteristic and that Spanish architecture will, over time, lose the unity and independence that has characterized its past (the beginning of understanding itself as part of a specifically Western culture). Still, this characterization prevails more than is usually thought, or more than can be shown in this brief review.

Eclectic rationalism
reason
discipline
composition
construction
city
diversity

Modern tradition
functionalism
modern language
modern construction
international style
spatialism

Traditionalism
history
type
academic
classic
vernacular
place

Neo- Modern
minimalism
conceptualism
stylism
idea
expansion of modern language

Post- Modern
scenography
historical language
emblem
image
caricature

Figurativism or neo- organic
formalism
naturalism
painting
sculpture
biological analogy
cult of the surface

Fig. 24. Antón Capitel. Schematic diagram of contemporary Spanish architecture, 1971-92.

The Architecture of Democratic Spain

Victor Pérez Escolano

Transformations of an Historic Period

In 1936 General Francisco Franco led a military coup against the Second Spanish Republic, sinking the country into a terrible civil war. During the almost forty years of his dictatorship, Spain reflected the important changes that were occurring internationally. Although Franco avoided openly entering the Second World War, his fascist policies and the Allied victory kept Spain relatively isolated from what was happening in Europe and America. Even after the Franco government was recognized by the United States during the presidency of General Eisenhower, Spain was slow to join the capitalist economic system and establish economic plans for technological development that was consistent with Western goals. Gradually, it allowed a more liberal cultural and professional permissiveness, and only at the end of the period was there a slight opening up of the political system, largely as a result of a tough, militant, anti-Franco struggle, an opposition fervently supported by the Communist party. Thus, the authoritarian regime that had survived the defeat of the Axis in 1945 little by little overcame its autocracy and absorbed the values of the free-market system of economy, later adding traces of freedom. These acts, along with the restoration of the monarchy in the figure of Juan Carlos I, prepared the country for a change; other acts, such as the assassination of Franco's right-hand man Admiral Carrero Blanco by the Basque terrorist group known as the ETA, exemplified a model of political transition that the majority of the country, including the Communists, opposed.

When General Franco died in November 1975, all of Spain (with the sad exception of the ETA) entered a process of pacific, social reconciliation and democratic development that was formalized in the new constitution of 1978. The first article of this constitution established fundamental democratic principles. The second article, while declaring the indissoluble unity of the Spanish nation, recognized and guaranteed the autonomous rights of the various nationalities and regions within Spain. Together, these main articles gave Spain its democratic, but "federalist," structure, ensuring solidarity among its autonomous provinces. The beginning of the 1980s witnessed the consolidation of the system, through the promulgation of new laws of autonomy of the nationalities and regions, the almost complete transference of powers that were to rest in the hands of these regional governments, and the subsequent elections that marked the sharing of power among different political parties.

To these internal factors must be added one external factor to understand better the path of recent Spanish architecture. The transition from dictatorship to parliamentary monarchy coincided with the serious effects of the 1973 oil crisis. The world economy suffered through difficult years, the consequences of which were felt in Spain until the end of the 1970s. Meanwhile, Spain became a member of the European Economic Community, which in 1992 will welcome free trade and free movement of people in all their productive and consumer activities. This economic unification, the preamble of a long-desired, but difficult, political unity of Europe, has been surprised on the eve of its accomplishment by recent events in Eastern Europe, the crisis of the socialist model of the Communist regimes, even now within the USSR itself, and the startling reunification of Germany. The European community is sure to experience a decade of major readjustment in the 1990s.

Urban and Regional Impact of Democratic Institutions

Spain, then, is constituted as a nation of autonomous regions; while the national government is responsible for certain public programs like the national highway system, some national museums, and the national theater restoration program, many other projects and decisions rest in the hands of the regional governments. During the 1980s, Spain developed a very large body of institutions and policies directly related to architecture and urban and regional planning, especially in regard to new laws, commissions, and financial agencies that have an enormous impact on the appearance of present-day Spain. Certain initiatives concerning areas of physical transformation were undertaken during Franco's dictatorship. It is enough to remember, for example, the efforts that were realized in relation to the primary sector of the economy, the improvement of agriculture in rural communities, and important advances in hydraulic engineering and water resources, with corresponding architectural efforts that achieved some notable successes. Equally, in the area of urban housing, promoted by the state institutions, architects had a central role, as much in the politics as in the management and design. Important works resulted, both quantitatively and qualitatively, which might constitute a series of the best examples of Spanish architecture of the 1950s and 1960s. Among the architects still active who participated in these projects are two of the patriarchs of the current panorama of Spanish architecture, Alejandro de la Sota and Francisco Javier Sáenz de Oiza, both of whom began their careers with housing projects or with public housing initiated by the government. Together with these works, others for the central government, such as the 1949 offices for the official trade unions in Madrid (designed by Francisco Cabrero and Rafael Aburto), represented a certain line of innovative architectural production that ran parallel to the historicism or populism that by-and-large characterized the regime.

Centralism remained the most apparent characteristic of the Franco era, and the official architecture and urban planning were produced according to this system, although specific operations, such as postwar reconstruction and recolonization, were carried out through decentralized technical services. Nevertheless, the one factor that was considered was the municipal tradition, which, even within a political framework, offered some urban competitions and public services that allowed the development of significant architectural practice. The municipal housing developments might be seen as an example of this work, even though the common denominators of this system, especially during the last decade of the regime, would reflect the absurd growth of our cities, and the destruction of the urban architectural heritage of so many historic villages and of the natural heritage of our coasts, as these were submitted to a savage

Fig. 1. José Luis R. Noriega and Emilio Tuñón. Teatro de Rojas, Toledo, 1984. Interior view.

tourist expoitation. One must not forget, however, that the incipient action of clandestine political organizations, citizen's movements, and professional organizations (particulary the associations of architects) united in their critique of the system and in the creation of a specific political culture that supported the rise of leftist efforts in numerous administrations, especially in municipalities after the 1979 elections.

Between the promulgation of the new Constitution in 1978 and the overwhelming victory of the Spanish Socialist Worker party in the general elections of 1982, the actions of the new democracy had its first effects within the architectural sector. The governments and parliaments of the regional autonomies assumed substantial power previously held by the central authority. As the 1980s progressed, a profound judicial and administrative transformation occurred, with a mark of particular relevance to everything related to publicly funded architecture. The central administration saw its power, and consequently its economic authority, drastically reduced. Its accommodation to the new state of affairs followed along predetermined lines, for example, in the grand cultural outfitting of museums, perhaps the most eloquent example being Rafael Moneo's

National Museum of Roman Art in Mérida, or in the systematic restoration of ancient theaters all over Spain with excellent results, such as the Teatro de Rojas in Toledo (fig. 1) by J.L. Rodríguez Noriega and Emilio Tuñón, the Principal in Zamora by Javier Vellés, and the Falla in Cádiz by J.A. Carvajal and J. Daroca, or, finally, in the construction of new auditoriums, such as those by the architect García de Paredes in Madrid, by Sáenz de Oiza in Santander (fig. 2), or by Juan Navarro Baldeweg in Salamanca (see photographs and project description in Part II). Some of these works were actually produced during the period of the transfer of power, and they constituted a kind of swan song of state activity by Madrid, if not an initiation of new modes of cooperation with the autonomous regional administrations. The emblematic role of architecture assumed by the new state can be broken down into the three levels—central, regional, and local—with decided actions in many areas which can demonstrate the contribution of public architecture in Spain in the 1980s (see fig. 3). Each administration confronted, with greater or lesser success, the demand for comprehensive programs in health, education, and social services; in the new administrative services for sports and popular culture; and in the historic preservation of architectural heritage, whether in public spaces or in the design of new seats of democratic power. In addition, other areas of the government (the treasury, the armed forces, and

Fig. 2. Francisco Javier Sáenz de Oiza. Festival Auditorium, Santander, 1984-91.

Fig. 3. Victor López Cotelo and Carlos Puente. Town hall, Valdelaguna, Madrid, 1983-86.

the television and communication commissions) have been particularly relevant. For example, the central state bank, the Bank of Spain, has produced a new chapter in the history of its architecture, from the proposal for the expansion of its headquarter in Madrid by Rafael Moneo (fig. 4) to the realization of new and excellent provincial centers in cities like Gerona by Lluís Clotet and Ignacio Paricio (see photograph and project description in Part II).

The municipal councils, provincial administrations, autonomous governments, and the national parliamentary bodies, under formulas of cooperation and assistance, have counted on architecture for the betterment of everyday life or for solutons to exceptional challenges. The results have been uneven, but numerous examples of unequivocal quality could well represent the decade of work. These architectural achievements usually form part of a strategic plan, which may involve planning and policy decisions affecting innovative urban planning efforts, the coordinated modernization of the country's obsolescent highway, railway, seaport, and airport systems, and other copious investments in communication networks that have been long deficient in comparison with the rest of Europe. If we add to this the challenges represented by other areas of planning, such as the updating of the land-use laws in the coastal regions and, to a lesser degree, in the major river valleys, we can understand how a fistful of examples of good architecture are but the visible face, albeit beautiful, of an extraordinarily complex body of work that largely goes unseen. Another consideration must be added here. The general operations represented by ordinary planning, regulated by the common factors of the regions and cities of Spain, have been complemented by what could be considered a string of concerted strategies at an exceptional time, an era of extraordinary events planned for 1992: the Olympic Games in Barcelona, the World's Fair in Seville, and the designation of Madrid as the cultural capital of Europe. These three commitments, without doubt of varying magnitude and significance, have propelled Spain to modernize quickly and become a full member of the European community.

Municipal Governments and Architecture

The potential for the development of public architecture in Spain gained its strength following the 1979 elections, when the leftist parties (particularly PSOE and PSE) conbined to win control of municipal governments in almost all the important cities and in a majority of the smaller owns and cities of Spain. From a political point of view, these 1979 results foreshadowed what would happen three years later in the national elections, which proved to be an overwhelming victory for the Socialists. We can consider these political victories a preamble to the decade of the 1980s, a new era of urban and architectural cultue in Spain. Perhaps not all municipal governments experienced a similar trajectory, but it was, in general, a time of optimim and euphoria, with a willingness to confront the problems of the quality of social life. With a euphoria typical of the founding moments of a new era, new policies were established to satisfy old needs such as solutions to chronic infrastructure problems, the demands for basic urban services (especially for the disadvantaged), and the regulation of speculative building financed by the private sector.

Fortunately, there appeared at this time, by way of Italy, a much-needed alternative to the message of urban opulence which had dominated the Western world in the 1960s. The tendencies of neo-capitalist success with its emphasis on renovation and its sometimes savage substitution was challenged by an excellent analytical and suggestive line of investigation on the significance of historic centers that was most effectively represented by two books: Aldo Rossi's *The Architecture of the City* (1966) and the practical guide to the city of Bologna (1973) by P. L. Cervelatti and R. Scannarini. Aldo Rossi established strong followings in Barcelona, Galicia, and Andalusia. The patrimonial cities of Spain found, throughout Europe, great examples of the partnership of economic and urban interests that favored cultural heritage. These examples demonstrated the formulas for success, whether in the conservation of monuments, or in the rehabilitation of architecture and urban spaces, as well as different methods of intervention (under the auspices of the

Fig. 4. Rafael Moneo. Proposal for the expansion of the central offices of the Bank of Spain, Madrid, 1980. Model.

rules of restoration, for example, or a sensitivity to how one constructs over the constructed), which so ably joined the dialogue between inherited architecture and new architecture.

This new urban movement had as its flagship Barcelona, the Spanish city that was most open to Europe even in Franco's time. Following study groups such as the Urban Planning Laboratory at the School of Architecture in Barcelona, the city was able to put in place two valuable instruments that would give it an advantage in facing issues related to urban architecture: the Metropolitan Master Plan and the designation of important municipal historic districts. To these, Barcelona was fortunate to add the imaginative and brilliant implementation of plans at the hand of Oriol Bohigas, who headed the municipal team established by the city's mayors as the Department of Architecture and Urban Planning. Bohigas's discourse was skillful, coherent, and, finally, hegemonic in the new Spanish urban concert. Barcelona was a complete city, endowed with the financial means to realize urban designs that Franco-era infrastructural engineering had omitted. New plazas, enclaves, and streets defined the character of the city, with architecture that emphasized the modern urban European condition, while satisfying the need for services and facilities that it was deficient in. Through a plan that was defined by some as enlightened despotism, Bohigas gave play to the best architects, who, in the previous years, had been forced to keep their professional and cultural talents hidden.

The declared objectives to transform Barcelona have met with extraordinary good fortune. No other example of urban commitment in Spain has achieved, even remotely, the success and publicity of Barcelona. Many books and magazines, together with other official initiatives, have disseminated the ideas and municipal accomplishments. Bohigas has expressed it in texts written over many years with eloquent and polemical phrases: he declared in 1981, for example, that "urban planning is not possible" and that all urban action should be called "public works." More recently, in his conversations with Oscar Tusquets published under the title *Dialegs a Barcelona* (1986), he has reiterated the principles of Barcelona's established directives: "the reconstruction of the built city" would encompass the water's edge, the contact with the mountain, Montjuïc, the area around the transit stations, the communications system, the service infrastructure, and much more, down to the most minute problems. The city has sought to incorporate professionals in tune with the new horizons of urban design, dedicated to recovering the themes of urban tradition, the treatment of public space, of monuments, and of public parks.

This orientation bore fruit in numerous places throughout Barcelona during the decade. To cite only the ones favored by Bohigas: the Plaça del Països Catalans in front of the Sants Station (Albert Viaplana and Helio Piñón), the Industrial Park of Spain (Luis Peña Ganchegui), the Moll de la Fusta by Manuel de Solà-Morales (fig. 5), the Palmera Plaza (by a municipal team headed by Pedro Barragán and Bernardo de Solà), the restoration of the Plaza Real (Federico Correa and Alfonso Milá), the gardens of Villa Cecilia (Elías Torres and José Antonio Martínez Lapeña), and Picasso Street (Roser Amadó and Lluís Domènech). Others that could be added are the small plazas in the Gracia district (Jaune Bach and Gabriel Mora), the reconversion of the Via Julia (by the municipal team with de Solà and Julía), the Bach de Roda-Felipe II bridge (Santiago Calatrava), the coverings of Parets (Enric Miralles and Carme Pinós), and the Creueta del Coll Park (Josep Martorell, Oriol Bohigas, and David Mackiy).

The new master plans of the 1980s exhibited these principles: first, that the various "projects" were points of departure for a city "as it should be"; second, that these projects made a political contribution through their ability to shape the city; third, that they would overcome the disconnection between plan and actualization; and fourth, that they would incorporate a new, broader concept of public works, superannuating the conventional reduction to highway systems. This change of focus toward the idea of what a city "should be" was especially important in the Master Plan of Madrid, created by the team led by Eduardo Leira and promoted by Eduardo Mangada during the mayoral tenure of Enrique Tierno Galván. Recognized as exemplary among plans of the period, it opposed the social segregation of the city's center along with zoning ordinances that restricted residential development in the central city, and it favored the reduction of inequalities through provisions for new social services and accessibility, and it favored publicly held land and the protection of the city's architectural heritage. It was a leftist plan imbued with the general characteristics of the moment. While the circumstances of each municipality would lead it to assumptions and emphases of one or another aspects of the model, the common denominator, nonetheless, was that, finally, almost all municipalities realized that they had to be the catalyst for these urban projects, as the expression of an alternative vocation of the new municipal urbanism.

In the first professional Spanish publication on the theme of new municipal urban planning (the September-October 1981 issue of *Arquitectura*), the first projects in Barcelona that appear are the volumetric ordering of open space, office buildings, residences, and historic buildings in the neighborhood of Raval known as the Seminary Lyceum by Lluís Clotet and Oscar Tusquets; and the new ordering of the Paseo de Colón and the Plaza de Palacio by Manuel de Solà-Morales for the Moll de la Fusta. The latter two works reveal the strategic plan to rebuild the city and open it to the sea. In the same publication, Seville offered other magnificent works revealing future intentions and difficulties: the project designed by Guillermo Vázquez Consuegra for the Plaza de la Encarnación, which political jealousies were to frustrate, is an example of a series of planned interventions in that historic city; and the new partial plan of Pino Montano by Antonio Cruz and Antonio Ortiz altered the polygonal model of blocks in favor of perimeter streets and a type of housing with ample courtyards for communal use, plans that were immediately executed in apartment buildings by the Sierra brothers (see fig. 6), and by Antonio Barrionuevo and Francisco Torres, among others.

During the 1980s the Spanish economy became more robust, with positive GNP figures, partially as a result of liberal policies similar to those of more developed countries, that were paradoxically put into practice by the Socialist governments. This economic upturn permitted the realization of the more ambitious objectives of public investment, as much through the ordinary channels as through strategies of an extraordinary nature. For example, the idea of a lasting urban economic crisis that assumed that our cities would not grow was overthrown. The politics of the construction of public housing had suffered a loss of vigor that was recovered immediately in many cities; in Seville and Cádiz, Guillermo Vázquez Consuegra realized developments of extraordinary quality (see fig. 7), and in Madrid there were many examples in districts such as Palomeras, with projects by Manuel and Ignacio de las Casas and the team of Javier Frechilla and J. M. López-Peláez (see fig. 8), and at Carabanchel, by Luis Peña Ganchegui, Cruz and Ortiz, and the de las Casas brothers, and along the borders of the M-30 highway with the most polemical of the housing developments created by Francisco Javier Sáenz de

Fig. 5. Manuel de Solà-Morales. Renovation of the wharf area known as Moll de la Fusta, Barcelona, 1985-88.

Fig. 6. José Ramón Sierra and Ricardo Sierra. Housing blocks in Pino Montano, Seville, 1981-84. Perspective drawing.

Building in a New Spain: Contemporary Spanish Architecture

Oiza. In a number of new urban works or "new towns," one common feature has been the will to emphasize their location, to endow them with an identifiable character, for example, occasionally of a certain classicized style (such as in the French housing projects of Ricardo Bofill), when not reminiscent of the anti-modern urbanism of the 1930s and 1940s.

Public space, at many different levels, was the principal architectural objective during the 1980s. The initiative of the government of Barcelona and its public acceptance became contagious in an extraordinary way in numerous Catalan towns and in Spain in general. The small Ampurdanese town of Ullastret, Gerona (fig. 9), that was planned by José Luis Mateo in collaboration with Carlos Fuente, or the Plaza del Castillo of Santa Coloma de Queralt in Tarragona by J. M. Rovira, or the Besòs Park in Sant Adrià de Besòs in Barcelona by Albert Viaplana and Helio Piñón, are notable examples of public work on different scales of space. Similarly, this has been echoed in other Spanish cities, for example, in Zaragoza, where, in the very large and difficult spaces of the plazas of Pilar and de la Seo (fig. 10), Ricardo Usón and J. M. Pérez Latorre, respectively, have created some of the most courageous projects to date. Scale reaches its greatest potential, however, in Catalonia: in Lérida the public work has been decisive in the configuration of the city's historic center, for in the project of El Canyeret (fig. 11), designed by Roser Amadó and Lluís Domènech, the great retaining wall (547 meters long and almost 22 meters high) and the tower of the funicular that vertically connects the upper and lower parts of the city, along with other works, create a landscape of exemplary value, perhaps unique in the last half of this century "among comparable treatments of historic areas in Europe," according to Ignasi de Solà-Morales.

A completely different example on a grand scale is the so-called Garden of Túria in Valencia, created in a dry river bed that runs through the city. This project was spearheaded by Mayor Ricard Pérez Casado, and its execution, beset with difficulties and not a few frustrations, covered the whole decade of the 1980s.

Fig. 7. Guillermo Vázquez Consuegra. Housing development, Cádiz, 1986-91.

The overall plan was done by the architectural firm of Ricardo Bofill, and it elicited national and international attention because of his well-known personality. Nevertheless, only two sections were built according to the classicist ideas of his "atelier" (see fig. 12). The remaining sections were reinterpreted or simply abandoned. The most brilliant example, produced in a section designed by the Valencian team of Vetges Tu i Mediterrania, evoked a certain presence of water that had also motivated Santiago Calatrava's design for the neighboring Ninth of October Bridge.

After decades of disinterest and abandonment, urban rivers, like the waterfronts, are having a special impact on the renewal of the cities of Spain. In addition to Valencia, other cities with rivers are undertaking projects, such as Córdoba

74

or Seville on the Guadalquivir, or along the embankments of the Ebro in Zaragoza, or in the planning of the left bank of the Tormes in Salamanca. These building programs are frequently the result of architectural competitions, with modifications required by the water authority. On the other hand, the character of a maritime city is excellently shown in the old and beautiful almost-island that is Cádiz. Its maritime coast is being systematically reworked, with successes and some frustrations: the chromatic treatment of the facades facing the sea, by A. Cabrera and O. Rodríguez, the unfortunate abandonment of a projected auditorium by Juan Navarro Baldeweg, or the rehabilitation of the sea-wall area known as the Baluarte de la Candelaria as the Maritime Museum, designed by Cruz and Ortiz (see Solà-Morales, fig. 4).

Other examples of strategic urban interventions could be cited in which symbolic will is expressed very directly. The internationally known sculptor Eduardo Chillida has contributed to a series of urban projects: *The Comb of the Wind* in the Plaza del Tenis (fig. 13; done in collaboration with the architect Luis Peña Ganchegui), the end of the Concha Beach in San Sebastián, and the Monument to Tolerance at the edge of the Guadalquivir in Seville on the site where the Inquisition had its castle.

Occasionally and less desirably, the large scale transcends the strictly urban framework. It seems logical that this should happen in Galicia, where a project in a natural environment was well planned and completed by the Galician government. This occurred with the magnificent work on the mount of Santa Tegra, at the mouth of the Miño River, a true geographic and historic landmark of Galicia. The project was conceived by a team led by César Portela, the architect of interventions of great synthesis with the surrounding landscape, such as the Carballeira de Santa Miña in Brión, La Coruña (fig. 15), or on the island of San Simón in the Vigo estuary.

Nationalities and Regions in Progress

While their administrative reforms have not overcome some of the asphyxiating bureaucratic vices, the autonomous governments have produced beneficial effects in their attention to public works. Public health, the bastion of social politics, still represents the principal measure of the power of the state in general and of the autonomous communities. Some of the autonomous governments have made great efforts in particular areas of public health service such as primary care. During the 1980s a large body of works were built in towns and in the heavily populated neighborhoods of cities—hundreds of centers dedicated to supplying the residents' most immediate medical needs, whether in Catalonia or in Madrid, in Andalusia or in Navarra, in the Basque country or in the Valencian community. Excellent examples of clinic architecture in Catalonia include centers for primary care (CAP) by some of the better architects, such as those in Mora la Nova, Tarragona, by Jordi Garcés and Enric Sòria, Sant Hipólit de Voltrega by Albert Viaplana and Helio Piñón, or in Ripollet, Barcelona, by Josep Llinás. Larger buildings include the hospital of Mora d'Ebre, Tarragona, by Elías Torres and

Fig. 8. Javier Frechilla, José M. López Peláez, and various architects. Housing in Palomeras, Madrid, 1981-83.

Fig. 9. José Luis Mateo with Carlos Fuente. Plaza of the church, Ullastret, Gerona, 1982-85.

Fig. 10. José M. Pérez Latorre. Plaza de la Seo, Zaragoza, 1989-91.

Fig. 11. Roser Amadó and Lluís Domenech. El Canyeret, Lérida, 1982-90.

José Antonio Martínez Lapeña. Some of the best architects have worked in the Basque country and in Navarra as well: for example, José Ignacio Linazasoro in Segura, Guipúzcoa, or Manuel Iñiguez and Alberto Ustarroz in Lesaka, Navarra.

But it could be said that health care architecture has been eclipsed, in a certain measure, by educational buildings, that other great arena of public intervention in the fundamental needs of society. In educational architecture one would have to choose the Catalan examples of Bach and Mora (at Torre Balldonna, Santa Coloma de Gramenet); and Enric Miralles and Carme Pinós's conversion of a factory into the La Llauna school in Badalona (see Solà-Morales, fig, 6); or among the "ikastolas" (Basque language schools) of the Basque country, the pioneering example of Hondarrabia, Guipúzcoa (fig. 14), by Miguel Garay and J. I. Linazasoro. Other smaller service buildings, such as cemeteries, markets, or basic administrative offices, have met the needs of democratic societies.

Because of their importance, nationally and internationally, Spain's public museums have not been totally handed over to the regional governments, and this situation has at times led to conflicts. Nonetheless, some exceptions should be pointed out: in Barcelona—where the museums are of municipal origin—Jordi Garcés and Enric Sòria (the architects also of the extraordinary reconstruction of the Museum of Navarra in Pamplona; see photographs and project description in Part II) produced brilliant works during these years, such as the Science Museum or the extension of the Picasso Museum; and in Madrid, where there are national museums such as the Prado. Those regional governments that have been most sensitive to the contemporary figurative culture have known how to face the challenges with positive results. Beyond the Mérida and Navarra museums, we must note three very significant examples of buildings for art. First by chronological order, ambition, and result, is the Valencian Institute of Modern Art, with its Julio González Center, designed by Emilio Giménez and Carlos Salvadores; second, F. J. Sáenz de Oíza's Atlantic Center of Modern Art in Las Palmas; and, third, the hope of the magnificent project for the Galician Center of

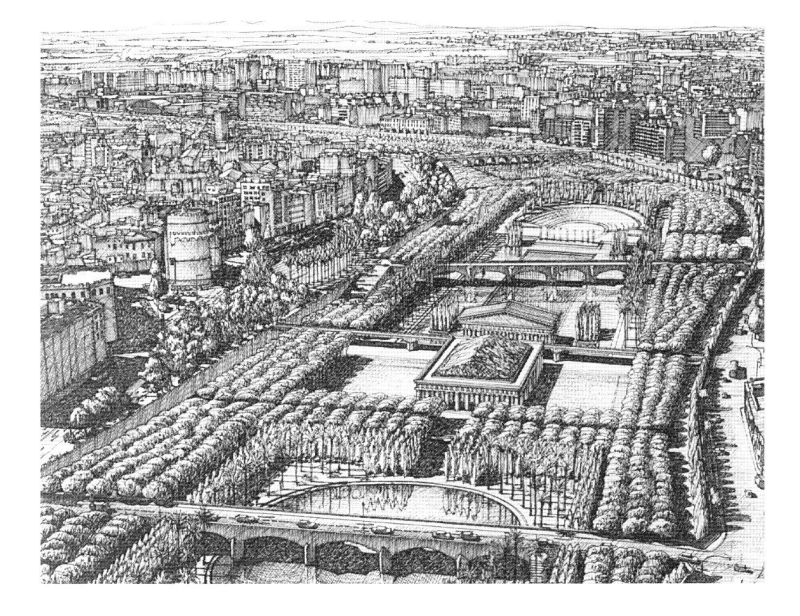

Fig. 12. Ricardo Bofill and Taller de Arquitectura. Garden of Túria, Valencia. Sections 10 and 11. Bird´s-eye view drawing.

Contemporary Art by Alvaro Siza Vieira in Santiago de Compostela.

The autonomous regions of democratic Spain, however, have also had to face the need for new institutions, such as regional executive government seats and corresponding legislatures. The autonomous parliaments have given architects numerous opportunities for essays of varying focus and quality. Frequently historic structures have been reused and adapted so that the region's governmental functions take place in buildings of appropriately noble character and monumentality, although this may require innovations and expansions, such as those created by Manuel Portaceli and Carlos Salvadores in the Valencian Courts in the Palace of Benicarló (fig. 16), or by Antonio Reboredo for the seat of the Galician parliament in the ancient quarter of Hórreo in Santiago de Compostela.

The seats of regional governments are still in the planning stage in many communities, but some examples of notable

13. Luis Peña Ganchegui, architect, and Eduardo Chillida, sculptor. Plaza del Tenis, including The Comb of the Wind, (El Peine del Viento), San Sebastian, 1976.

quality are the seats of the Ministry of Agriculture headquarters for Andalusia in Seville (fig. 17)—in which the architect Antonio González Cordón transformed what was the cotton mill of Tabladilla into a brilliant articulation of new buildings—and the Ministry of Agriculture headquarters for Castile-La Mancha in the historic center of Toledo (see photographs and project description in Part II). The creation of the complex of San Caetano for the Galician executive branch (fig. 18), designed by Manuel Gallego and others, is another excellent example of an orientation especially prevalent since the first half of the 1980s, which sought the eloquence of new interventions in extant buildings.

The most powerful example of the alternative way, the construction of a new and grand building that could contribute to these expansive processes is the Triana Tower in Seville (fig. 19), which will house various functions of the Andalusian government. This is a building marked by a monumentality that is the trademark of Sáenz de Oiza's later work, more intense and unencumbered than ever. At the border of the World's Fair and in a strategic visual location from the Guadalquivir River, the Triana Tower has come to be, inexorably, an outstanding element in the urban landscape of Seville. Its construction reflects the will to symbolize a new materialized autonomous power in the capital of Andalusia that the commissioner of public works, Josep Maria Montaner, and the director general of architecture, J. A. Moreno, believed that Sáenz de Oiza could accomplish better than any other Spanish architect.

Spain Redefines Itself

In democratic Spain at the end of the twentieth century, architecture, not without great contradictions, occupies an important role. Unlike the situation in France, where President François Mitterand acts as an architecture-loving monarch, personally determining plans for monuments that reaffirm the place of Paris as both the capital and the center of the nation, in Spain neither the King nor any of the governmental presidents has shown much special interest in architecture. Moreover, it could truthfully be said that the most decisive of our chiefs of state, President Felipe

González, does not have a personal feeling for architecture. Likewise, the presidents of the autonomous governments, along with most Spanish politicians in general, have not been known to have an affection for it. Nevertheless, some architects (among them, Oriol Bohigas, Eduardo Mangada, and Josep Maria Montaner) have enjoyed enough lasting confidence to be able to act or have been in positions of responsibility long enough that since the death of Franco there has been a ready architectural culture waiting and hoping to have an effect on the transformation of this country. The certainty of the democratic process has taken root, not without conflicts and failures, but facilitating the expression of this sensibility.

The effort to recover lost time has given architectural activity in Spain an added fervor, as it has created more architecture of a higher quality than in many other European countries during this time. If 1992 is going to be the *annus mirabilis* in which, through such initiatives as the Olympic Games in Barcelona, the World's Fair in Seville, or the European Cultural Capital in Madrid, a better knowledge and understanding of the peoples and cultures of the world and, equally, between the peoples and cultures of Spain, is achieved, then Spain faces a very difficult challenge. A particular idea of history, plural and complex in its truths and falsehoods, also manifests itself in the extraordinary plans for 1992. History is viewed as a method of reflection, and patrimony is understood as its particular manifestation in architecture. Within the most dynamic, innovative, and opulent aspects of many of the works incorporated in the urban economy of recent years, precisely at the hour of

Fig. 15. César Portela. Carballeira de Santa Miña, Brión, La Coruña, 1985-86.

major ambition in the projects of 1992, the attention to and intervention in the restoration of Spain's architectural heritage has remained a substantial component of the overall culture, precisely because architecture means so much for a country so old and so rich in examples of its past.

It is not surprising that the 1933 patrimony law, which governed architecturally and historically significant works, survived during the forty years of Franco's dictatorship. It was a very good law for its time, and with its reduced ideological, material, and human means, Franco's government thought it sufficient to live up to this policy on monuments. Not until 1985 did the Socialist government promote the parliamentary approval of a new, national general law on historic buildings, which was to be accompanied by specific regulations in some autonomous regions. Before the power to intervene was transferred, a new policy of profound impact on the role of architecture in the areas of restoration, rehabilitation, and planning of buildings, archaeological remains, historic boundaries, and groups of buildings was put into motion. Through the Ministry of Culture and the Ministry of Public Works, employing many distinguished architects like D. Hernández

Fig. 14. Miguel Garay and José Ignacio Linazasoro. Public School, Hondarrabia, Guipúzcoa, 1974-78.

Gil, J. M. Hernández de León, Antón Capitel, Antonio Humanes, Antonio Vázquez de Castro, Manuel de las Casas, and Amparo Precioso, important initiatives were established that, with uneven results, were later implemented by the autonomous administrations. But in some institutions, the commitment to intervention in historic architecture was singularly developed. For example, in the Provincial Deputation of Barcelona, headed by the architect Antonio González Moreno-Navarro, a systematic and efficient effort was solidly established, especially notable in the restoration of medieval architecture, such as Sant Cugat del Gavadons, Sant Vicenç de Malla, and the Tower of the Manresana.

On the other hand, the symbiosis between monuments and their environment has been a common concern at all levels of public administration, and today it is a special focus of the regional governments, such as the General Plan for Cultural Buildings of the Junta of Andalusia. But one must not forget to refer to some examples of broad-based activity on urban sites in diverse cities such as Alcalá de Henares, Madrid, where alterations were made to the city walls, urban spaces, and numerous monuments such as the church of the Colegio Máximo de la Compañía de Jesus. One could add many examples of integrated rehabilitation plans, oriented toward the recovery of historic buildings and residential neighborhood environments in numerous cities in Spain, such as the Jonquet of Palma de Mallorca or Puerto Real, Cádíz; or unique projects such as those required by world-class historic sites, such as the Alhambra and the Generalife of Granada.

As part of the vast spectrum of the Spanish architectural panorama, there is also a trend toward "non-intervention," perhaps prompted by the rehabilitative excesses of institutions that attempt to ennoble themselves with the monuments that they occupy. A few concrete examples of the diversity of restorations can be seen in monastic complexes, many of which had largely fallen into ruin before the interventions: the restoration of the Monasterio Premostracense de Santa María la Real in Aguilar de Campoo, Palencia, for example, was done with great fidelity by José María Pérez González, founder of the craft schools now diffused all over Spain. One might also recognize the "reverse-renovation" of the Cistercian Monastery of Carracedo, León, by Salvador Pérez Arroyo. Among the largest projects of the time in Spain, the ancient area known as La Cartuja de Santa María de las Cuevas in Seville has become an impressive complex that has remained as the heart of the area of the 1992 World's Fair (fig. 20). The complex has been worked on by at least five architectural teams in different areas, and it shows a combination of diverse methods of treating inherited elements with analogous reconstructions and new additions.

The assistance given by the state, including the regional governments, to preserving the architectural heritage of the

Fig. 16. Manuel Portaceli and Carlos Salvadores. Valencian Courts, Palacio de Benicarló, Valencia, 1988-90.

Fig. 17. Antonio González Cordón. Ministry of Agriculture headquarters for Andalusia, Seville, 1989-92.

Catholic Church has been impressive. The cathedrals, great basilicas, and episcopal palaces of Spain have been the object of a broad range of interventions from the See of Zaragoza (J. M. Pérez Latorre) to the Cathedral of Granada (P. Salmerón), from that of Córdoba (Rafael Moneo, Gabriel Ruiz Cabrero, and G. Rebollo) to the Basilica of San Francisco the Great in Madrid (Feduchi brothers), or the museum-like intervention in the Episcopal Palace of Tarazona (Luis Burillo and Jaime Lorenzo) and the project of Alejandro de la Sota for the extension of that of León. In ancient churches of very diverse character especially significant renovations have been made, for example, the unusual transformation of the small chapel of l'Hospitalet in Ibiza (Elías Torres and José Antonio Martínez Lapeña; see Solà-Morales, fig. 1), the completion of the Church of Our Lady of Montserrat in Madrid (Antón Capitel, C. Martorell, and A. Riviere), or the impressive reinterpretation of the ruin of the Church of Santa Cruz in Medina de Rioseco, Valladolid (fig. 21), by José Ignacio Linazasoro.

Other building types have been affected by this same expansion of options. One of the most beautiful recent interventions, a paradigm of the doctrine of the pursuit and recovery of the inherited patrimony, is the conversion of the Palacio de los Condes de Benavente in Valladolid into a public library, a project of Manuel de las Casas and Jaime Lorenzo. This could be accompanied by a good handful of sensible interventions of diverse magnitude, such as the subtle renovation of the Palacio del Marqués de Campo as a Museum of the City of Valencia by M. Portaceli and J. J. Estellés. Some projects have taken place in medieval buildings, such as the castle of Puebla de Sanabria, Zamora, by Javier Vellés and Francisco Somoza, in those of the eighteenth century, such as the Segura River mills in Murcia (see fig. 22) by Juan Navarro Baldeweg, or in the restorations of twentieth-century buildings, such as Gaudí's Parque Güell by Antonio González or the Government Building of Tarragona by Alejandro de la Sota.

To be brief, I will add only some references to the interventions in Roman theaters in Spain, which alone offer an excellent example of the diverse attitudes and positions that are taken in preserving the country's architectural and archaeological heritage. Since the Roman theater of Mérida was reconstructed and adapted for use in presentations, it became a point of reference for the application of theories regarding the treatment of ruins. At the theater in Mérida, the architect, D. Hernández Gil, chose to protect the original

Fig. 18. Manuel Gallego and various architects. Government seat of Galicia in the complex of San Caetano, Santiago de Compostela, 1984-85.

structure from the destructive effects of use by superimposing pavements of fiberglass and polyester and by substituting replicas for original statuary. Others have taken the path of reconstruction, though with quite different sensibilities. This can be seen at the theater in Itálica, Seville, which was renovated by the architect Antonio Jiménez using reconstructions and simulations. While the projects in the theaters of Segóbriga in Saelices, Cuenca, or Acinipo in Ronda, Málaga, were done with taste and modesty, Córdoba has seen the vestiges of its extensive Roman ruins emerge in the works of its new railway station, producing the most pronounced situation of perplexity between preservation and progress. Using architecture as an instrument, Spain continually attempts to define these terms as it reckons with its past.

The Events of 1992

The importance that the year 1992 holds for Spain has already been mentioned. The conjuncture of the quincentenary of the discovery of America and the foundation of European unity in that year has been translated into an accumulation of international commitments of enormous transcendence: the Olympics, the World's Fair, and the European cultural capital in Barcelona, Seville, and Madrid, respectively. Although not equally felt in all three cities, these accomplishments have operated as vectors, as directional elements oriented and disposed to accelerate the pace of anticipated transformations, but also to constitute themselves as strategies for the future that are quantitatively and qualitatively unthinkable without the contemporary urban history of our cities. This history relies on such precedents as the 1888 World's Fair in Barcelona or the International Exposition there in 1929, both of which were definite factors in the urban transformation, as well as the celebration, in Seville, of the Ibero-American Exposition also in 1929.

In order of magnitude, of the volume of specific investments generated by the event, Madrid has felt the least far-reaching impact and has, one might say, continued to extrapolate the objectives of its general plan. The Master Plan of Madrid of 1985 had as one of its most ambitious aims the search for a relationship of equilibrium between the city's northern and southern halves: a North placed in pleasant hills with clean water and a clear sky, offering the highest standard of living, versus a South where factories and migrant workers were decanted. For this reason, in a winning proposal of urban solidarity, three of the five great structures of the plan were placed in the central cradle of the capital of Spain: the park along the Manzanares River; the distributor highway and new southern access; and the remodeling of the area immediately contiguous to the Atocha railway station, the true point of arrival, adjustment, and departure of the masses of migrant workers from Andalusia. Attention has also been given to the Vallecas district, through hundreds of housing blocks on 280 acres; or, in metropolitan scale, to the development of Carlos III University, the third university in Madrid, situated in Getafe as a counterpoint to the position of the Autonomous University in Tres Cantos in the northern half of the city. A similar political philosophy is reflected in

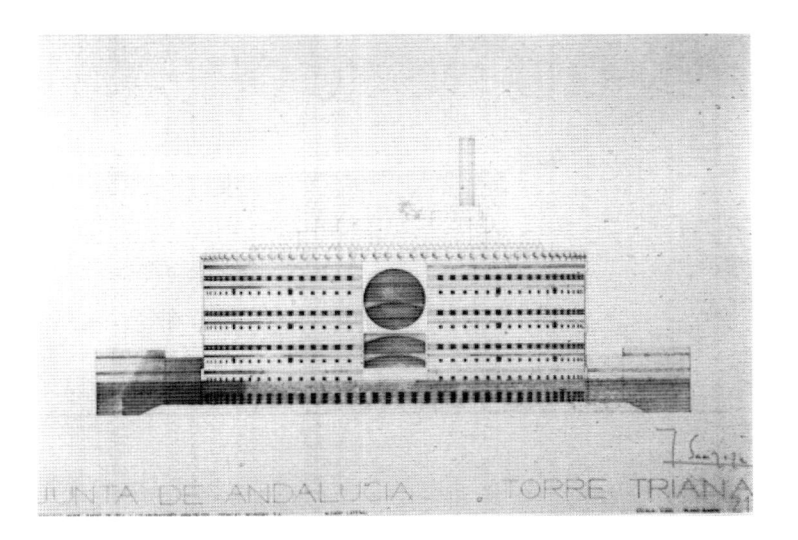

Fig. 19. Francisco Javier Sáenz de Oíza. Triana Tower, government seat of Andalusia, Seville, 1989-92. Perspective drawing.

Fig. 20. Roberto Luna and Fernando Mendoza; Francisco Torres; José Ramón Sierra and Ricardo Sierra; Guillermo Vázquez Consuegra. La Cartuja de Santa María de las Cuevas, Seville, 1987-92. View of the complex.

the decision to initiate the establishment of a high speed train in Spain through a new route that unites the capital city with Córdoba and Seville.

Of all the above, there has been a special emphasis on the remodeling of Atocha Station (fig. 23). The new station, the fruit of a transformation of the existing one, its expansion as a new building nearby, and its place as the interchange of public transport, were all part of one of the most important competitions of the 1980s. Rafael Moneo received the commission for this large and difficult architectural operation. But Atocha turns out to be much more than the most complex directional center of human transportation in Madrid. Its position at the foot of the Paseo del Prado, symbol of the enlightened urban planning of Carlos III, contributes to the larger cultural strategy in which the offer to serve as cultural capital of Europe in 1992 is based.

In effect, a so-called triangle of art would be constituted by the renovated Prado Museum, the neighboring Villahermosa Palace rehabilitated by Rafael Moneo to house the Thyssen Collection, and the immense Reina Sofía Center of Contemporary Art, remodeled to the plans of Antonio Fernández Alba, first, and Antonio Vázquez de Castro, second. The program of cultural centers and theaters composes a complex system, with both new and remodeled institutions. In the area of sports, Madrid can boast new installations such as the velodrome of La Latina or the great new community stadium and its related installations, a project designed by Antonio Cruz and Antonio Ortiz. These and other installations, such as the new fairgrounds by Sáenz de Oiza and five new parks, bringing the total park land to 8,500 acres, or the completion of the M-40 highway, establish for Madrid some dynamic objectives of doubtless urban relevance, although they could be seen as insufficient to satisfy all the requirements of the everyday life of the Madrilenes. Political changes during recent years have, as a consequence, generated contrary attitudes, dissatisfactions, and alternative objectives.

Although Seville also experienced changes in its municipal government in 1991, the conditions of the World's Fair project and the consolidation of the greater part of its large urban operations in an accomplishment of such breadth has made the local government circumstances irrelevant. The reality is that Seville takes on the last world's fair of this rank in this century, and it does so being the most compact city, the smallest, the one of greatest historical patrimony, and the least developed of those considered. The award, made at the end of the 1970s with the approval of King Juan Carlos I, was made firm between 1982 and 1983. Thereafter followed extraordinarily complex modifications, some of which are pertinent to mention: for example, the delay in the decisions of President Felipe González (who, after having first named Ricardo Bofill, later proposed Manuel Olivencia as first commissioner for a year); the unusual determination of its general design with a competition that produced two antithetical solutions, one by Emilio Ambasz, and another by Jerónimo Junquera, Estanislao Pérez Pita, and J. A. Fernández Ordóñez (both later altered in an almost anonymous master plan); or the readjustments necessary at different moments to realize so complex an undertaking, like the creation of the public company for Expo '92, the naming of Jacinto Pellón as director of the works, or Olivencia's resignation as commissioner and his replacement by Emilio Casinello. Nonetheless, the uncertainties of the early years, along with the coincidental competitions for the Junta of Andalusia, resulted in a general design with conventional respect for the developmental traditions of previous expositions (Osaka and Montreal, for example), of strong impact on the urban and metropolitan structure of Seville, with the consequent

Fig. 21. José Ignacio Linazasoro. Restoration of the Church of Santa Cruz, Medina de Rioseco, Valladolid, 1985-88.

Fig. 22. Juan Navarro Baldeweg. Hydraulics Museum, Murcia, 1983-88.

need of articulating a group of decisions necessary to structure a vast and precarious territory, incurring copious investments on the order of $100 million. Some of the results of these efforts include: almost doubling the arterial highway network, extending it by seventy-five kilometers; building a perimeter highway, then non-existent; completely modifying the railway network, raising its course along the river, burying its urban branches, and creating a new and magnificent station (designed by Antonio Cruz and Antonio Ortiz) to replace the two that were insufficient; building on the Guadalquivir River as it passes through the city with important hydraulic works complementary to those that originated the process of territorial localization of the Fair, and the subsequent urban renewal; the construction of seven new bridges (the works of the engineers José Antonio Fernández Ordóñez and Julio Martínez Calzón, Luis Viñuela and Fritz Leonhardt, and Santiago Calatrava being most impressive) in a city which had only had four; the realization of a new and compact airport (designed by Rafael Moneo); aside from diverse urban projects, such as the Opera Theater (designed by the firm of Marín, Pozo, and Yanes).

Seville is now a transformed city, better connected by air, highway, and rail, recovered from decades of a loss of willpower, after activities that have turned over 500 acres of the city into a site covered with buildings and pavilions of every type and condition, among which very few, as is always the case with these events, are of incontestable architectural quality. After some projects by important international firms such as Tadao Ando (Japan), Nicholas Grimshaw (Great Britain), Gae Aulenti (Italy), Vigier and Jodry (France) and a few others (regrettably, the United States did not select Robert Venturi's project for their pavilion), the Spanish contribution to the architecture of the World's Fair does not account for all that it should have been capable of, missing the opportunity that, with a little cooperation, could have produced a collection of the most relevant architects of the country. Perhaps the best pavilion is the one on navigation by the Sevillian architect Guillermo Vázquez Consuegra (see photographs

The Architecture of Democratic Spain Victor Pérez Escolano

and project description in Part II); in addition are notable projects such as the Pavilion of the Future (fig. 24) designed by Martorell, Bohigas, and Mackay, with Rice, Arup and Freixa; the experimental theater by G. Ayala; and the regional pavilions of Aragón (J. M. Pérez Latorre), Asturias (Muñoz and Sanmartín), Castile-La Mancha (fig. 25) by Manuel de las Casas, or Tierras de Jerez (Ignacio de la Peña).

For Seville, there will be the day after the Fair (see fig. 26). When six months of universal acclaim have passed and millions of visitors have left, the hour will come when the effects of the Fair will have to be measured. Potential benefits include the reconversion of the precinct of the Fair into a technological park, the lasting improvements in the the way of physical structures, and even better, in the light of day, the recognition of an historic city of the first magnitude and of its social, cultural, and economic vitality that have remained hidden to the usual avatars of contemporary progress. This concerted effort should heal not a few open wounds and should be accompanied by

Fig. 23. Rafael Moneo. Atocha Station, Madrid, 1985-92.

Fig. 24. Martorell, Bohigas and Mackay, with Rice, Arup and Freixa. Pavilion of the Future, World's Fair, Seville, 1992. Model.

other works, pending attention to the most small-scale necessities of the city's neighborhoods and to its cultural and architectural heritage.

The case of Barcelona is different. The 1992 Olympic Games have also been a singular stimulus that has galvanized the processes of transformation of the city, further, surely, than ordinary actions would have been carried within a systematic urban plan. The public and private investments in infrastructures and urban planning operations will have a direct economic impact on the order of $100 million and add an indirect impact of $240 million. The remodeling of the city, taking advantage of its qualities and the still available open spaces, was a point of departure, which only later (in October 1986) was articulated in the exceptional challenge of hosting the Olympic Games, the necessities of which were then faced under the principle of urban integration, betterment of its infrastructures, and the realization of grand projects. As is logical, this caused a shift in the scales of intervention, the contexts, the method of measurement, and its pace. The objectives and subtleties of some interventions of the early 1980s disappeared and others of greater size and more peripheral character appeared. The expression "the city as laboratory" has been used precisely to indicate the empirical and fragmentary method that has been used. The Games have merely been a medium to transcend it decidedly in a grand project of urban renewal localized in four Olympic areas in the four quadrants of the city proper (Montjuïc, Diagonal, Vall d'Hebron, and Nova Icària/Olympic Village), with the goal of their usefulness as urban service areas after 1992, "areas of a new centrality."

The new airport terminal (designed by Ricardo Bofill and the Taller de Arquitectura) or the Telecommunications Tower in Collserola (Norman Foster) are the symbols of a system of communications in Barcelona 1992, but from the point of view of everyday necessities of the citizens, the arterial highway network, in particular the perimeter belts and tunnels, is the primary system that the post-Franco urbanization needed. Nevertheless, the radical difference is in the definition of the highways, the design of which continues in accordance with the guidelines generated since the beginning of the decade. Barcelona could not but be strengthened as a city of art through prestigious initiatives, although problems may prevent some of these from being ready on time in 1992, such as the Museum of Contemporary

Art by Richard Meier; the Art Museum of Catalonia in the National Palace of the 1929 International Exposition, a project by Gae Aulenti and Enric Steegmann; the National Theater of Catalonia by Ricardo Bofill; or the alteration and enlargement of the Grand Theater of the Lyceum by Ignasi de Solà-Morales. Much of this large span of work has, however, already been excellently completed: the reform of the Museum of Archaeology by Josep Llinás, the Arts Center in Santa Monica (fig. 29) by Albert Viaplana and Helio Piñón, the Antoni Tàpies Foundation by Roser Amadó and Lluís Domènech, the reconstruction of the Barcelona Pavilion of Mies van der Rohe by Cristian Cirici, Fernando Ramos, and Ignasi de Solà-Morales, or the remodeling of the concert hall known as the Palau de la Música Catalana by Oscar Tusquets and Carlos Díaz, aside from the work by Jordi Garcés and Enric Sòria already cited.

Among so many initiatives and urban realizations, however, one sometimes forgets the essential sporting nature of the 1992 Olympic Games. The substantial portion of the architecture for its celebration constitutes a group of works built for the practice of sport: the Olympic Stadium at Montjuïc, a remodeling of the 1929 International Exposition stadium (which has been without a doubt a controversial issue) by Federico Correa, Alfonso Milá, Carles Buxadé, Joan Margarit, and Vittorio Gregotti (see fig. 27); near it the stellar realization of Arata Isozaki, the Sports Pavilion of Sant Jordi (fig. 28), as well as the National Institute of Physical Education of Catalonia by Ricardo Bofill; in the area of Horta, the velodrome by Esteve Bonell and Francesc Rius; in Vall d'Hebron the La Teixonera tennis courts (Tonet Sunyer) and the municipal sports complex (Garcés and Sòria); to which must be added the installations for archery designed by Enric Miralles and Carme Pinós (see photographs and project description in Part II), and in Badalona the basketball stadium also designed by Bonell and Rius (see photographs and project description in Part II). All these are primary edifices for the celebration of the Olympic events.

An accomplishment that necessarily brings us again to a final urban consideration, and one that exemplifies the leap

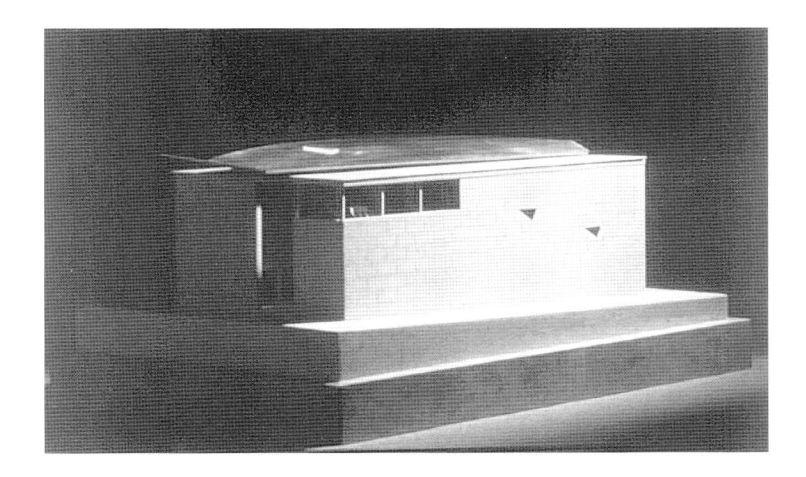

Fig. 25. Manuel de las Casas. Pavilion of Castile-LaMancha, World's Fair, Seville, 1990-92. Model.

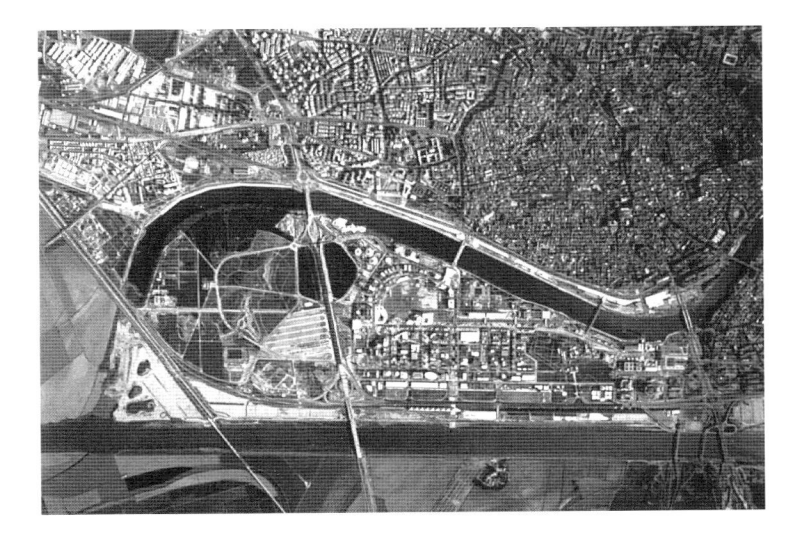

Fig. 26. Aerial view of the site of the World's Fair, Seville, 1992.

from a "completed Barcelona," according to an early 1980s expression, to a metropolitan and expansive Barcelona, a territorial paradigm between the Besòs and Llobregat Rivers, is the construction of the Olympic Village on 325 acres liberated from the old industrial area of Nova Icària or Poble Nou. This is an area, beyond the mythic limit of the Ciutadella that once constituted "another Barcelona." The Olympic Village is the principal touchstone for the anti-Olympics faction, and not just because of the elimination of important elements of the industrial character, since this is an urban renewal operation that cannot be equaled even by the major ones in the United States during the 1970s. Along with the projected 2,000 housing units and the Eurocity office buildings, the implantation of a great commercial center, the hotels, or the palace of congresses, became, according to Oriol Bohigas, "locomotors of concentrated and permanent activity" toward the end of reaching immediately the central value and the social destiny desired for the Olympic Village. The urgency at different moments of its design and management produced some questionable decisions: for example, according to Josep Maria Montaner, the morphology of the great blocks or the lack of connections among the various interventions; on the other hand, the decision to invite all of the architects who in the last thirty years have obtained an FAD (Fomento de las Artes Decorativas) prize—the most prestigious of those that exist in Spain—to participate in this immense undertaking, that decision is surely irreproachable. Among the other relevant buildings that should be mentioned, the authors of the overall design (Martorell, Bohigas, Mackay, and Puigdomènech) drafted Litoral Park; Juan Navarro Baldeweg designed the multi-sports pavilion in the area; Alvaro Siza Vieira and Joan Falgueras did the Ministry of Public Works and Transportation building and the Meterological Center; José Antonio Martínez Lapeña and Elías Torres were selected for the Conference Center; and Bruce Graham (of Skidmore, Owings and Merrill) designed one of the two private skyscrapers, mainly a hotel, which, at 153.5 meters high, will be the tallest building in Spain.

Fig. 27. Federico Correa, Alfonso Milá, Carles Buxadé, Joan Margarit, and Vittorio Gregotti. Olympic Stadium, Montjuïc, Barcelona, 1986-89. Aerial view of complex.

Fig. 28. Arata Isozaki. Sant Jordi Sports Pavilion, Barcelona, 1984-91. Aerial view.

Fig. 29. Albert Viaplana and Helio Piñón. Santa Mónica Arts Center, Barcelona, 1987-89. Interior view.

Conclusion

Joan Busquets has said that in any process of developing large projects contradictory phases always exist. There are numerous issues that demand our critical reflection, especially in regard to the great projects of transformation that are planned throughout Europe, for we have looked only at Spanish examples: their minimal dimension, their strategic location, the development of accompanying infrastructures, the innovations that affect necessary urban functions, the specificity of the operative competition, or the long-term contribution of these projects are some of these issues. The enormous undertakings in Spain, brought together by and for the year 1992, have responded to these parameters, but with what level of satisfaction? The equilibrium between innovation and its coherence with the existing city has not been satisfactorily maintained in equal measure in Madrid, Seville, and Barcelona. It is evident from what has been realized, especially relative to the scale of the city, and from their respective models of implantation and strategic process, that Seville has faced the most risky process of transformation, while Barcelona has operated with a greater intellectual consciousness. But in all of them there is recognizable, with certain pluses and minuses, large and small, and with architecture as its banner, the sign of historic changes occurring in Spain.

The Prodigious Decade

Ignasi de Solà-Morales

One of the more celebrated recent Spanish novels is Eduardo Mendoza's *The City of Marvels* (*La Ciudad de los prodigios*). The central character of this urban novel is none other than a city, in this case, Barcelona. Throughout the novel, through the vicissitudes of the other characters in it, Barcelona is transformed from a tranquil town of little more than 200,000 inhabitants at the turn of the century into a thriving metropolis of the 1930s. The success of Mendoza's narration lies in his having presented this process of change as a rosary of marvels, a fortuitous chain of events in which the most unforeseeable conjunction of apparently unrelated phenomena occurred. If we borrow the idea that certain leaps forward are often the consequence of an unpredictable conjuncture of events, we can analyze Spanish architecture of the last decade as a prodigious accomplishment, unexpected and exceptional.

In recent years the Italian historian Carlo Ginzburg has articulated the distinction between center and periphery in the analysis of cultural history. Ginzburg's theoretical model posits a relationship between a central space—the generator of new ideas, forms, and ways of living—and a peripheral one—dependent and receptive, and only able to act as a satellite to the center. In considering the events of the 1980s, however, it is clear that the appearance of a relationship between a dominating center and a dominated periphery is deceptive. In the midst of the cultural crisis that the Western world has experienced since at least 1968, the dynamic between center and periphery may, in fact, have changed. The mechanisms of hegemony are not so evident in the great cultural centers—London, Milan, and New York, for example, in the world of architecture—nor has peripheral design activity been so exclusively dependent that it can only be recognized as a provincial version of what was invented and developed in the centers.

Architecture and many other forms of cultural activity on the periphery are not, in fact, dependent upon the center, and can, instead, be shown to be independent and efficient (see fig. 1). The reasons for this are numerous: autonomous exchanges of creativity entirely from the non-dominant areas; different material conditions that allow an engagement of technical and human resources unavailable in the centers; the weight of local traditions substantially modifying a point of view or the way of understanding a problem; and interchanges between architectural communication and other forms of mass media. This is the case of the cultures supposedly peripheral to the international mainstream culture.

For these reasons, Spanish architecture in this prodigious decade can be read as a unique response to the general world crisis. If by the term "postmodernism" we can mean not simply the designation of a style in which an architectonic language is based on the substitution of forms of the modern tradition for those of the classical style, then we can indeed affirm that Spanish architecture of the last

Fig. 1. José Antonio Martínez Lapeña and Elías Torres. Restoration of a chapel, L'Hospitalet, Ibiza, 1982-85. Interior view.

ten or fifteen years constitutes a distinct "postmodern" form, different from that produced by the great centers. Furthermore, Spanish architecture is a response to a general crisis in modern architecture and of the languages and methods of intervention that have been used by all segments of Western culture since at least the end of the Second World War.

Spain's architectural culture has also effectively placed the orthodoxy of the modern tradition in a state of crisis. In the writings of architects Oriol Bohigas, Antonio Fernández Alba, or Rafael Moneo, and also in the evolution of the works of these same architects, as well as those of Luis Peña Ganchegui, Francisco Javier Sáenz de Oiza, or F. Correa and M. Mila, we can detect the changes that have taken place in the concept of progress, the confidence expressed in the successful transformation of abstract and supposedly rational languages, and the security of using historic building typologies in the face of the new urban growth.

What is different in the case of Spanish culture is the way in which these changes have been made. During the economic and cultural crisis of the 1970s, a corresponding and long-awaited political change took place in Spain. The transition from the dictatorship of Francisco Franco to a fragile democracy occurred precisely in these years of economic and cultural upheaval. What in other countries was merely disenchantment and a loss of confidence in the lofty ideals of change and progress had a completely different character in Spain. The democratic transition was not just political, because it also opened up all cultural areas as a consequence of the new democratic freedoms.

According to an image commonly held in America and most of Europe, Spain was seen as humble and backward, anchored in the past by the omnipotent rule of dictatorship. But this is not exactly the way things were. In art and architecture, as in literature and thought, development in Spain and contacts between Spain and the centers of world culture were more alive than appearances would lead one to believe, although it is no less true that the reflections and preoccupations of Spanish intellectuals were compromised by the slow arrival of political and civil change.

The new political situation created by democracy in the parliament, in the autonomous governments, and in the municipalities made the construction of public works a priority: those symbols, spaces, and monuments that are capable of representing the collective values so long awaited and so painfully achieved (see fig. 2).

Any architecture of merit that was created during the years of the Franco dictatorship always and invariably occurred in the private realm. Only in the beginning of the dictatorship did the public powers perceive the necessity of making itself visible and present through an architecture that would be representative of an authoritarian state. Throughout the 1950s and 1960s, which was a period of economic development and initial prosperity, it was in the private arena that sporadically innovative and creative architecture appeared. Private houses, structures for tourism, and residential developments on the outskirts of cities were the predominant types of private projects designed by Spanish architects during the dictatorship. In the 1970s, the economic recession, the first oil crisis, and the end of the dictatorship produced a Copernican revolution in cultural attitudes and objectives. Architecture was invited to participate in that revolution.

At this juncture, when a decline in the economic resources of the private sector met an emerging will to express the new forms of power in government, a shift occurred in the architectural emphasis from the private to the public realm. Suddenly, architects who were used to designing housing developments, elegant interiors, hotels, bars, or discotheques were being called upon to design new public spaces and to give shape to the new services that emerged from the democratic government (see fig. 3). While in many other countries the economic crisis of the 1970s manifested itself in the creation of an architecture that was drawn but never built, in Spain theorization and formal speculation had little to do with the work of reconstructing the country.

The Prodigious Decade

Moving from the third world to the developed world, Spain found itself enthralled by the new political situation. During these years, the preoccupation with the form that public architecture should take was the dominant issue for Spanish architects. In voicing this issue, they discovered immediately that public space and monumental architecture—that is, architecture representative of collective values—were absent, or at least ill-defined, in the modern tradition.

At the universities and in articles published in journals—notably *Arquitecturas bis*, *Arquitectura,* and *Quaderns*—the problem of public space and its configuration gained prominence over merely semantic debates. A revision of the modern tradition within this key forum brought with it a reconsideration of the traditions of the nineteenth-century bourgeois city and of subsequent movements like Civic Art and the City Beautiful. These movements supplied the support for important theoretical discussions and tentative projects in which no orthodoxy could be imposed, since the modern tradition was deficient in regard to the design of civic spaces and monumental public architecture.

Hundreds of public spaces—plazas, avenues, urban parks—dozens of institutional buildings—regional parliaments, government seats, councils, and all sorts of administrative buildings—and hundreds of buildings for public institutions—schools, hospitals, airports, train stations, museums, libraries, and sports facilities—these formed the bulk of the culturally relevant architecture of the last decade (see figs. 4-6). Of course, most of these projects and built works did not have a stylistic unity, nor did they proceed from a single urban or architectural plan. A quick review of an extensive catalogue of recently realized Spanish buildings shows a diversity of criteria, an absence of indisputable dogmas, and a variety of references, all of which clearly demonstrate the tentative, experimental character that the search for public architecture in Spain has displayed.

It may be illustrative to note that the process of defining public architecture in Spain has unfolded gradually over the last ten or fifteen years by the successive appropriation of

Fig. 2. Jaume Bach and Gabriel Mora. Bellaterra Station, Barcelona, 1984.

Fig. 3. Juan Navarro Baldeweg. Municipal Center for Social Services, Puerta de Toledo, Madrid, 1985-88. Interior view.

Fig. 4. Antonio Cruz and Antonio Ortiz. Conversion of the Baluarte de la Candelaria into the Maritime Museum, Cádiz, 1986-89.

projects from the small scale to the large scale and by the cumulative discovery of design solutions. These steps forward have provoked, in works more than in words, a progressive consolidation of architectural forces, increasingly accepted by politicians and citizens, as well as by the architects themselves. We can note at least three outstanding characteristics of these changes.

First, at the beginning of this period, there was an exaggerated interest in the adaptive reuse of historic buildings (see fig. 7). Among the more interesting projects of recent years we can note a great number of interventions in existing buildings. A certain lack of confidence in new architecture on the part of politicians and citizens and the necessity of giving priority to Spain's architectural patrimony in urban politics produced a paradoxical situation in which much of the better Spanish architecture in the 1980s took the form of intervention in the existing fabric of our cities.

An obsession such as the one we are describing (seemingly that of a conservator) provoked certain positive effects in the sense that the treatment of historic architecture was not given over to supposed specialists, but to architects who had much more creative and interpretive solutions to the problems presented by these projects. Currently, the treatment of the Spanish architectural heritage is a singular phenomenon, for it is difficult to find a parallel in other countries, where such work is controlled by much more rigid and historicist bureaucratic mechanisms. In Spain in past years, the reuse of historic buildings for new public functions has been a much more important creative opportunity than has normally been the case in other countries.

Second, there is an ascendant movement on the ladder of problems related to public architecture. From significant, specific operations, limited to very emblematic spaces and generally in areas of maximum urban density, there has been a progressive movement toward large-scale projects in peripheral, and consequently less densely urban, areas. With these projects comes the need to incorporate the values of culture and public sentiment that would not even have been considered in the modern tradition.

In the Spanish cities most sensitive to these questions, in Seville, La Coruña, Valencia, Madrid, and Barcelona, there has been an increasing number of innovative new projects. Consider that the projects to which we refer and which are included in this catalogue and in the exhibition it accompanies are also the consequence of a displacement of confidence in the public planning/private building partnership. Instead, there is a new process based on the public administration of building as a tool for the reorganization of spaces previously controlled by private development. While the architecture constructed by the government took on the task of recomposing the fragments of a city broken by separate private initiatives, the scale and complexity of these public commissions were gradually increased, in a process in which the new project and the built work would involve those whose responsibilities were formerly limited only to planning.

Third, the new conditions under which architecture is being practiced can be characterized by the incorporation of those habits and aspects of style that issue from the private tradition and are adopted in the creation of an architecture that communicates its public nature (see fig. 8). It is evident that the modern tradition lacks many examples of this sort. The great public projects of Le Corbusier, Oscar Niemeyer, or Louis Kahn do not serve as points of reference in the works of existing cities that are loaded with history, where all new activity must be produced over a previously woven fabric. This may explain why the most common response of Spanish architects, when faced with these questions, has been the effort to capture the essence of public architecture, especially in large spaces (both interiors and exteriors), by combining scale with rich details, and with the almost obsessive attention to finish that has become such a characteristic of the decorative splendor of recent Spanish architecture.

It would be difficult to explain Spanish architecture of the last decade through programmatic manifestoes, for in the transformation that has occurred, the positions that have been taken have reflected, first and foremost, concrete projects rather than theoretical formulas. But it is not true that there has not been a critical and reflective debate about architectural design, just as it is not true that the unfolding of recent architecture has been created without debate or confrontation with other positions. Perhaps what has happened is that the channels through which the new positions have been communicated are dispersed in certain university curricula and in the prestige gained by those professors who have been the well-known designers of innovative new projects. A similar change has also taken place in publications: edited collections and architectural journals have clearly become more influential in the area of

Fig. 6. Enric Miralles and Carme Pinós. Conversion of the La Llauna factory into a secondary school, Badalona, Barcelona, 1984-86. Interior view.

Fig. 5. Luis Burillo and Jaime Lorenzo. Museum of Tarazona, renovation of the Episcopal Palace, 1982-83. Interior view.

Fig. 7. Jordi Garcés and Enric Sòria. Expansion of the Picasso Museum, Barcelona, 1981-86. Interior view.

ideas and are no longer merely informational. Furthermore, the daily press has, in recent years, given an unprecedented amount of attention to the built projects and to the architects involved. This recognition indicates that the once widespread indifference to architecture has been transformed into an abiding interest and sensitization, promoted, without doubt, by the public character of culturally significant buildings and monuments.

It appears, therefore, that recent architecture has defined itself more from the particular to the general than vice versa. The architectural profession in Spain has had, and continues to have, an important technical component that is construction-oriented. The architect is not only he who designs and plans, but he who also builds the buildings, supervises construction on site, decides on the details, and is legally responsible for the quality of the building. This tradition, sustained by the professional method of teaching architecture, makes itself apparent in the notable realism of actual works. The Spanish architect is always linked to the reality of his construction and to its logic, durability, and economy, more than to its form, style, or historic associations.

Together with this strong link to function and construction, Spanish architecture also reveals the distinct characteristics of a culture that has not been a cultural leader. Spanish architecture has always been an eclectic discipline. Despite this condition, Spanish architects are now well-informed, curious about what is happening in the world, sensitive to innovation and modernity, so their capacity to choose is not limited by a previously set forth ideological program, nor by theoretical experiments distant from actual practice.

It is no surprise, as Kenneth Frampton has indicated, that in the past decade the most interesting architecture is to be found, in good measure, in countries peripheral to the history of modern architecture—countries such as Japan, Finland, France, and Spain. In differing degrees we find that the recent architecture of these four countries demonstrates an original combination of the three apparently diverse components. On the one hand, there is the weight of the built environment as the place in which the primary architectural discourse occurs. Then there is also the peripheral condition, mentioned at the beginning of this essay, which easily translates itself in design decisions most linked to the languages and styles with which the architectural text is made legible. Finally, there is the indubitable weight of tradition, which distances contemporary Spanish architecture from what is built elsewhere.

The postmodern crisis has provoked the reconsideration of all forms of architecture not strictly modernist, just as it has posed the question of tradition and local values in the face of the abstraction and temperament of the modern tradition. Interest has been revived in marginal figures of this century such as Adolf Loos, Josef Plecnik, Carlo Mollino, and Gunnar Asplund. There have been incursions into the academic architecture of the eighteenth and nineteenth centuries, from that of the Enlightenment to planning theories for the design of the modern city by Karl Friedrich Schinkel, Hermann Muthesius, Camillo Sitte, and Werner Hegemann.

A counter-model, however, has been sought after in the popular, the vernacular, the volkgeist, the anonymous, and the genius loci. It has also been recovered, and has been seized by the vanguard as an antidote to the indiscriminate use of building forms, gestures, and types exported and imported from place to place via an ever-faster communications network that places all architectural culture in the global village prophesied by Marshall McLuhan.

Does Spanish architecture possess a special and potent vernacular component? In my judgment, no. But it is no less true that the conditions of our cities, the dimensions of the projects, the weight of historic context, the efficiency and

Fig. 8. Albert Viaplana and Helio Piñón. Sants Station plaza (Plaça dels Països Catalans), Barcelona, 1982-89.

economy of certain local materials and construction methods, and the taste for color, density, and luminosity are present in a different way in Spanish architecture than in that of other countries.

More than an identifiable regionalism, what can be detected as the common denominator of a large number of the more interesting examples of Spanish architecture is the uninhibited continuity of certain traditions and certain methods of creating architecture. This issue is important to consider since the reading of Spanish architecture in the vernacular obscures many of the values of contemporaneity and continuity with the modern tradition, and these values are, without a doubt, much more important. Currently, maintaining an architectural tradition does not appear to be a value explicitly sought after. Fortunately, Spanish architecture is not driven by the question of its own identity. On the contrary, what appears dominant is the search—more project-oriented than theoretical—for solutions to problems that are outside the scope of what is actually built, problems that have to do with the city and its population, with civic society and its institutions (see fig. 9).

The presence of brick or ceramics, the adoption of a certain brutal style, the limited incorporation of "light" technology rather than highly sophisticated solutions—these constitute the conditions, the points of departure, or, if you will, the limits within which the architect works. Nevertheless, it would be a grave misunderstanding to presume that these physical limitations are the characteristics of Spanish architecture, or that they are the goals toward which the project is aimed.

Identity and difference certainly constitute the two poles between which, as contemporary thought has well pointed out (e.g., Gilles Deleuze or Jacques Lacan), all definition of the signified moves. When our contemporaries look at Spain, they tend to emphasize our unique identity. Spanish architecture in recent years can be seen as the last chapter of a particular history: that of Spanish culture made of El Grecos, Goyas, Gaudís, Picassos, and García Lorcas. But a definition of Spanish culture that makes these extraordinary figures into stereotypes circulates a Hispanicism that is most impervious to the winds of modernity.

In actual Spanish architecture this identity can be seen—in the genius of the Alhambra and the Escorial, in Mudejar art, and in Latin American colonial architecture. But I sincerely do not believe that any of these has been a dominant preoccupation of Spanish architects of the last decade. The tradition exists—it would be ingenuous to deny it—but I think that currently it does not constitute in itself the end toward which the efforts of young Spanish architects are aimed. Indeed, all indications point in exactly the opposite direction. After many years, perhaps centuries, of isolation, Spanish culture—architecture as well as current

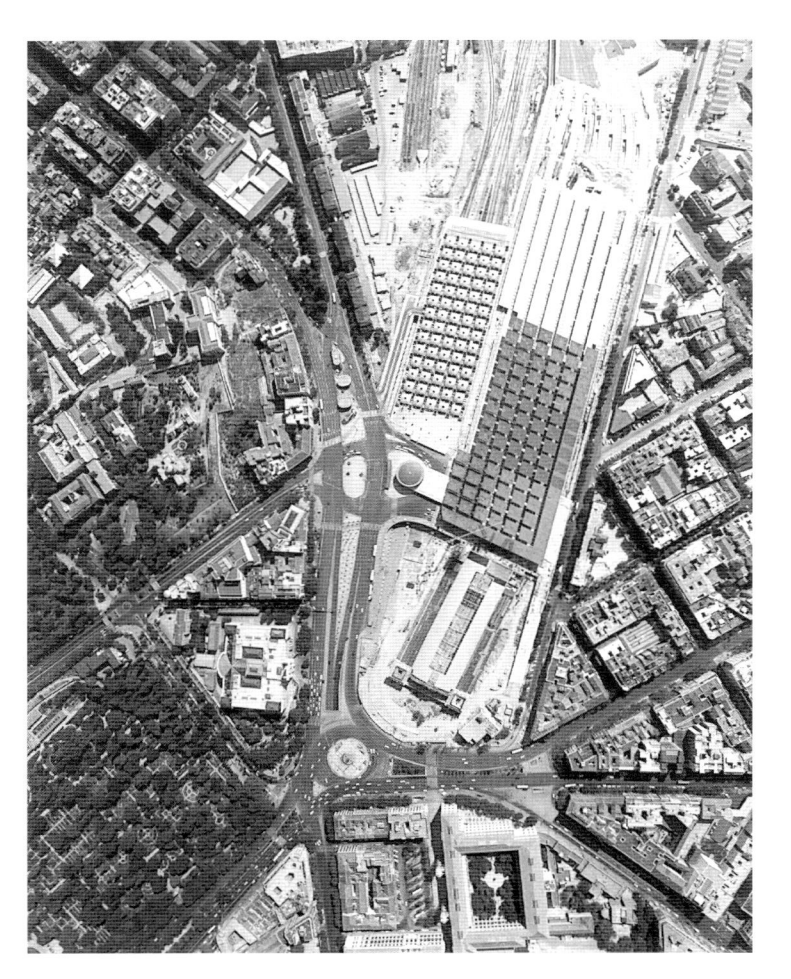

Fig. 9. Rafael Moneo. Atocha Station, Madrid, 1985-92. Aerial view.

Fig. 10. Santiago Calatrava. Bach de Roda-Felipe II Bridge, Barcelona, 1984-87.

trends in philosophy and in artistic creation—appears to be more concerned with the dynamic of the difference than with an absorption in its own identity (see fig. 10).

Spanish architecture is fed by what seems to me to be a real ideological transformation, stemming from a departure from Spain's borders, an opening to new ideas and suggestions from anyone and anywhere, and a belief in being more European than Spanish, more citizens of the world than villagers. Certainly, objective conditions, traditions, and limits exist. But these limits, however, are not felt to contain the experience. As Eugenio Trías has recently written in his insightful book *Lógica del límite*, all cultural aesthetics exist between two boundaries—that of the *center*: bureaucratic, powerful, stable; and that of the *exterior*: undefined, barbarous, and troubled, and lacking any other identity that is not negative.

To speak of present Spanish architecture as an activity within limits is to understand how different it is from traditional and historic architecture. To say that the best contemporary Spanish architecture is an architecture of limits means that its essence, its principal characteristics and significance, arises from its ability to escape its own specific local conditions, as well as to escape the arena of international, theoretical architecture of images on paper. In the tension between the local and the international, one finds not a passive situation that is well-defined, self-referential, and exportable, but an abiding responsiveness to function, specific needs, and concrete problems.

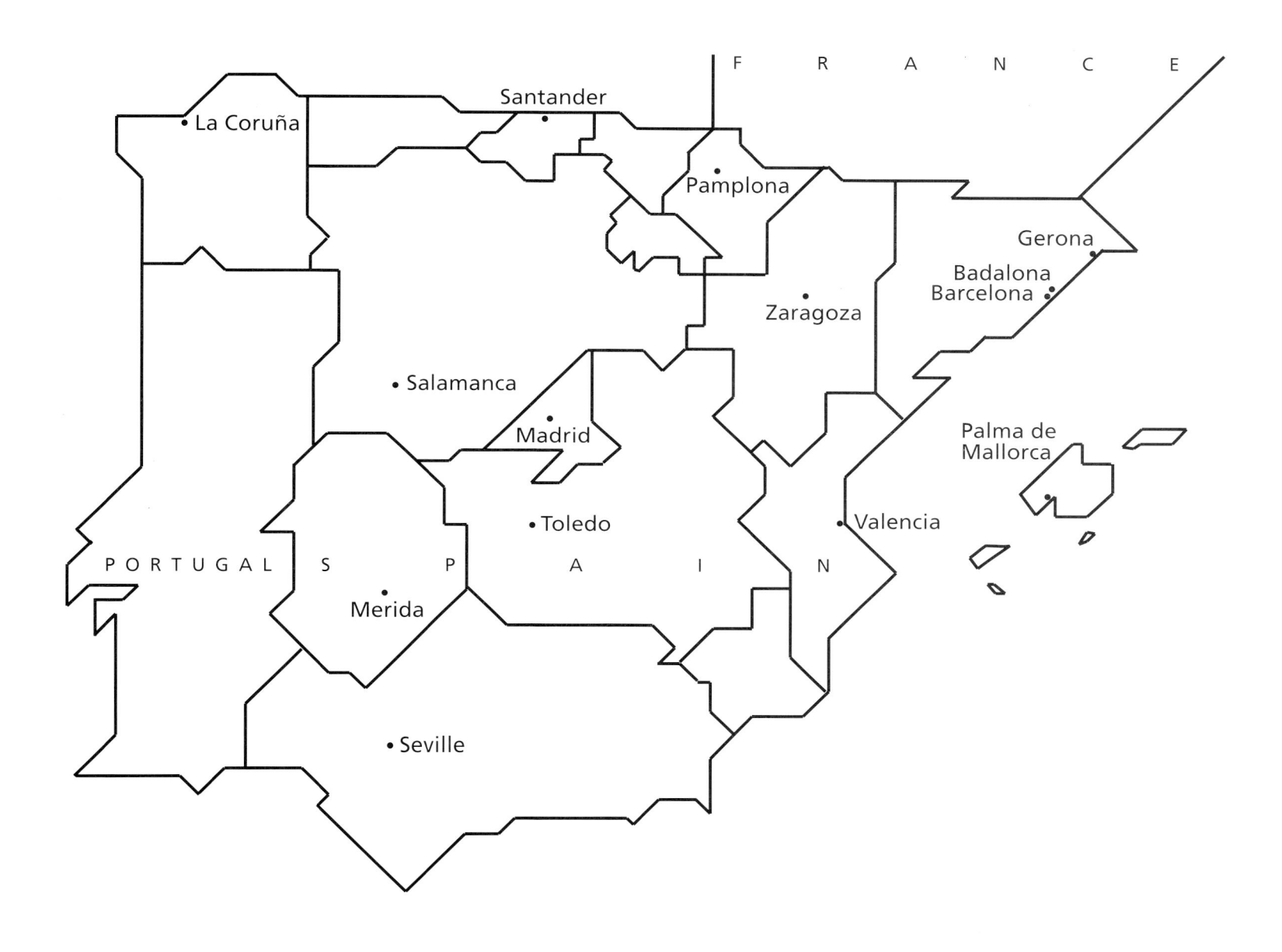

Part II   **Contemporary Spanish Architecture**

Bank of Spain

Gerona

Architects
: Lluís Clotet
Ignacio Paricio

Collaborators
: Joan Sabaté, architect; Jesús Jiménez, Alfonso García, civil engineers; G. Barrena, R. Rexach, technical architects; M. Correa, E. Manino, D. Andreu, A. Orbañanos, J. Ruiz, P. Cárceles, M. Riera, A. Miquel, P. López, and M. Quintanilla

Project
: 1982-85
Construction
: 1986-89
Commission
: National Bank of Spain

The tension created by the combination of a complicated site and relatively simple space requirements was the driving force behind the search for the basic form of the new bank building in Gerona. For security reasons, the bank had to be freestanding and separate from adjacent structures. Given the nature of the commission, the building had to have a strong design that would reflect the institution, even though the dimensions of the site were small, about 3,000 square meters. At first, the building's minimal needs—a few offices, vaults, a meeting room, and a service area for the public—seemed as though they would limit its potential strength. The result, however, shows a skillful combination of forms, the creation of dramatic spaces, and a clear understanding of the representative nature of the building, all of which exemplify the successful design solution of the architects, Clotet and Paricio.

The site occupies a corner lot on an angle of the Gran Via de Jaime 1, a position that allows motorists and pedestrians a long view down the street to the bank. Requirements for the design demanded that the unattractive walls of some nearby buildings had to be hidden, while the scale of other, neighboring buildings that have been designated historically significant, had to be respected. An urban park recently designed by the team of José Antonio Martínez Lapeña and Elías Torres is across the street from the site, and the bank design was also supposed to address this new park. From the beginning the architects decided to use a cylindrical shape for the main portion of the building; it seemed a logical form as it would provide varied perspectives, both from the inside and the outside. The bank rises to a height of 18 meters, with the exterior wall of the cylinder extending above the roof line.
This exterior wall adds further height and monumentality to the structure and conceals the buildings behind it. The lower rectangular building that hugs the cylinder creates a dialogue with the surrounding low-rise structures. The perimeter wall encompassing the bank establishes the transition between the tall cylinder and the scale of the street and makes the building complex appear larger.

In the interior, the monumentality of the cylinder and the unity of the design, hinted at from the exterior, are achieved in an open public banking space that rises from the ground to the third floor. The cylinder's walls are 45 centimeters thick and are supported by buttresses that are visible on the interior. Natural light has a dramatic effect as it enters through the large vertical windows placed in the upper level of the curved wall. The building is organized as a semicircular space, which is divided in half by the tellers' windows. This area, for public banking

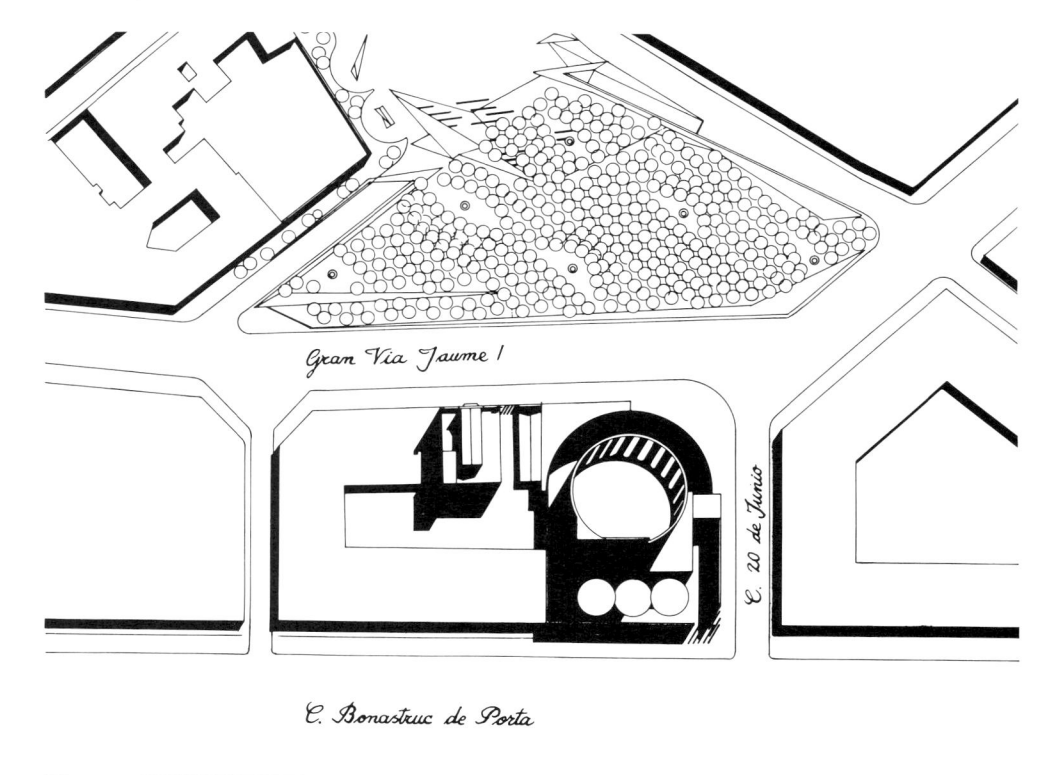

Site plan

View from 20 de Junio street

services, flows into a more regular rectangular space, used for offices, meeting rooms, and other needs. The superposition of layers, or walls, creates varied views and allows an understanding of the entire interior. These layers are pierced by arched openings or circles—forms that the architects consider the most "natural" for openings created in brick construction. Metal pillars, painted white, as is the entire interior, support the upper walls at the points closest to the banking areas and enhance the lightness and transparency of the interior design.

Although the Bank of Spain seems to be very elaborate in its details and furnishings, and perhaps even somewhat mannerist in its architectural style, the design process commenced with a strong concept that progressed through many phases, some even more complex, to arrive at the final building design, which is controlled and masterfully integrated. The elegance afforded by the use of a single, long-lasting material—red brick—and the high quality of construction ensure that the building will age with grace.

Bank of Spain
Gerona

First floor lounge

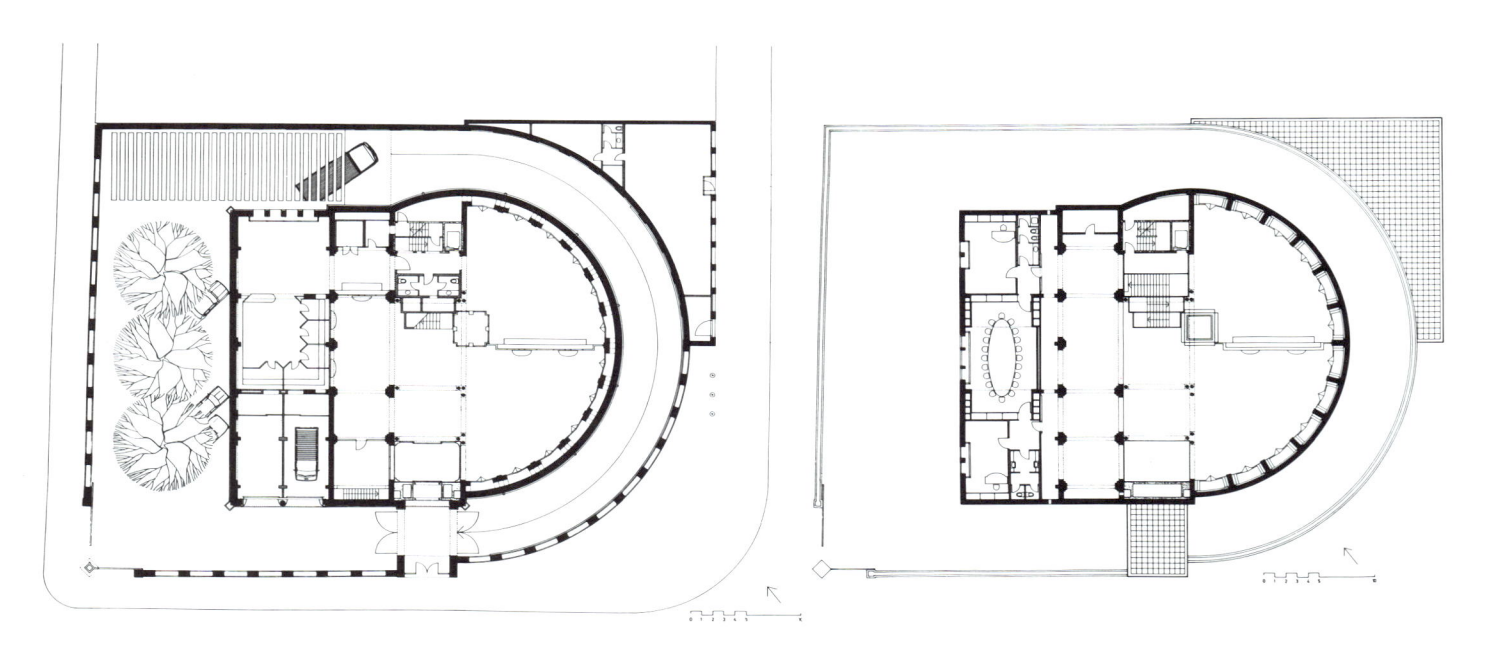

Ground floor plan

First floor plan

Bank of Spain
Gerona

View from intersection of Gran Via de Jaime I and 20 de Junio streets

Bank of Spain
Gerona

Main banking area

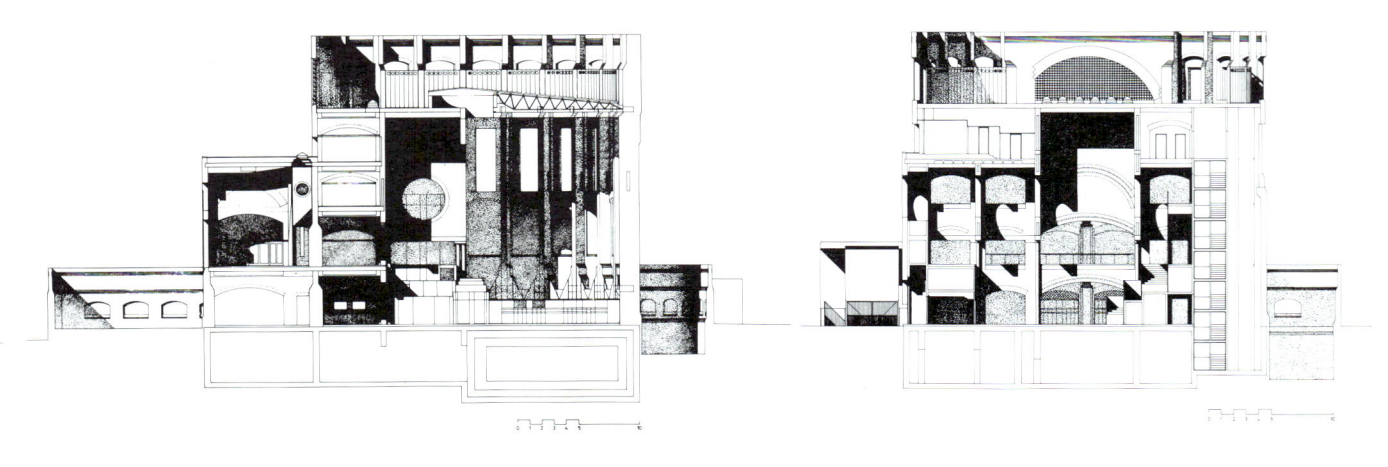

Longitudinal section

Cross section

Bank of Spain
Gerona

Perimeter wall

Museum of Navarra

Pamplona

Architects: Jordi Garcés
Enric Sòria

Collaborators: Montserrat Bou, Rafael Soto, architects; Estudio BGM and Anna Miquel

Project: 1986
Construction: 1987-90
Commission: Regional Government of Navarra and Principe de Viana Institution

The Museum of Navarra is located at the edge of the historic district of Pamplona, so, in renovating the existing museum to create the new structure, Garcés and Sòria remained within the architectural style of the original buildings, if only on the exterior. The original museum was created from a sixteenth-century hospital; in their renovations, the architects allowed the church next door, with its elaborate entrance, to remain intact and incorporated it into the new museum design. As the church and the museum are close to each other, the architects modified the museum's main entrance in order to unify the two facades. Garcés and Sòria created a more monumental entrance to the museum, in keeping with the church's, by placing the original ornate portal against a plain, modern, stone facade, which is simply engraved with the words "Museo de Navarra," as is the portal itself.

The major renovations, however, are in the interior. The architects wanted to design a new interior that was powerful enough to hold its own against the original architecture and with dimensions that were large enough to suggest the public nature of the building. A new, almost-oval entrance hall was developed from what was the central courtyard between the hospital and the church. The only straight side of this central hall is formed by a glass wall that allows light to enter and also provides a view of the exterior wall of the adjacent church, where mosaic fragments are hung. The hall is connected to several arched entryways that lead visitors to the collections. The arches are painted a brilliant blue in contrast to the natural stone and muted colors used throughout the museum. In their building renovations, such as the Picasso Museum in Barcelona, Garcés and Sòria often combine old and new architectural elements in ways that allow visitors to experience new qualities as independent entities while they also appreciate the old ones.

Most of the galleries of the four-story 7,500-square-meter museum are accessible from a main staircase. (The only exceptions are a subterranean gallery of prehistoric objects, which lies beneath the church courtyard and is reached by a wedge-shaped staircase at the rear of the building, and the adjoining church, where seventeenth- and eighteenth-century religious art is displayed. Visitors can enter the church directly from the street or through the

Main entrance

Cross section

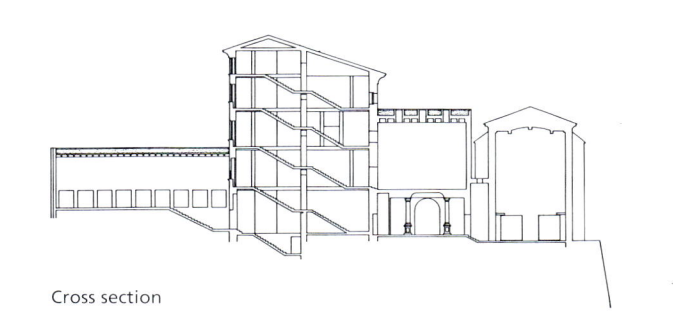

museum.) The museum's main staircase employs a modern architectural vocabulary with subtle iron detailing for the banisters and balusters.

Garcés and Sòria also designed the installation of objects in the galleries, which has allowed them to carry out completely the architectural objectives of their project. They worked closely with the staff of the museum, selecting the objects to be displayed and planning their placement so that they have sufficient space to be properly viewed and to create a dialogue among them.

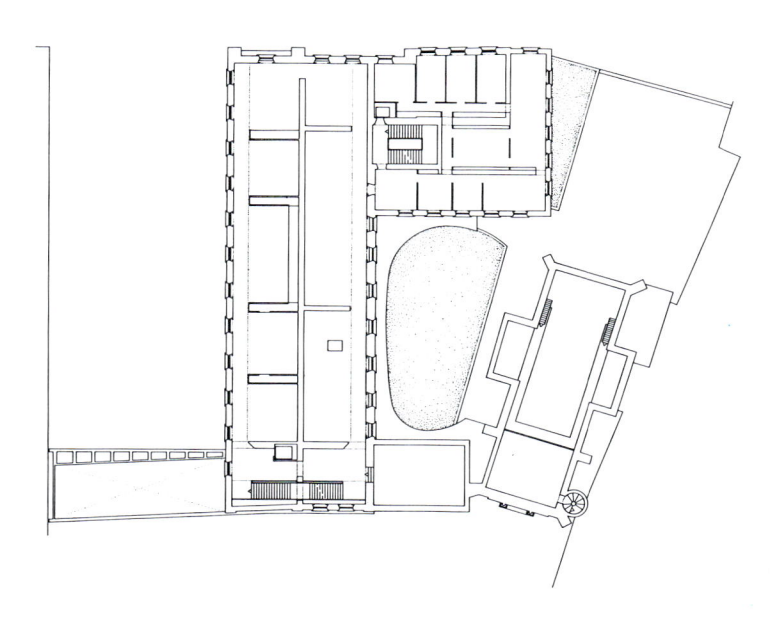

First floor plan

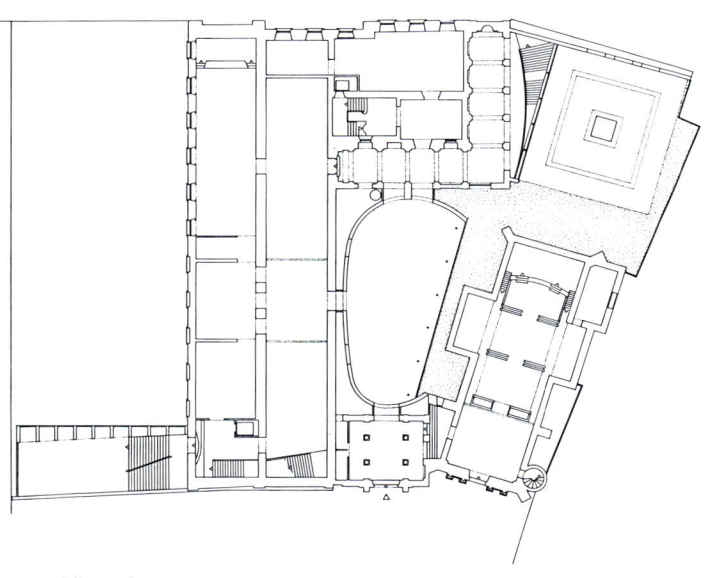

Ground floor plan

Main lobby

Staircase leading to exhibition galleries

Exhibition gallery

Museum of Navarra
Pamplona

Exhibition gallery

Museum of Navarra
Pamplona

Detail of courtyard with mosaics

Museum of Navarra
Pamplona

Arched corridors

Public Library of Aragon

Zaragoza

Architects: Victor López Cotelo, Carlos Puente

Collaborators: F. J. García Delgado, architect; J. M. Fernandez Alvarez, civil engineer; J. A. Valdés Moreno, P. Urroz Lasuén, R. Ruíz Mesa, technical architects; M. Burkhalter, R. Medina Iglesias, J. Pascual, J. Milla de Marco, G. Navarro Jiménez, and I. Mira Pueo.

Project: 1984-86
Construction: 1986-89
Commission: Ministry of Culture

The main library for the city of Zaragoza is in a residential area, a factor that made it necessary for the design to be appropriately monumental so that the building might be recognizable as a public facility, without overpowering its surroundings. The zoning regulations allowed only a small, low building to be built next to the existing apartment blocks. To circumvent this restriction, the planners decided to construct a larger library building by annexing an adjacent housing site. The zoning was not changed, so the architects created two adjoining buildings for the facility rather than one large building. The taller section, faced on one side with high-density plywood panels, is similar to the architectural style of the nearby housing units, so similar, in fact, that it's as if the existing blocks had been severed down the middle to make room for the new library. López Cotelo and Puente accepted both the contradictory zoning requirements and the position of the new library in the middle of a row of apartments; then, through the use of materials and the rhythm of the facade they connected the building to its environment.

To suggest the solid, civic character of the whole structure, gray Calatoroa stone was chosen to cover the base of the entire library building. The lower volume of the library is finished with light-colored stucco, a permanent material with long-standing

Side view

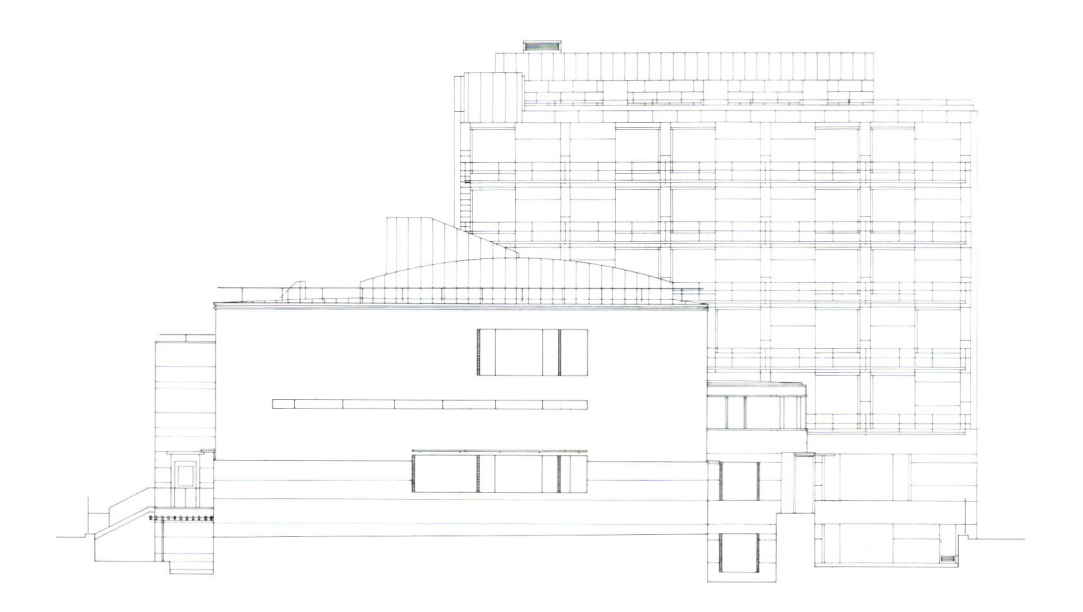

West elevation

Main entrance

historical connotations. Finally, it is crowned with a copper roof that works as a fifth facade as it can be seen from the neighboring buildings. The oversized windows also add a monumental quality.

The smaller section, only three stories above the ground, is set back from the street, in marked contrast to nearby structures. As visitors approach the entrance, they encounter a transitional space with perspectives that change as they move from the busy roadway to the library. The broad brick-paved entryway gently slopes up from the street, requiring visitors to advance gradually as they leave the noisy street

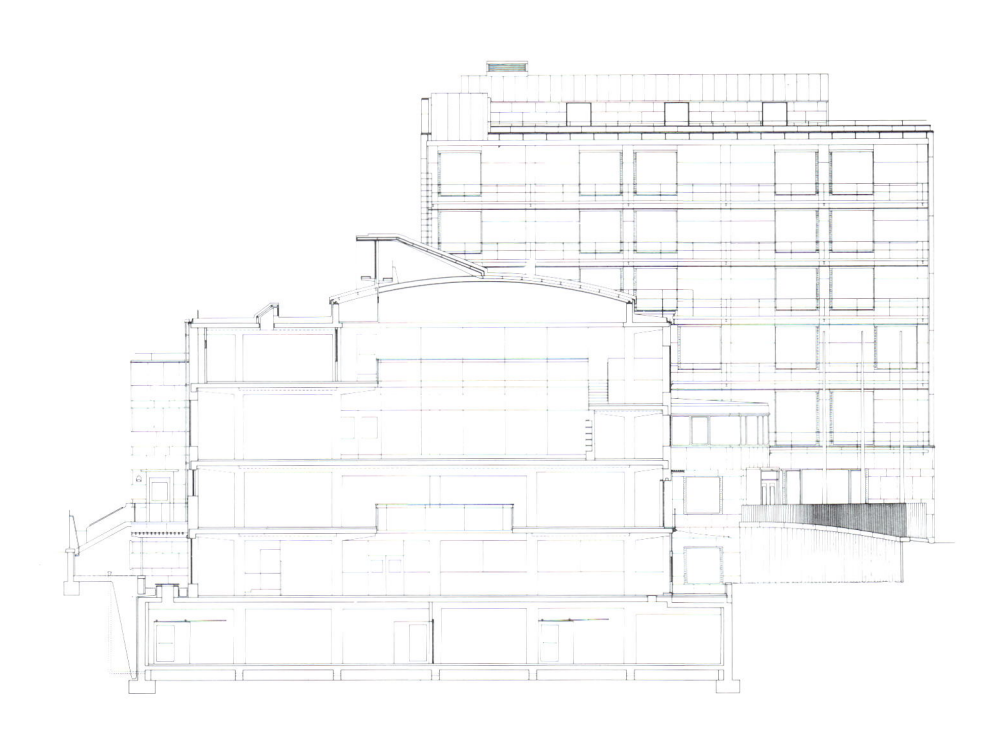

Longitudinal section

Public Library of Aragon
Zaragoza

behind before entering the quiet space of the library.

The interior space does not reflect the fragmentation of the exterior. The two buildings, which appear to be separate structures from the exterior, are unified on the interior. The stacks are located in a sub-basement; the children's library and the auditorium are in the basement, with access to an English-style patio outside; card catalogues, open stacks, and user services are on the ground floor, and the main reading room is up one floor with additional reading rooms above it. The top stories house the audio-visual department, offices, and the Aragon regional library.

The architects sought to create an inviting, intimate atmosphere in the interior. They were especially careful to allow natural light to illuminate as many parts of the building as possible, in spite of the great depth of the building. Large glass windows that open onto the sunken patios allow daylight to penetrate into the basement. The furniture, some of which was designed by the architects, is largely made of natural wood and has a straightforward, somewhat Scandinavian style.

As in all the work of López Cotelo and Puente, the architecture seems to be the natural result of the clients specific requirements, the existing conditions, the immediate surroundings, a firm budget, and the well-examined needs of the users. No architectural element is superfluous. When all the existing concerns are considered, their design seems to be the only one possible. It takes into account all the facets of reality in a functional, elegant, and subtle way.

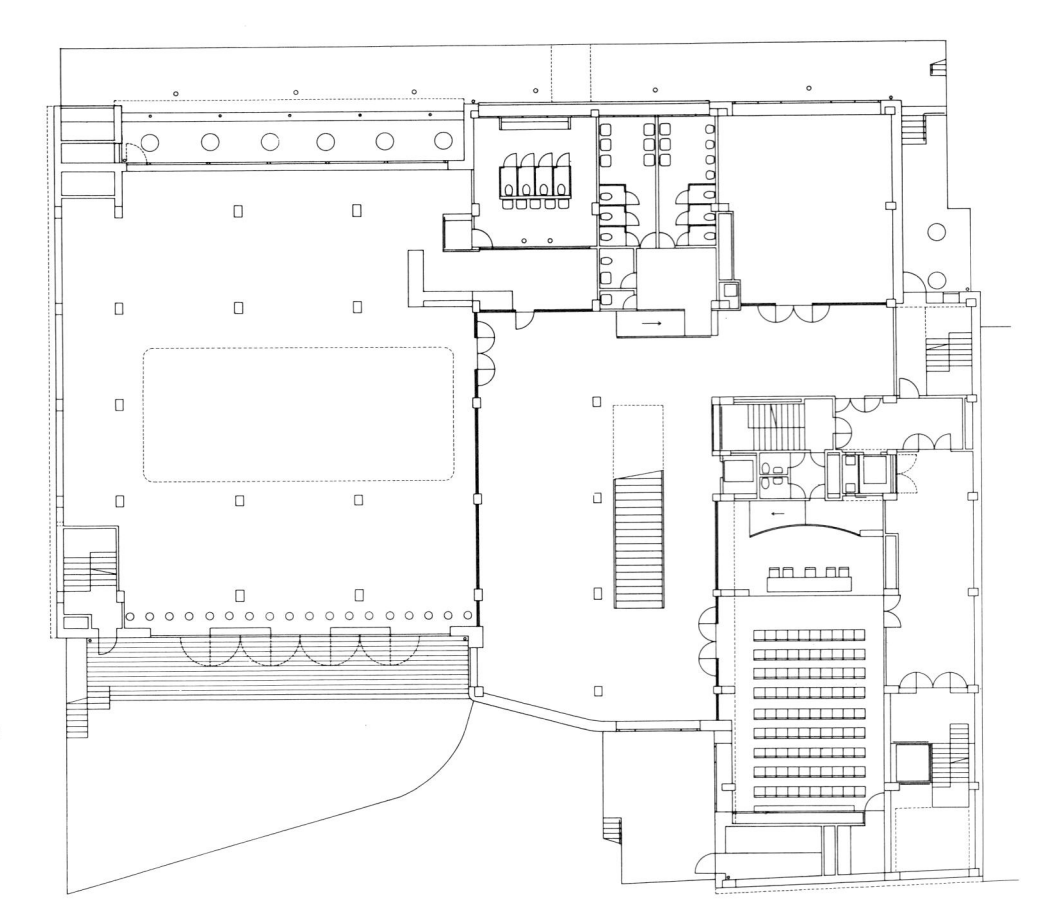

Ground floor plan

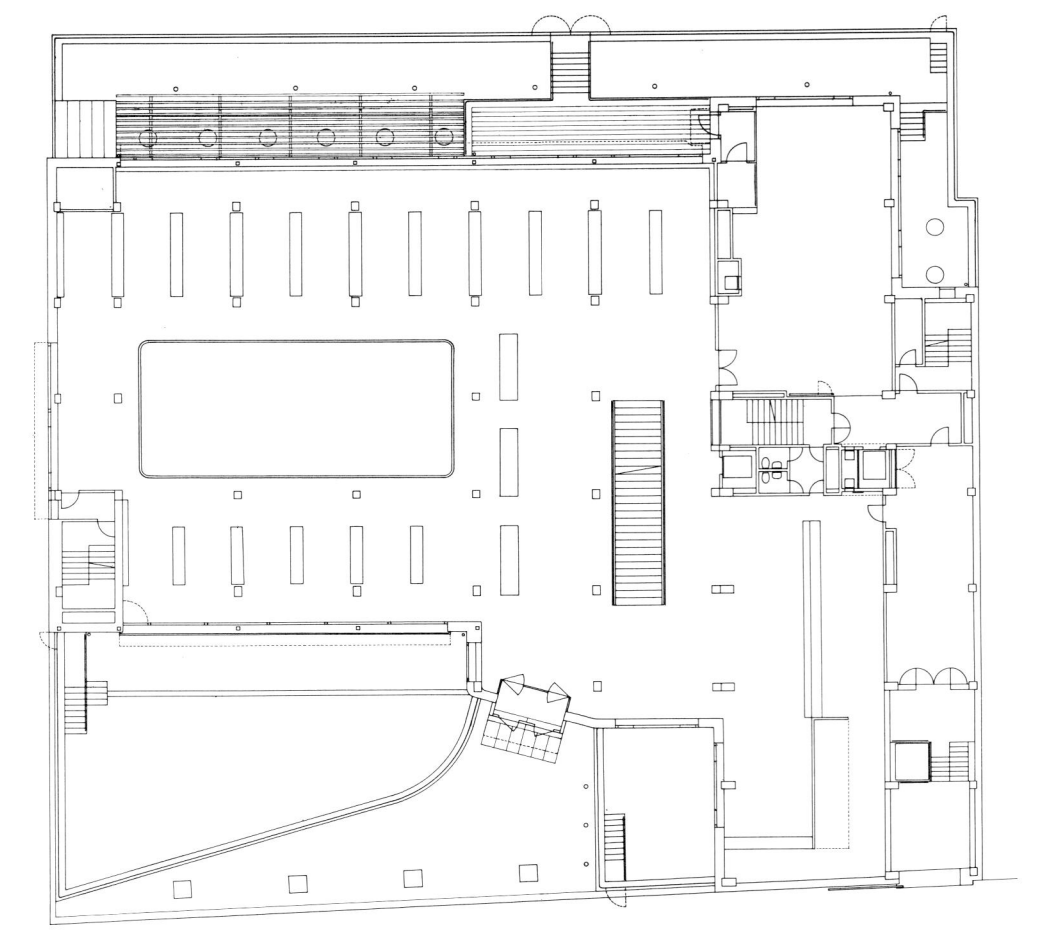

Sub-basement plan

Public Library of Aragon
Zaragoza

Rear facade

Hallway

117

Public Library of Aragon
Zaragoza

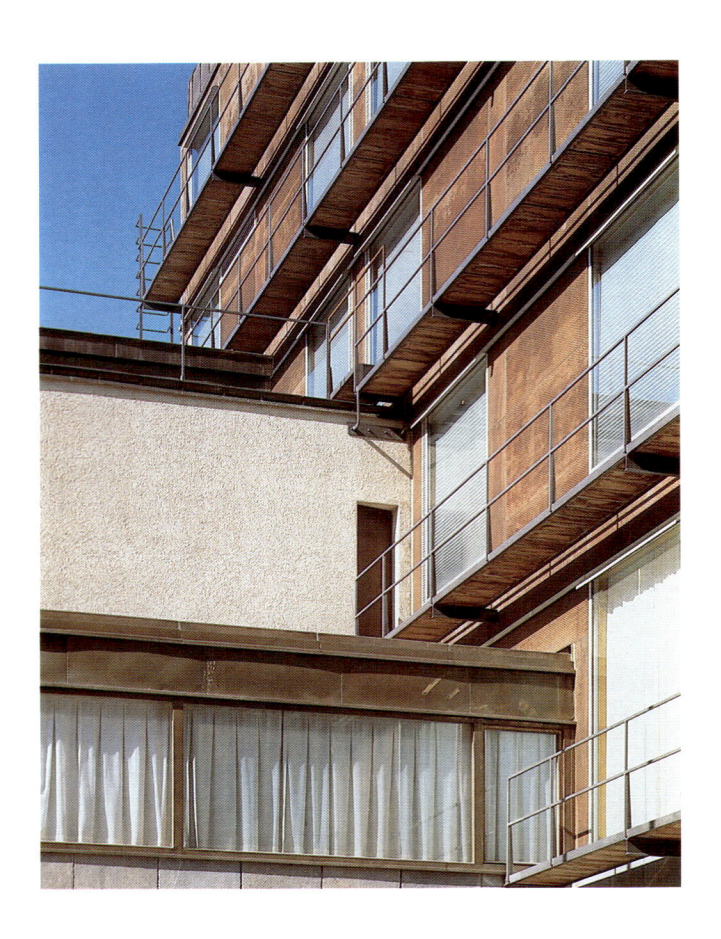

Detail of balconies on west facade

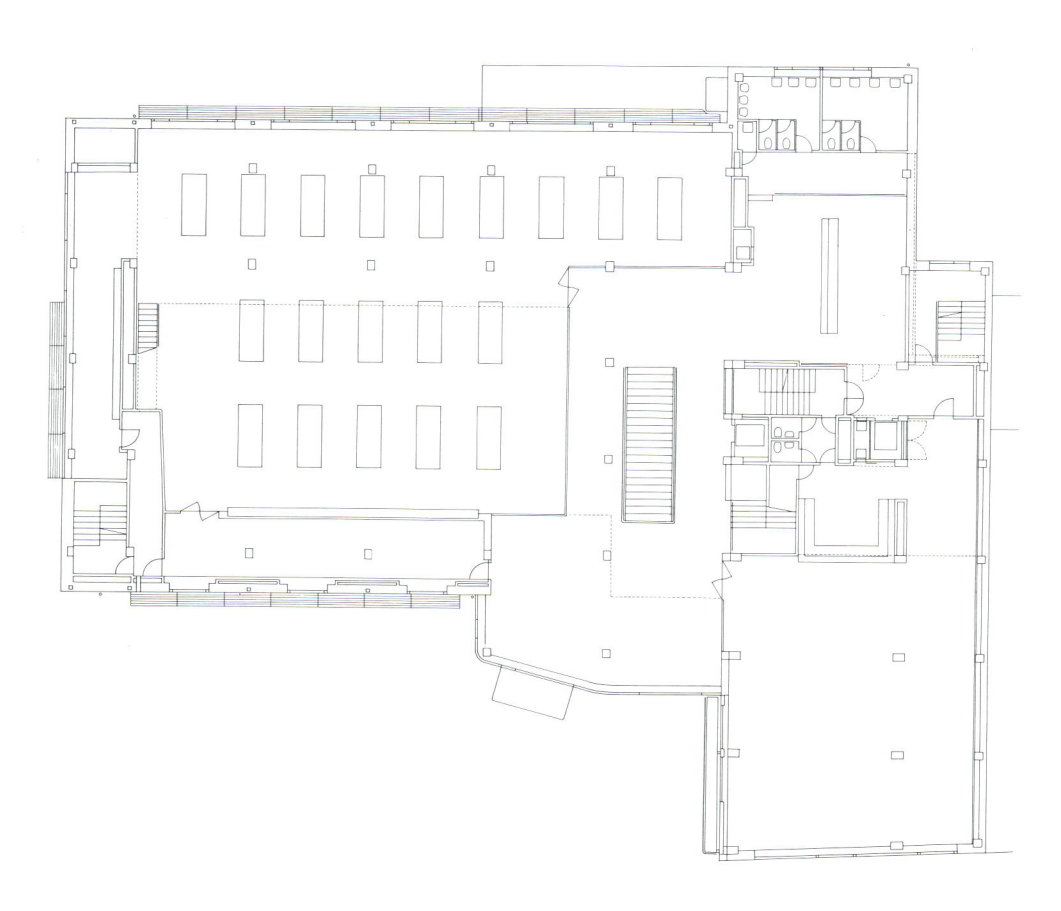

First floor plan

Main reading room

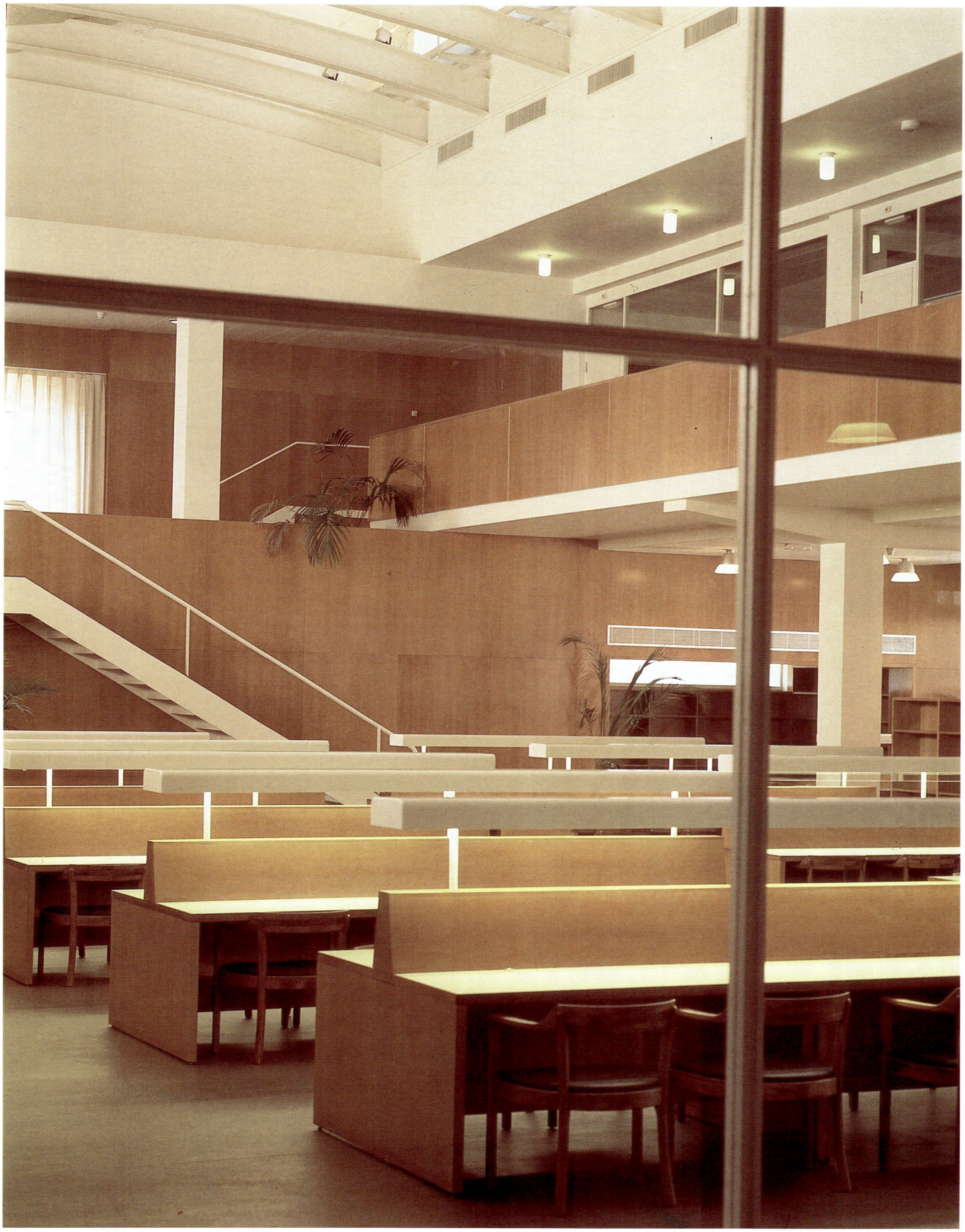

Housing for the Olympic Village

Barcelona

Architects	Albert Viaplana Helio Piñón
Collaborator	Ricard Mercadé, architect
Project	1988
Construction	1989-91
Commission	Nova Icària, S.A., a semi-public development corporation

The construction of the Olympic Village is part of a transformation project for a 320-acre seafront area of Barcelona called Nova Icària. The village, which will include housing, sports facilities, services, and open spaces, will be integrated into the city, and after the 1992 Olympic Games, it will become a residential neighborhood. Historically, there have been many attempts to reclaim this formerly industrial area along the sea for the city, and now, with the incentive of the Olympics, it will finally be renewed.

The master plan established for this area laid out a coherent pattern that is based on the existing grid layout of the city as decreed by the engineer Ildefonso Cerdà in his 1859 *Ensanche,* a plan for the enlargement of Barcelona. The Olympic Village is based on a new definition of Cerdà's "superblock," which had originally established a 100-by-100-meter grid for each city block. Under the new master plan, some of the superblocks are larger in size and irregular in shape, although they maintain the traditional character of the "corridor street" and the regular facades of the Cerdà plan. In the interior of each of these new superblocks, however, different types of housing have been built, thus breaking with the original Cerdà concept.

The firm of Viaplana and Piñón was commissioned to build 133 housing units in a modified U-shape with a highrise structure on the interior. The master plan was very restrictive, defining alignment of the new building and its volume, surfaces, number of units, height, materials for the main facade (brick), and cornice height. These norms were implemented so that the entire complex would be harmonious and unified even though many architectural firms, some of the most outstanding in Barcelona and the world, were commissioned to work on the project. With so many limitations, the architects' task was difficult. Innovative ideas were sometimes sacrificed to accommodate the requirements. It is not yet apparent whether the laudable goals set down in the original plan have been achieved.

In spite of all the restrictions dictated by the master plan, Viaplana and Piñón have designed attractive, highly functional housing units. Their first step was to break the given U-shape into separate buildings. Two of the four structures of their portion of this superblock are perpendicular (on Icària and Pamplona avenues), and they are joined to achieve a beveled corner, an element prescribed by the Cerdà plan. The floor plan of each unit of these six-story blocks organizes all the rooms around a central hall, with the bedrooms facing Icària Avenue and the living room and kitchen facing the interior of the city block. The spatial objective of this layout is to unite the apartments, transversely, from

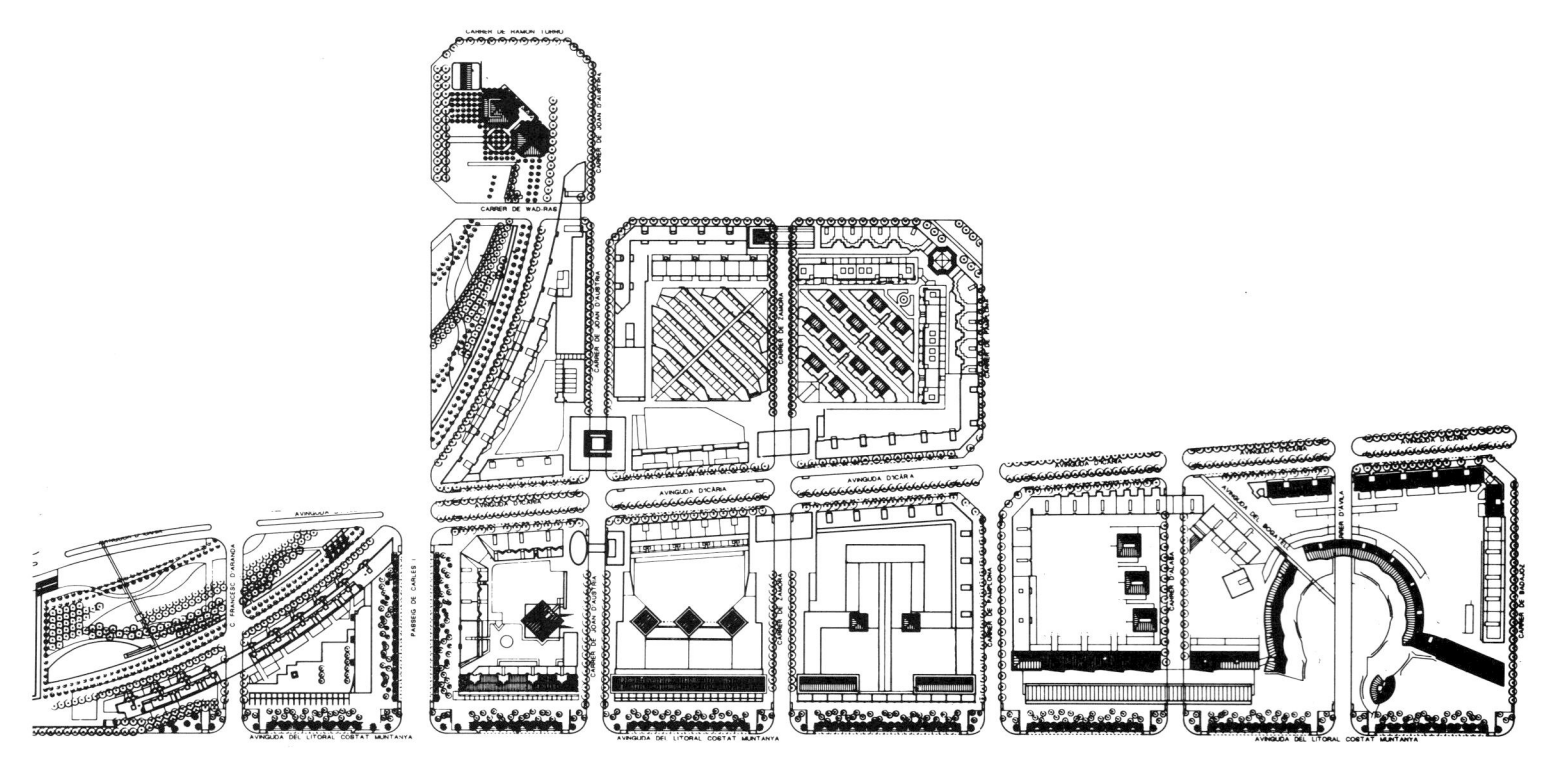

Plan of the area of Nova Icària

the open space in the interior of the apartment block, through to the balconies on Icària Avenue. A third, slightly smaller building completes the U-shape, although it is disconnected from the others and is aligned with Bogatell Avenue. The fourth structure is an entirely separate, freestanding, ten-story highrise, which contains only 19 units with its own underground parking.

The architects enlivened the exterior of the apartment block by repeating a regular geometric pattern of windows across the facade, even though the floor plans of each two-unit group are inverted and mirror each other around the main staircase. This arrangement of windows, then, does not reflect the interior arrangement of space. The dissonance that results from this discontinuity is made more emphatic on one side by the addition of terraces of varying depth. The terraces form an imaginary line that is parallel to Icària Avenue, while the building itself follows the parallel layout of the main street behind, Litoral Avenue. The architects took advantage of any liberties they had and did not use the materials required for the exterior facade on the apartment block's interior facade. The public side on Icària Avenue is faced with two tones of brick, and the more private interior space is faced with small ceramic tiles and has wooden overhangs and balconies. On the interior facade, a compositional exercise using different scales is apparent.. The window pattern corresponds to each apartment, and a wooden lattice shades every two apartments on the top floor, while the balconies from the upper-story apartments shade the lower units. The continuous concrete pillars placed at the stairwells of each building highlight the vertical structure and overall height of the building and add to its stylistic rhythm. The architects, using a subtle and abstract language, have stretched the building restrictions to achieve clever, sometimes tongue-in-cheek, and always eloquent solutions to difficult design problems.

View of Icària Avenue facade

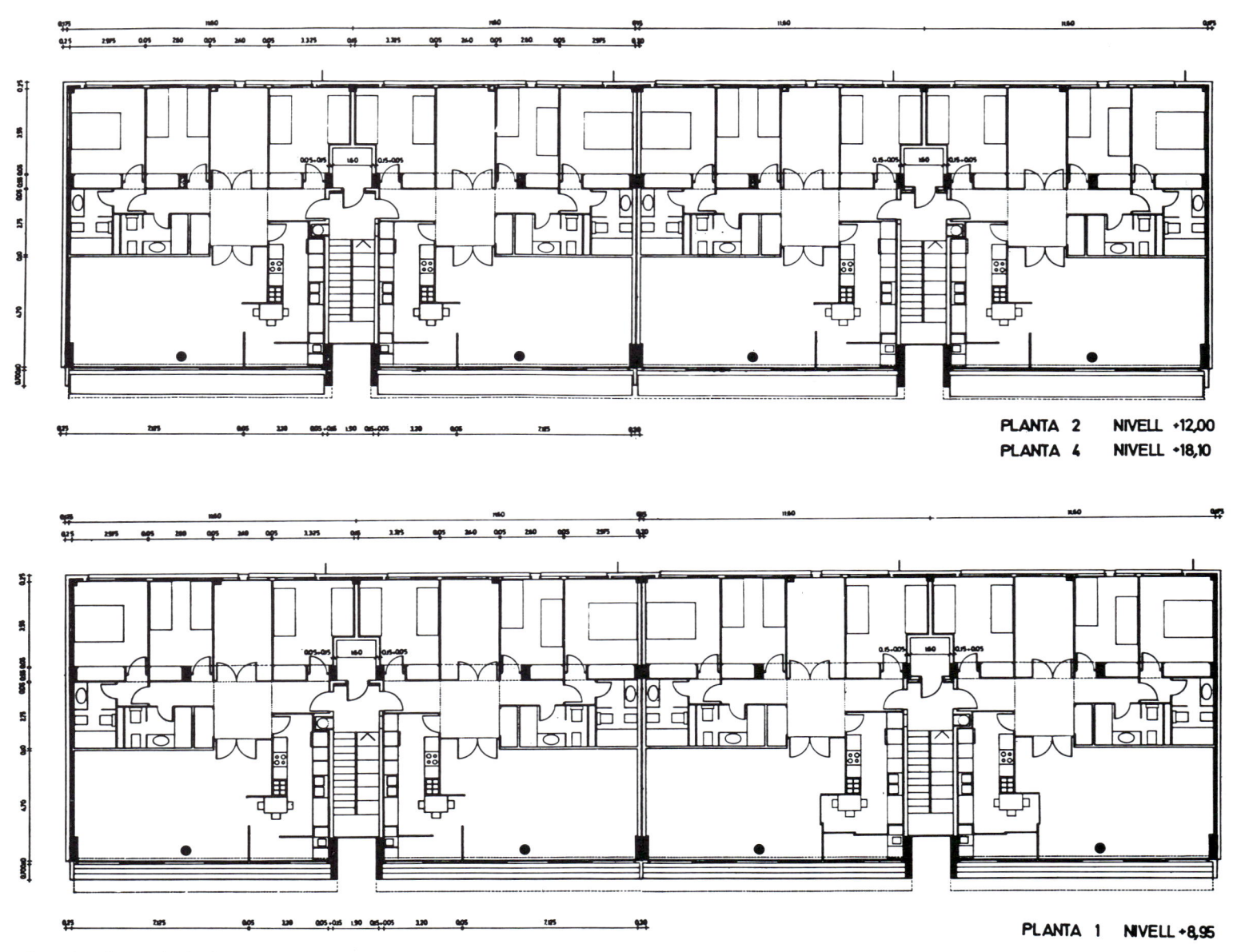

PLANTA 2   NIVELL +12,00
PLANTA 4   NIVELL +18,10

PLANTA 1   NIVELL +8,95

Floor plans for standard units

View of high rise housing block

Detail of balconies on Icària Avenue

Plan

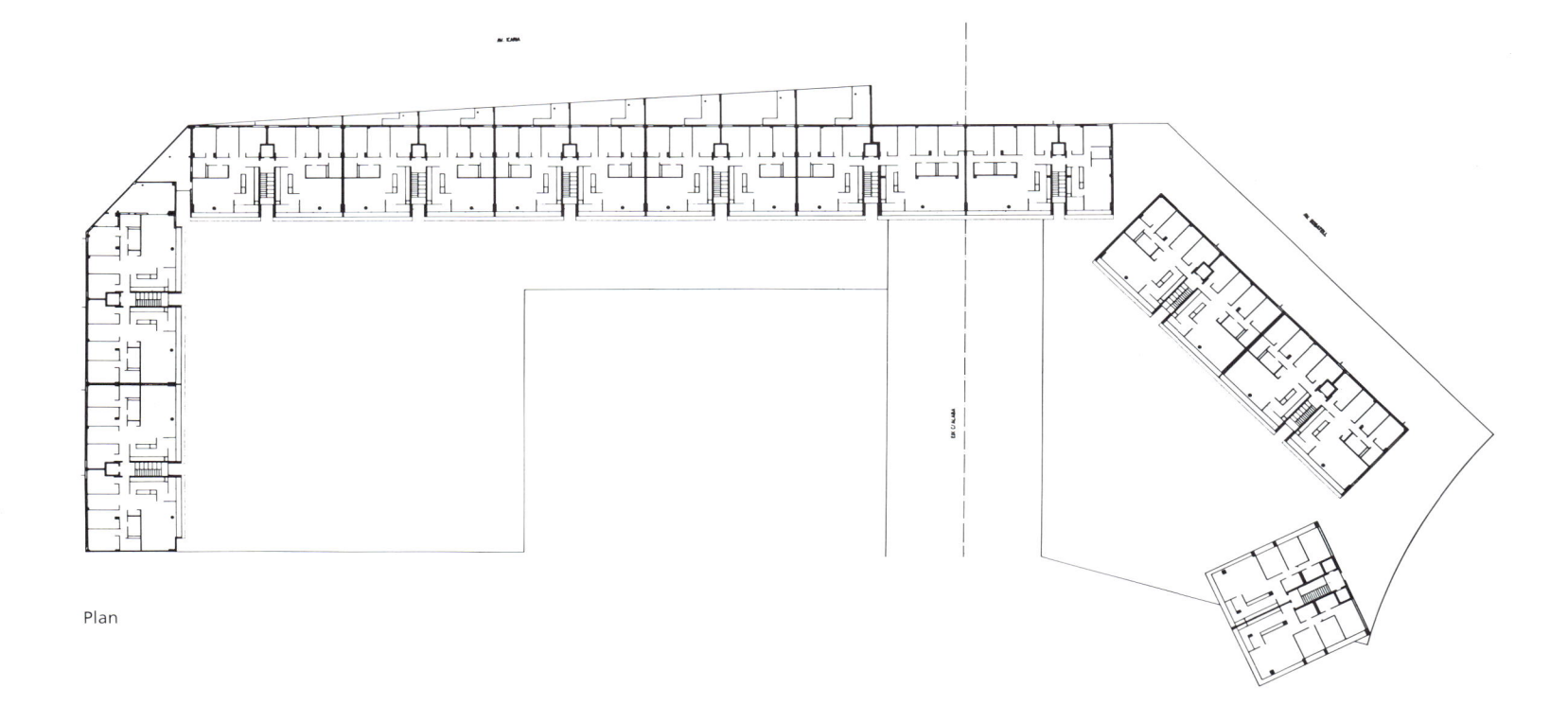

Detail of corner

123

Interior facade and through street

124

View of interior facade

Detail of balcony of interior facade

Olympic Archery Ranges

Barcelona

Architects Enric Miralles
Carme Pinós

Collaborators Rodrigo Prats and Silvio Martínez, architects; Brufau-Obiols-Moya, consulting engineers; and Edetco, S.A., technical architects

Project 1989
Construction 1990-91
Commission COOB '92, S.A. - The Olympic Organizing Committee of Barcelona '92

The project brief for the Olympic archery ranges called for the design of two separate buildings and adjacent fields, one for training purposes and the other for official competitions. Each structure will include changing rooms, showers, restrooms, a cafeteria, and other support facilities, in addition to the open-air shooting ranges. After the 1992 Olympics, however, the fields and accompanying facilities will be used for soccer and rugby.

In spite of the apparently modest scope of the project, the architects have created a visually surprising structure. An important aspect of their design is the modification of the site's topography. The architects mounded earth taken from the archery ranges to form a raised area at the rear of the service facilities. An irregularly shaped retaining wall around the earth mound forms the back wall of the service buildings. The front portion of the service buildings overlooks the archery ranges.

The competition archery range, which is built of precast concrete, houses the dressing rooms and shower units. Parking is located above the fields, on the fabricated hill. Spectators can walk down a path to a viewing platform, which is defined by a metal pergola and pierced by freestanding concrete and glass structures that function as skylights and illuminate the service building below. The dominant image of the building is a long, horizontal, curved concrete structure that is

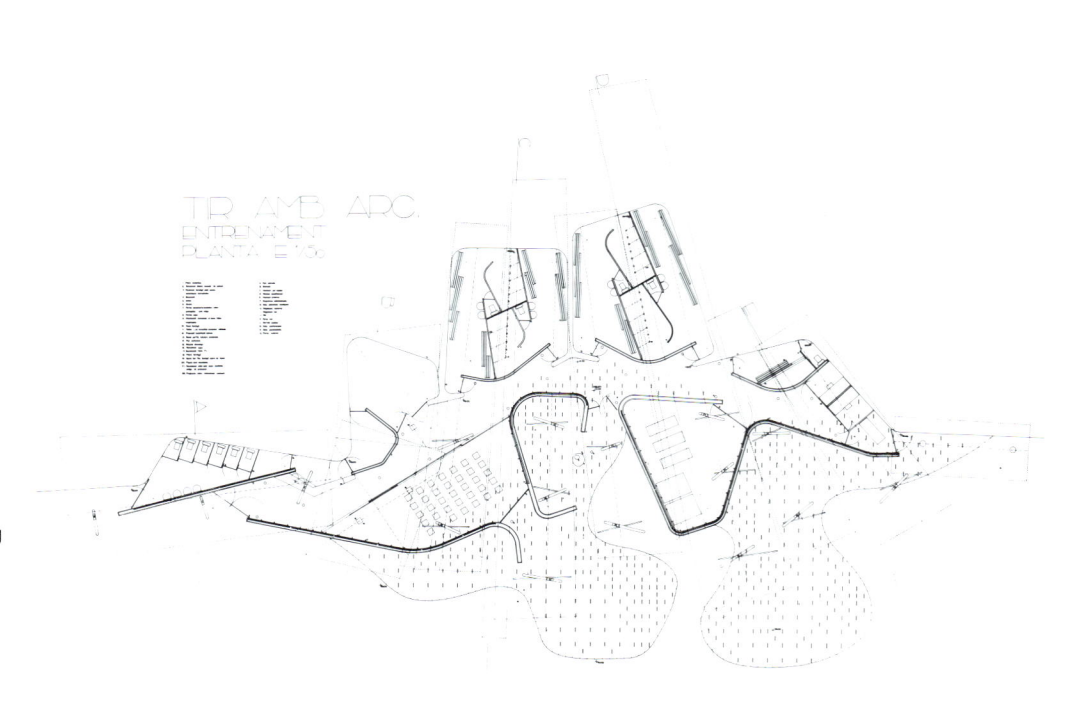

Ground floor plan, service building, training area

Service building, competition area

Detail of roof, training area

Service buidling, training area

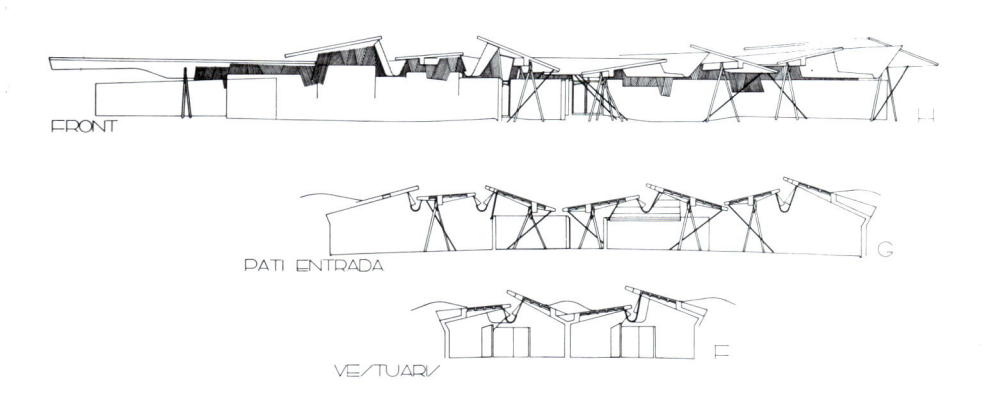

Sections and elevation, training area building

Olympic Archery Ranges
Barcelona

punctured by repeated rows of small triangular windows.

Although the two ranges have similar functions, Miralles and Pinós differentiated the two parts (training and competition), which are separated by a road that passes through the site. The architects employed different forms and materials for each structure. For example, the training range structure has mostly brick walls, in contrast to the competition range building's concrete walls, and a great concrete and tile roof of inclined planes juts out from the embankment behind the training building.

The visual and textural aspects of the architects' work are especially important. The forms are daring, often fractured and intentionally misaligned, and they appear to be pieces of sculpture embedded in the earth. The materials often seem rough, almost primitive, although Miralles and Pinós used contemporary technology in the structure. The architects' attention to detail is evident in the decorative metalwork, such as the initials TA (i. e., Tiro con Arco, literally, shoot with bow) that were incorporated into the design of the doors. A sense of naturalness is enhanced by the play of light and shadows. Their architecture creates new landscapes yet fuses with the terrain.

In the architects' plans, the distance between graphic representation and realized architecture can seem great. Each line in their architectural drawings, however, contains potent and complex ideas. Their refined and minimalist drawings represent a summary—like a compacted archive on a computer disk—that reveals the strength and meaning of the whole work when it is expanded to its full potential.

Detail of entrance, training area building

Exterior, competition area building

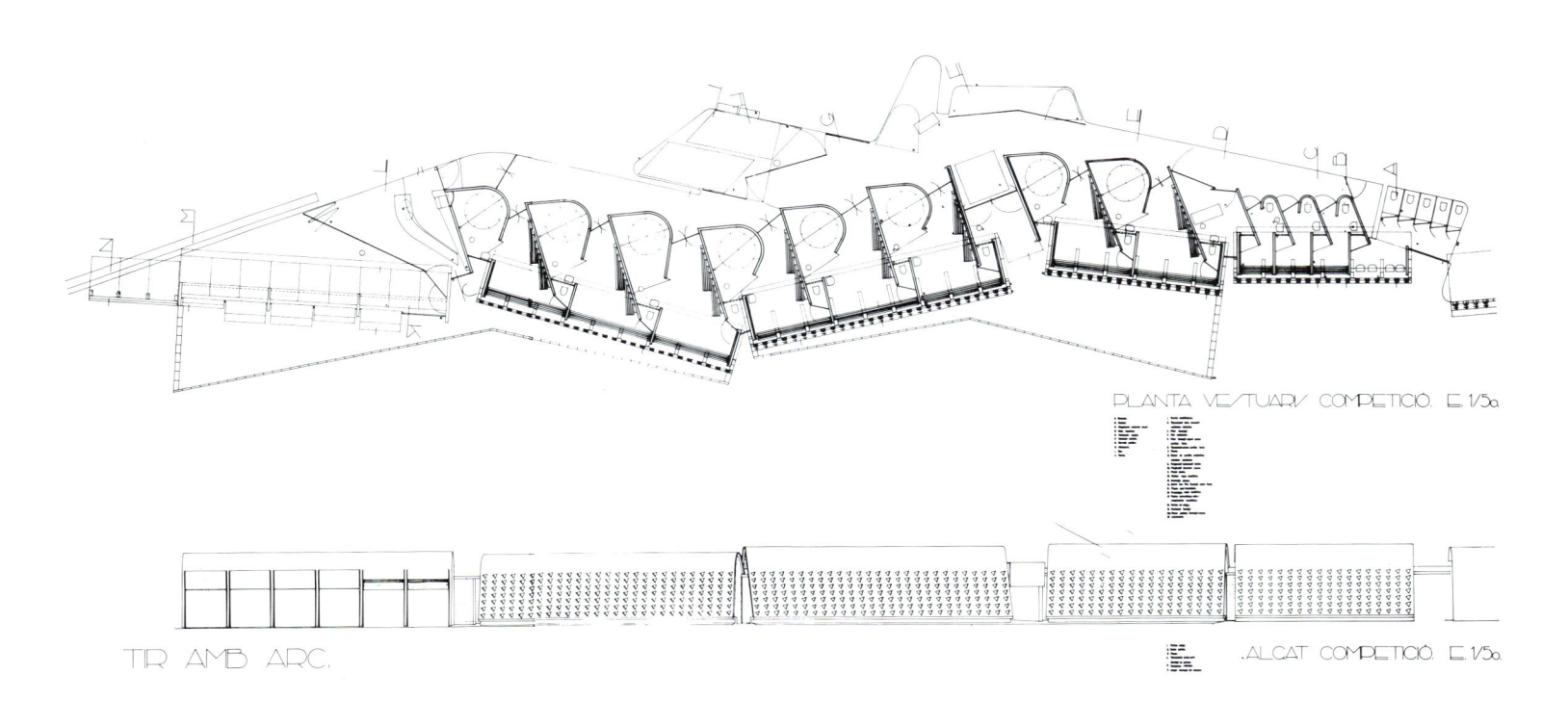

Ground floor plan and elevation, competition area building

Olympic Archery Ranges
Barcelona

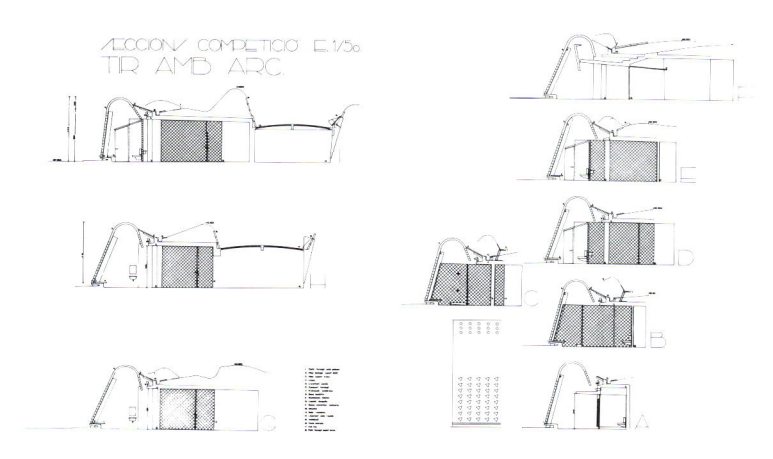

Sections, competition area building

Entrance, competition area building

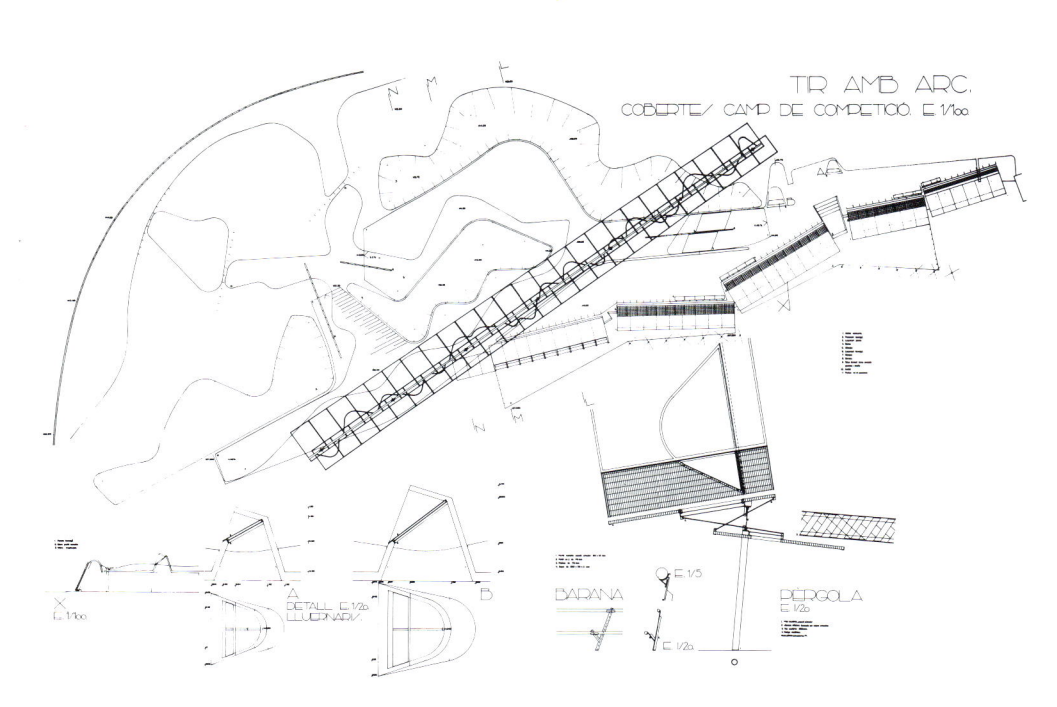

Pergola and details, competition area

131

Municipal Sports Stadium

Badalona

Architects: Esteve Bonell, Francesc Rius

Collaborators: Enric Rego and Pere Rius, technical architects; Brufau-Obiols-Moya, consulting engineers; C. Aubry, N. Bongard, J. Calsapeu, F. Khun, T. Lussi, D. Mas, and A. Mee

Competition: 1987
Project: 1989
Construction: 1990-91
Commission: Badalona Municipality; COOB'92 S.A. - the Olympic Organizing Committee of Barcelona '92; and the Generalitat de Catalunya

The enormous formal strength and the fine construction are two outstanding qualities of the new sports stadium in Badalona, just northeast of Barcelona. The architects Bonell and Rius were first-prize winners in the competition for the commission to design the new sport arena, which will house up to 12,000 spectators of basketball games for the 1992 Summer Olympics.

The slightly modified elliptical form is successful despite the difficult urban setting. The facility, set on a slightly raised platform, quietly dominates the mundane surroundings, which include a busy highway and rather prosaic blocks of housing. The main entrance, facing one corner of the site, opens toward an urban plaza across the street. This entrance adds an air of ceremony for those attending the sports competitions, for spectators must walk up wide granite steps to arrive at the entrance of six sets of double doors through which they get an immediate view of the arena inside.

The building appears to be anchored solidly to the ground, its solidity emphasized by the dark gray stone base. Changes in materials, color, and architectural vocabulary contribute to the lighter quality of the upper part of the structure. The main section is covered in a lighter gray stone and is punctuated by windows and ten exits placed at regular intervals around the structure. The steel roof seems to be held down (rather than held up) by delicate white metal columns and is completely different from the classical main volume. The stadium resembles an industrial building, due to its sawtooth roof; seven skylights placed in the angular roof provide the stadium with natural light during daytime games. Although the architects were not able to finish the roof in copper as they had wished, the green corrugated steel used instead approximates the interesting color and texture of copper as it weathers.

Overall view

The interior plan is simple and clear. Each of the two main tiers of seating are easily accessible. Visitors can approach the lower level through an interior hallway encircling the building. They can reach the upper level by ascending staircases along the exterior wall to an open-air hallway that also encircles the stadium. This hallway opens onto the upper seating sections. The main circulation area, where concessions, restrooms, and other services are located, has a certain intimacy, despite the large dimensions of the whole complex, due to the skillful combination of concrete, brick, and travertine marble. The architects have fully utilized the lowest level, under the seats, for changing rooms, two practice courts, medical facilities, and other support services.

Side view

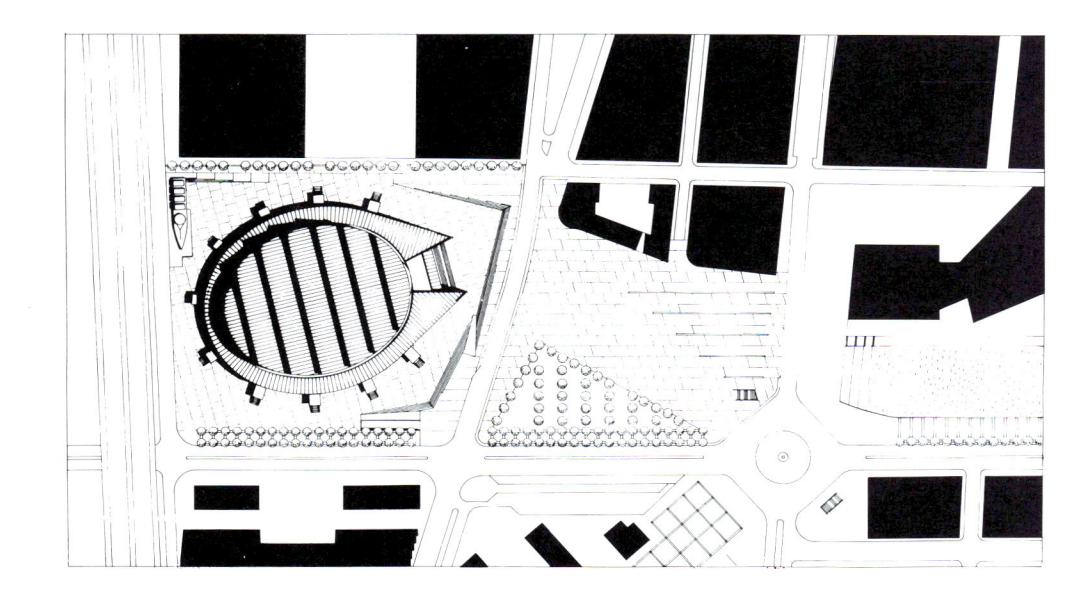

Site plan

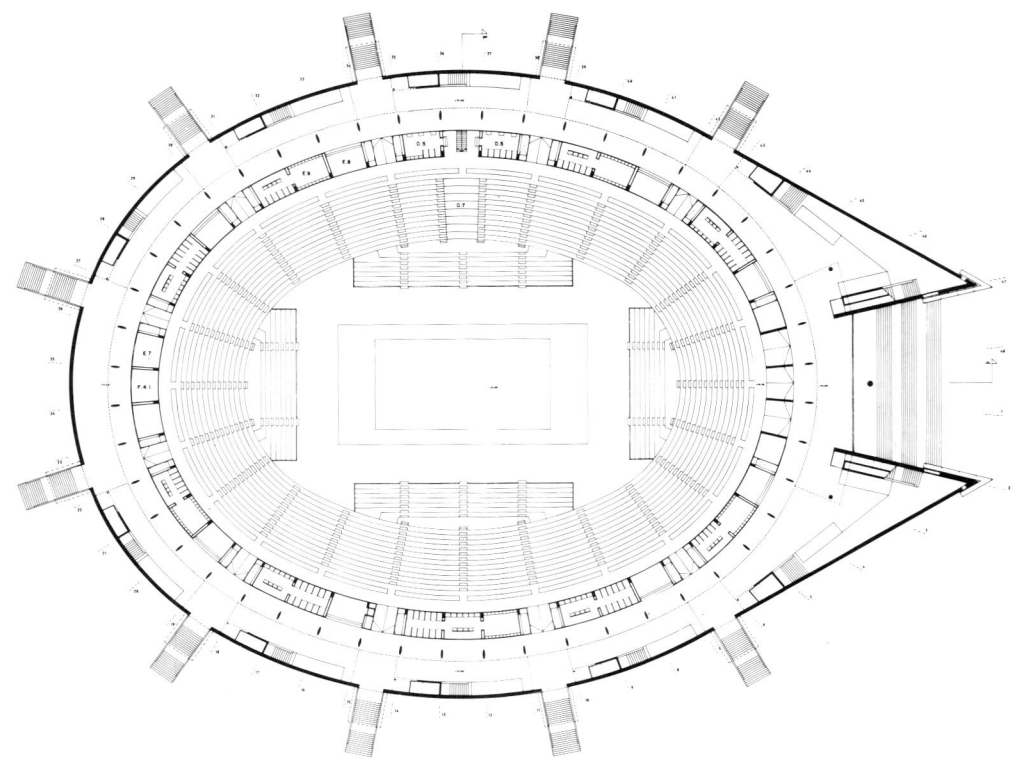

Plan

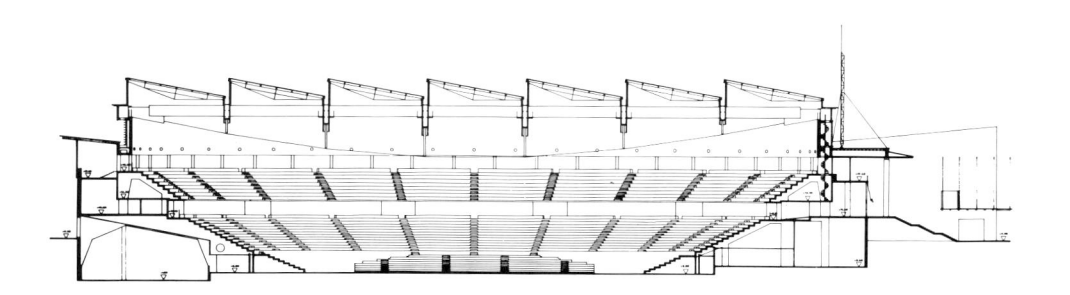

Longitudinal section

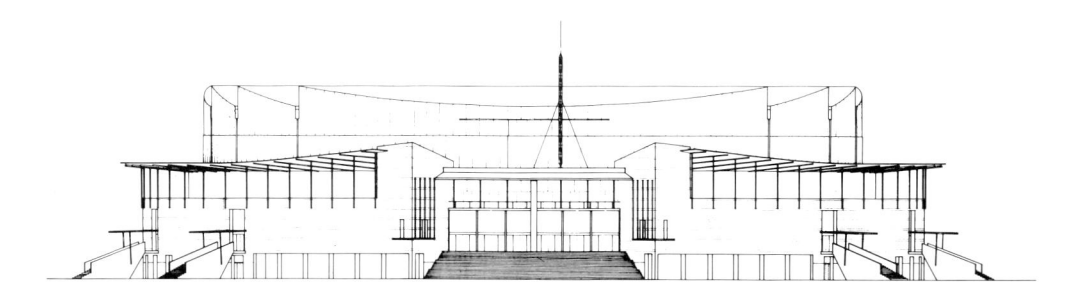

Front elevation

View of arena

Detail of entrance

Municipal Sports Stadium
Badalona

Detail of exterior staircase

Municipal Sports Stadium
Badalona

View of practice court

Convention Center

Salamanca

Architect: Juan Navarro Baldeweg

Collaborators: Julio Martínez Calzón, engineer; Eduardo González Velayos, technical architect; F. Antón Carbonero, C. Barreiro Sorrivas, F. Bucher, G. Clarimon Sandoval, L. Enseñat Benlliure, J. M. Merce Hospital, S. Schmutz, J. Serna Garrido, and P. Soler Serratosa

Competition: 1985
Project: 1986
Construction: 1988-1992
Commission: Regional Government of Castile-Leon

The work of Juan Navarro Baldeweg nearly always embodies two fundamental concepts: first, a deep understanding of the issues of architectural context and the dialogue among existing structures, topography, and new construction; and second, a constant concern for the recognition of natural phenomena. In the convention center of Salamanca, Navarro Baldeweg's fascination with gravity is relected in his design of the center's seemingly weightless, floating dome, which was inspired in part by the work of the nineteenth-century English architect Sir John Soane.

The site for the new convention center is a valley not far from the Tagus River in Salamanca. The valley forms the natural edge of the old city, a delineation that is further reinforced by the surrounding wall built from the remains of an ancient Roman wall. The architect has not attempted to make the new construction rise above or compete with the existing monuments and skyline of the historic city. The new building is clad in the natural golden stone of Salamanca, as are the majority of buildings in the city.

The strength of the convention center is derived intrinsically from its form. The new complex is composed of two buildings that are organized around an outdoor plaza placed at an intermediate level, which is reached by a staircase. From this plaza it is possible to enter the convention center, or the smaller exhibition hall, or an exterior arena designed for open-air activities. The larger building houses two auditoriums, one with a seating capacity of 1,300, the other for 400. Although the auditoriums are independent, each has a side vestibule with double-height ceilings, thereby keeping the overall design consistent. The smaller building, more delicate in appearance, functions as the center for exhibitions, seminars, and meetings. The exhibition spaces are connected by ramps that gently flow into one another.

The interior space of the main building can be thought of as architecture within architecture. It houses an enormous concrete dome, weighing some 1,500 tons, that seems to float above the main auditorium. The dome is suspended from 16 wedge-shaped concrete beams that project from the load-bearing perimeter walls. The arches within these walls carry the enormous weight of the dome, eliminating the need for columns or other supporting elements, which would have broken up the interior space. The formal and structural solutions were developed simultaneously. Natural light, entering both from the center oculus of the dome and from perimeter skylights, bathes the interior walls and emphasizes the complete separation of the dome from the walls. The arches placed

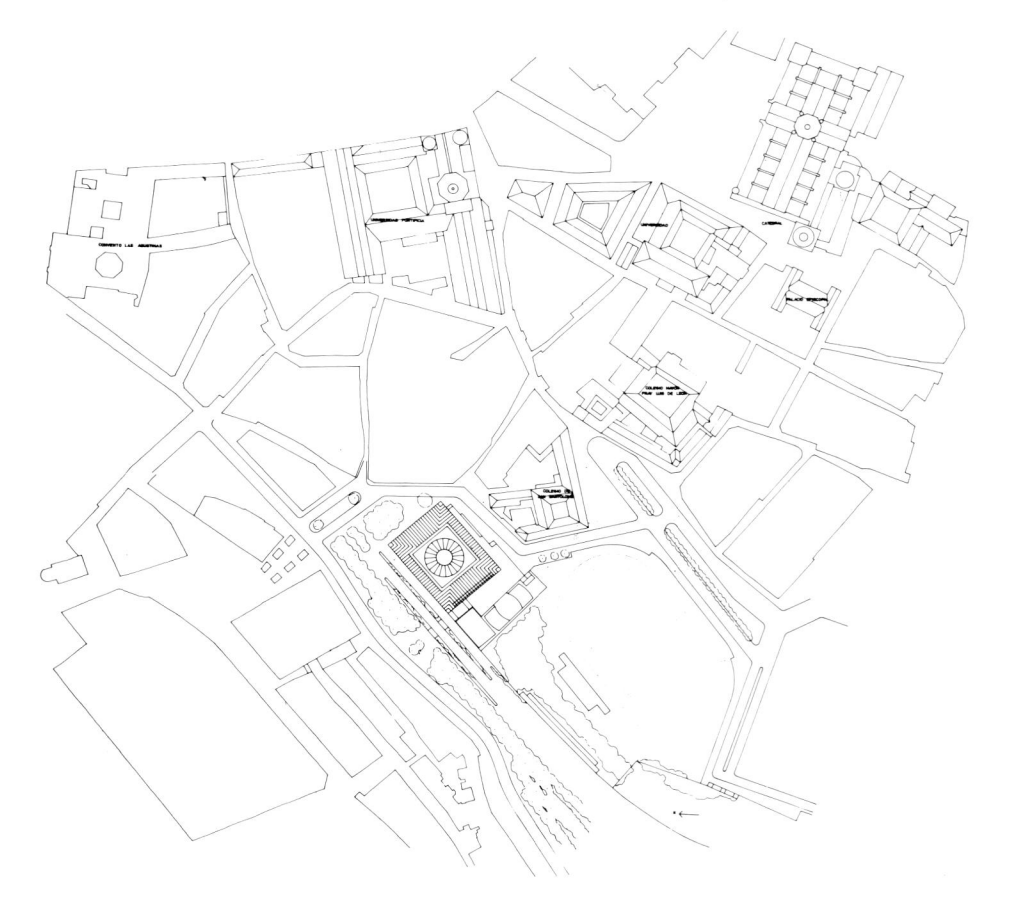

Site plan

on each of the exterior facades suggest the presence of the dome within, for it is otherwise essentially invisible from the outside.

Navarro Baldeweg's domed spaces are dramatic and awe-inspiring, yet they remain human in scale and intimate. Owing to his use of light, his structures often seem poetic, and the materials and textures he employs contribute to this lyrical quality. The architecture of Navarro Baldeweg is like a whisper uttered within the perfect dimensions of a Roman amphitheater. It is subtle and pure and has a resonance that is heard clearly everywhere..

Entrance plaza

Overall view

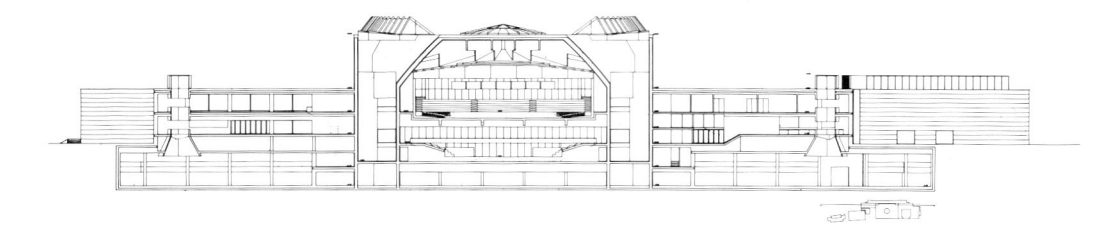

Cross section

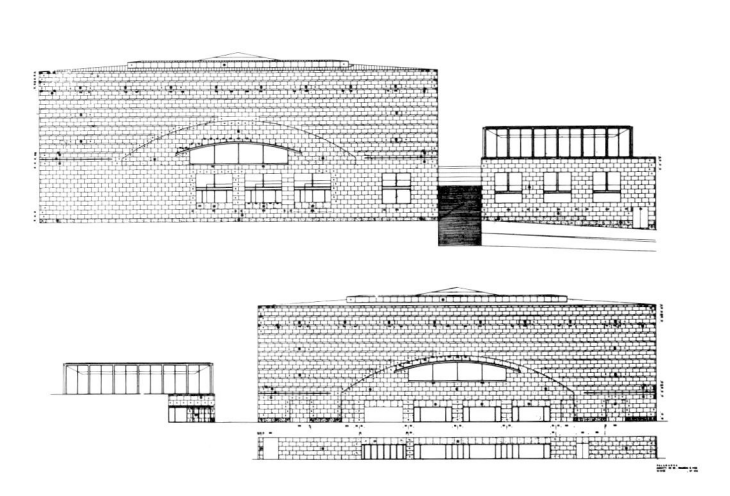

Elevations

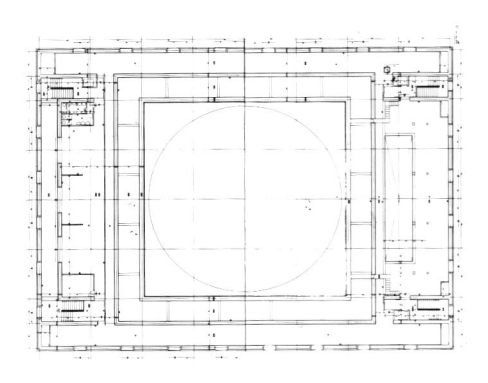

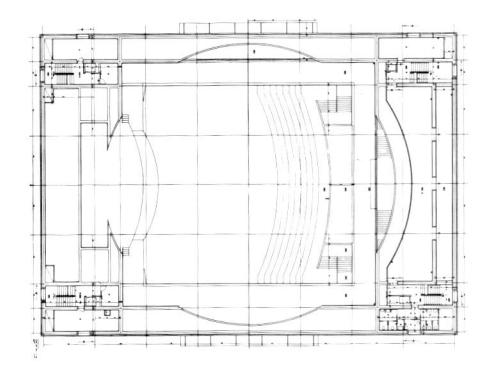

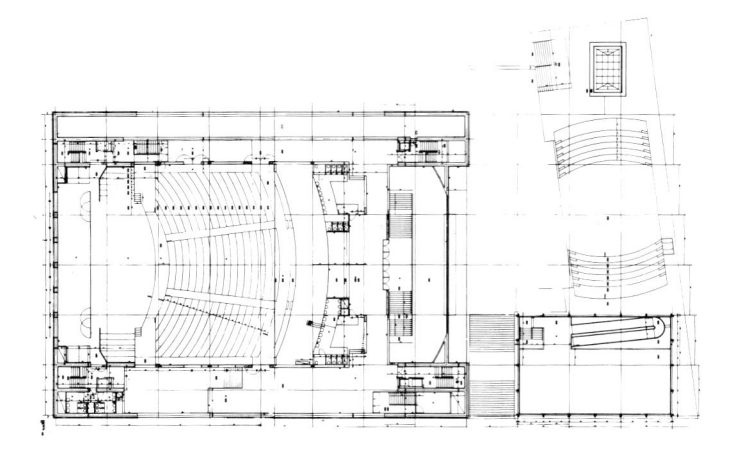

Floor plans

View from lobby towards exhibition building

Entrance to main auditorium

Side vestibule

Convention Center,
Salamanca

Auditorium and dome

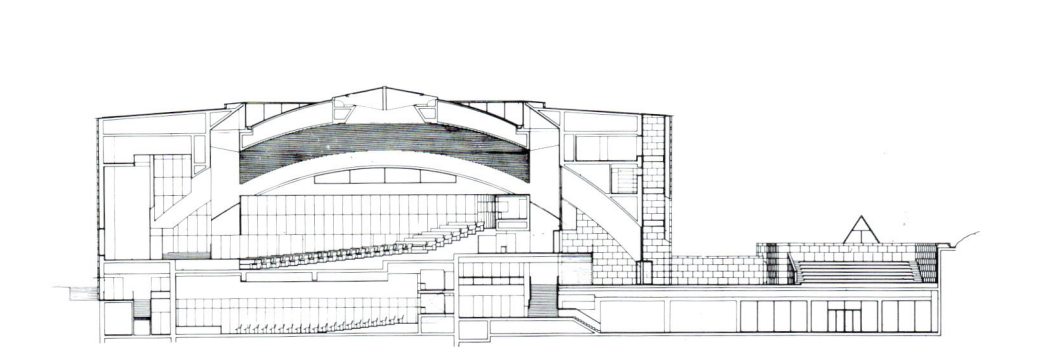

Section

Detail of roof

142

Convention Center,
Salamanca

Detail of entrance

Stairway leading to main entrance

Main entrance

Ministry of Agriculture Headquarters, Castile-La Mancha,

Toledo

Architects: Manuel de las Casas
Ignacio de las Casas
Jaime Lorenzo

Collaborators: Antonio de las Casas, civil engineer, Felicidad Rodríguez, artist (painter?)

Project: 1989
Construction: 1990-92
Commission: Regional Government of Castile-La Mancha

Spanish laws that control building in historic centers usually require architects to follow the paths of restoration or imitation of historic models. In the case of the new headquarters for the Toledo office of the Ministry of Agriculture, regional government officials applied a clause that permits exceptions and commissioned the architects to create a modern office building in the old city of Toledo. The administration should be commended for taking a daring and forward-looking position.

The architects accepted the challenge and sought a solution that was respectful of the structure of the old city and its buildings, yet they employed an abstract vocabulary in their design. The final result is a construction of almost 7,000 square meters comfortably and rather unobtrusively placed on a steep slope located between the old Jewish quarter and a group of convents.

The traditional architecture of the city consists mostly of small, tightly packed housing or monumental, religious structures. Toledo's historic monuments, enclosed by high walls, are usually simple volumes that are combined in such a way as to leave open space between them. The street pattern is a rich mixture of public and private spaces. Some public spaces, such as the *adarbes*, or short, dead-end streets, are really treated as semi-private. On the other hand, some private patios contribute to the public surroundings outside when their vegetation spills over the walls that contain them. The interplay of the concepts of solid and void, public and private, hidden and revealed were especially important in designing the new Ministry building.

Within this roughly triangular building, behind the main facade, runs a continuous corridor that functions as a walkway. The structure itself is a series of five modules separated by patios that run from front to back. The three center modules are parallel rectangles, while the ones on either end are irregular in shape and modified both to conform to the topography and to fit in between adjacent buildings. The patios are patterned after the scale and structure of the streets of Toledo, and the public can pass through the building to the street behind. The different areas of the Castile-La Mancha region will be represented by the vegetation in the patios: holly, orange, myrtle, chestnut, and prune trees.

The main facade of the complex is enclosed by a solid wall, which also takes its cue from the traditional character of the city. It is possible, however, for visitors to see the Tagus River valley from the building. The main entrance and library are marked by a pyramidal tower that blends well into the skyline of Toledo, as the city's numerous towers rise up to form an interesting collage. The lead roof and skylight of the tower make it the most distinctive feature of the building.

It was important to cover the building with a material that would age well, that would be appropriate for government offices, and that

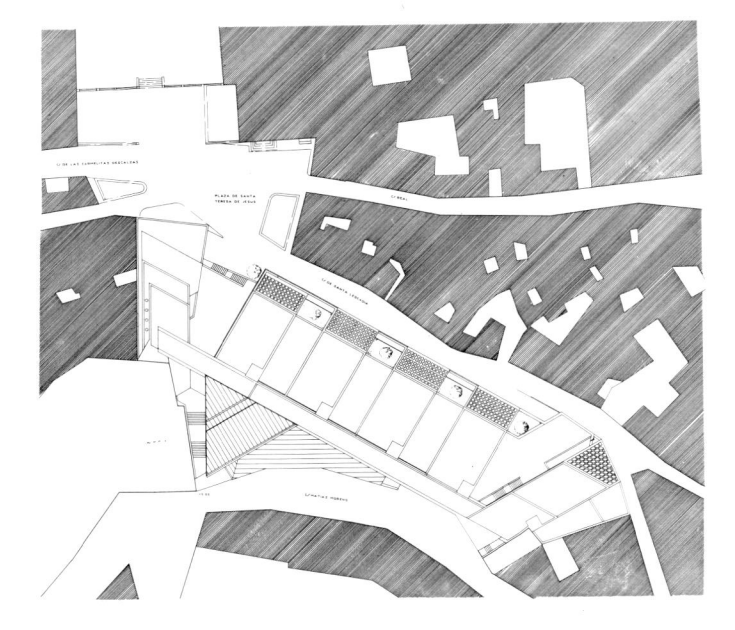

Site plan

Overall view

would also be in harmony with the rest of the area. The stone traditionally used in Toledo buildings, which was taken from nearby quarries, is no longer available. The architects chose, instead, a Galician stone of a golden-beige color that had been used in a seventeenth-century structure adjacent to the Ministry building site.

On the interior, the architects were able to diverge from local traditions. They covered the floors with polished black slate and made the stairs and window frames from natural wood. Both exterior and interior walls are extremely thick, almost sixty centimeters, so that all of the building's mechanical equipment (computer lines, air conditioning, etc.) could be housed within them. These thick walls, a characteristic of classical architecture, have, in turn, influenced the placement of openings for windows.

View from courtyard

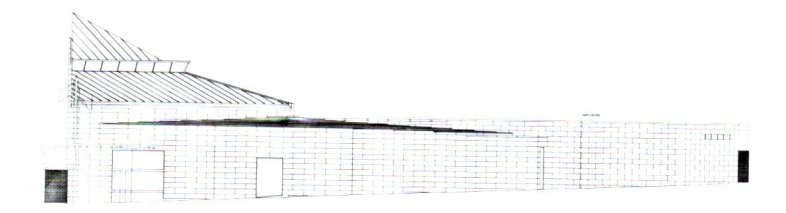

Ministry of Agriculture Headquarters, Castile-
La Mancha, Toledo

Front elevation

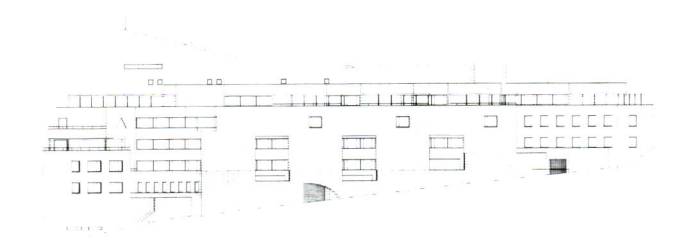

Rear elevation

View from rear balconies

146

View of entrance tower

Ministry of Agriculture Headquarters, Castile-La Mancha, Toledo

Rear facade

Detail of rear balcony

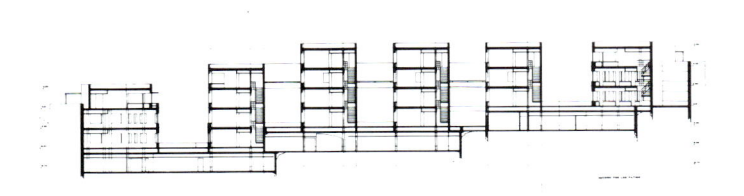

Section

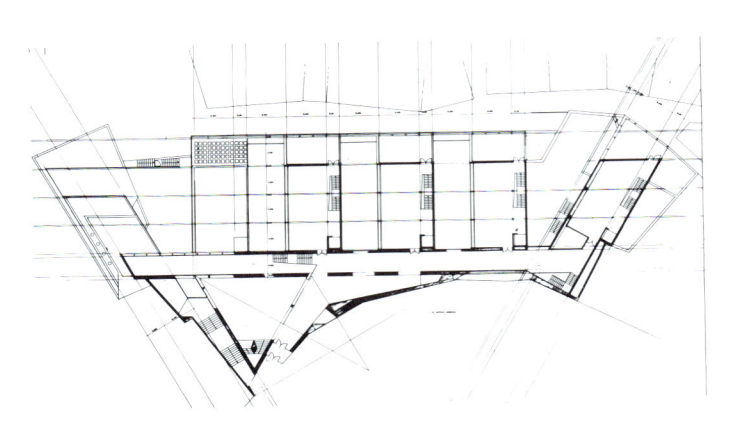

Plan

Ministry of Agriculture Headquarters, Castile-La Mancha, Toledo

Detail of exterior corridor

Navigation Pavilion, 1992 World's Fair

Seville

Architect	Guillermo Vázquez Consuegra
Collaborators	Marco Vázquez Consuegra and Carlos Vázquez Tatay, technical architects; Jorge Vázquez Consuegra, technical engineer; R. Aladio, A. López, G. Carty, R. Parr, and N. Gartnier
Project	1988-89
Construction	1990-92
Commission	State Commission for the Universal Exposition Seville '92

The Navigation Pavilion is one of the buildings constructed by the Expo '92 Committee as a theme pavilion. After the World's Fair is over, the 15,000-square-meter structure will permanently house Seville's Maritime Museum. Located at the edge of the Guadalquivir River, the building has two visually distinctive elements that are immediately apparent: the large curved roof and the nearby two-part observation tower that stands in the river. More specifically, the main complex is formed by a large rectangular building that will be used for exhibitions, a covered ramp of generous proportions that leads from the Plaza of Discovery down to the river, and a smaller service building for restaurant facilities. The ramp guarantees the unity of the project, permits the building to create its own harmony between the interior and exterior spaces, and reinforces the connection of the pavilion with the Guadalquiver.

The curved roof, because of its large scale, its copper cladding, and its relationship to the surroundings, acts as the main facade of the building, granting it its emblematic character. It curves down towards the river, thereby making a natural transition from the pavilion's main entrance, located on one side, to the river located at a lower level, on the other. At the same time, the pavilion recalls industrial buildings that are associated with port activities.

The exhibition building is organized as two parallel volumes of different sizes, which are separated by a space that forms an interior street. The public exhibitions will be in the larger, open volume, while the much smaller one will be used for storage, workshops, and offices. The circulation pattern within the exhibition space, which is based on the ramps and walkways around the perimeter, is designed to be highly functional and comfortable even with the large number of visitors and long lines that are expected during Expo '92. Visitors can exit the exhibition space through an 11-meter-high glass opening onto a platform that extends the length of the building and creates an observation deck with a view towards the river and the city of Seville beyond.

The construction solutions adopted by the architect, Guillermo Vázquez Consuegra, are also noteworthy. The enormous curved wooden beams that are the primary structural components of the roof had to be built in two pieces for their transport to the building site. These beams, which span 40 meters, are like the ribs of a ship's hull. The beams are supported at only two points: by concrete columns on one side and again, as they pass through the concrete platform facing the river.

The design for the two-part tower underwent many changes, some due to economic limitations, before the definitive solution was reached. The two sections of the tower—one in concrete and the other in steel; one appearing to ascend, the other appearing to descend—form a strong contrast with each other and with the horizontal strength of the pavilion. From their 60-meter-height, visitors have a striking view of La Cartuja de Santa María de las Cuevas and the entire city of Seville.

The architectural references to navigational themes enrich the pavilion's multiple levels of meaning, and these poetic elements are elegant, never slipping into kitsch: a great curved hull, a lighthouse, the building's location near the river, the observation platform that functions as a deck, and the void that separates the building from its surroundings. The atmospheric quality of the spaces enhances the subtle references. As the visitor experiences the building, passing from space to space, more of this symbolic architecture is revealed. Within the setting of the World's Fair, with so many new buildings competing for attention, the elegance and thematic integrity of the Navigation Pavilion stand out.

Aerial view

Observation tower

Detail of covered ramp and exhibition hall

Exhibition hall

Detail of roof facing Plaza of Discovery

Navigation Pavilion, 1992 World's Fair
Seville

Detail of hallway overlooking exhibition space

Promenade facing Guadalquivir River

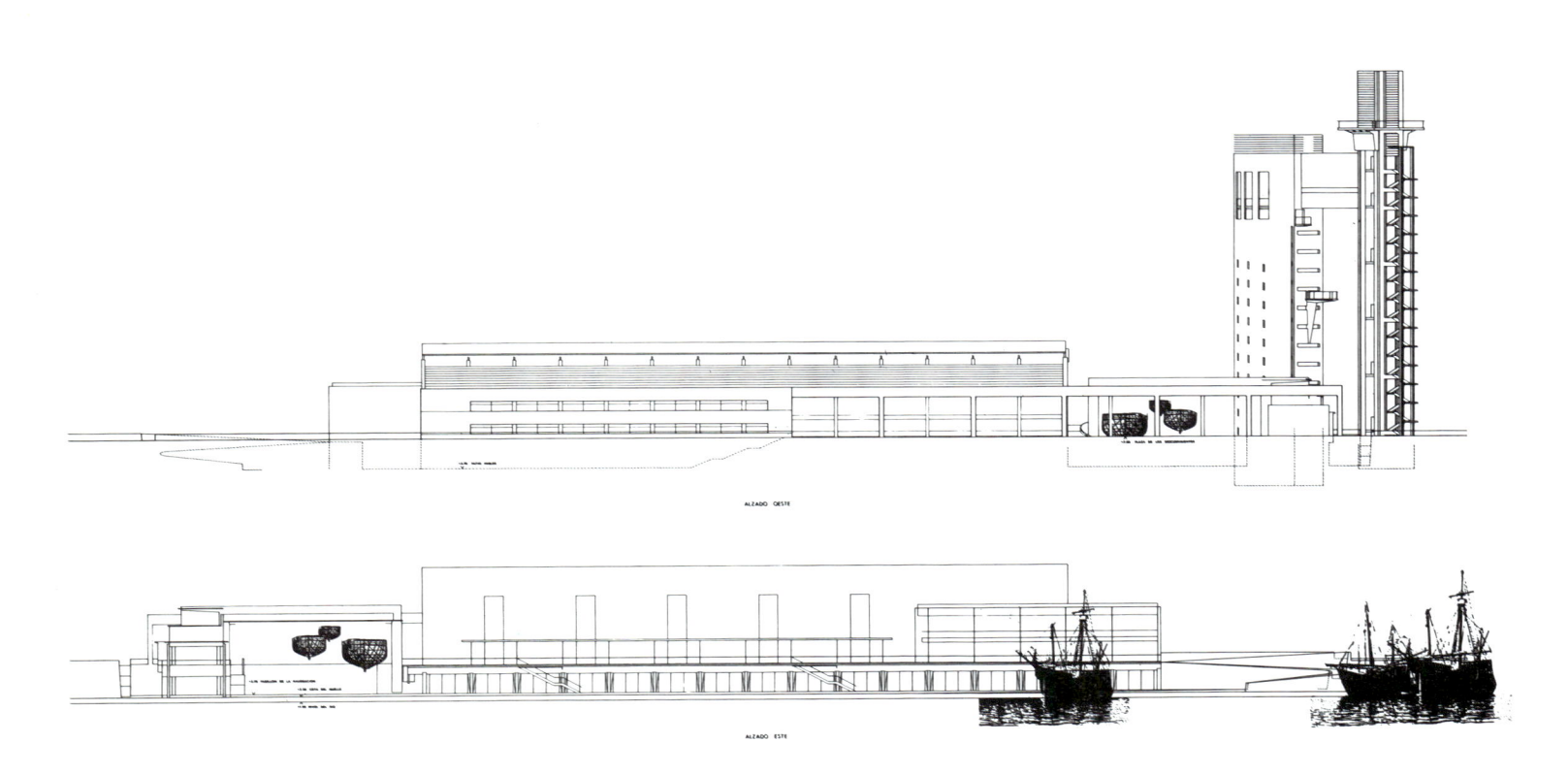

East and west elevations

Navigation Pavilion, 1992 World's Fair
Seville

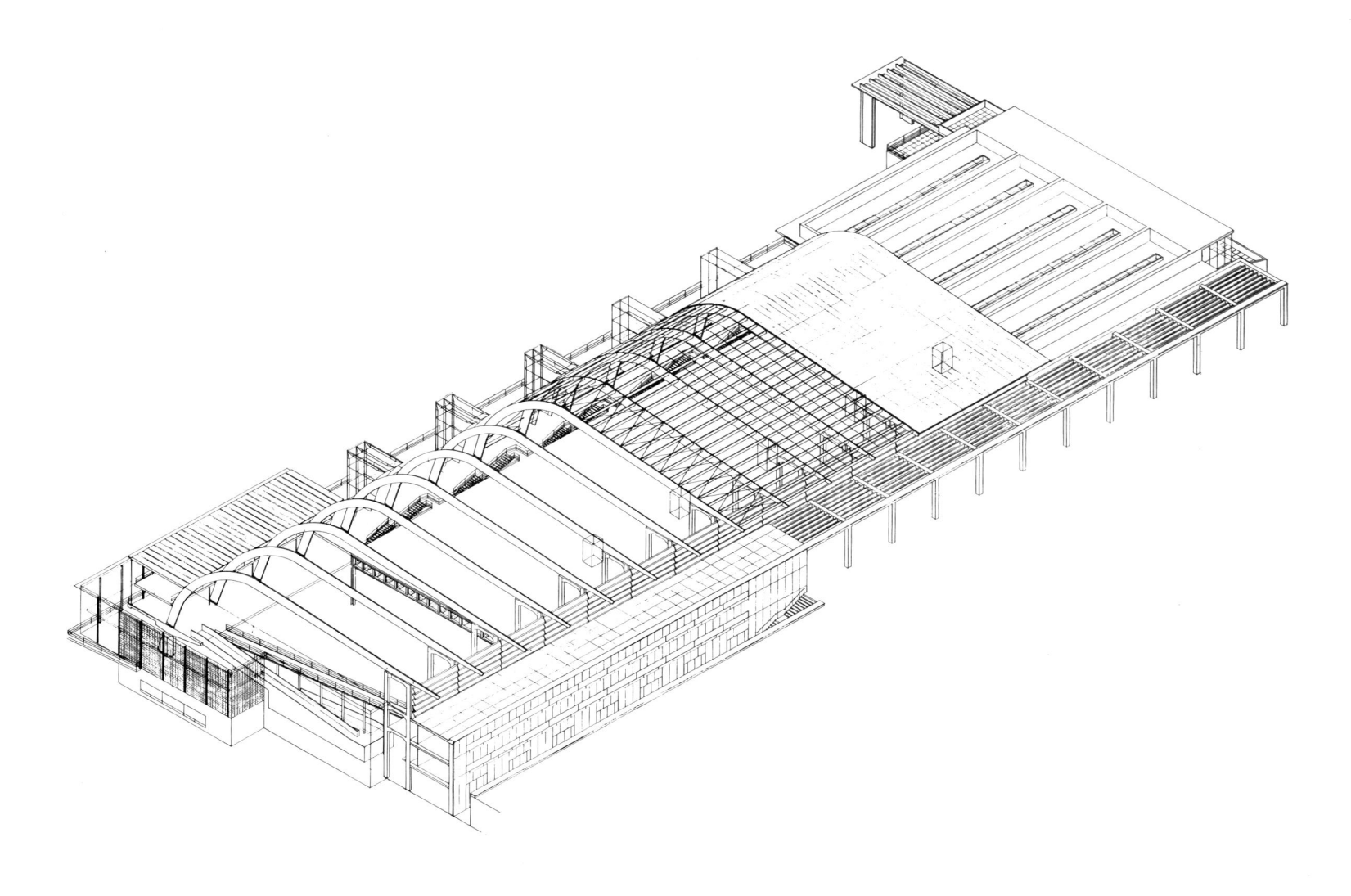

Axonometric drawing showing roof construction

Navigation Pavilion, 1992 World's Fair
Seville

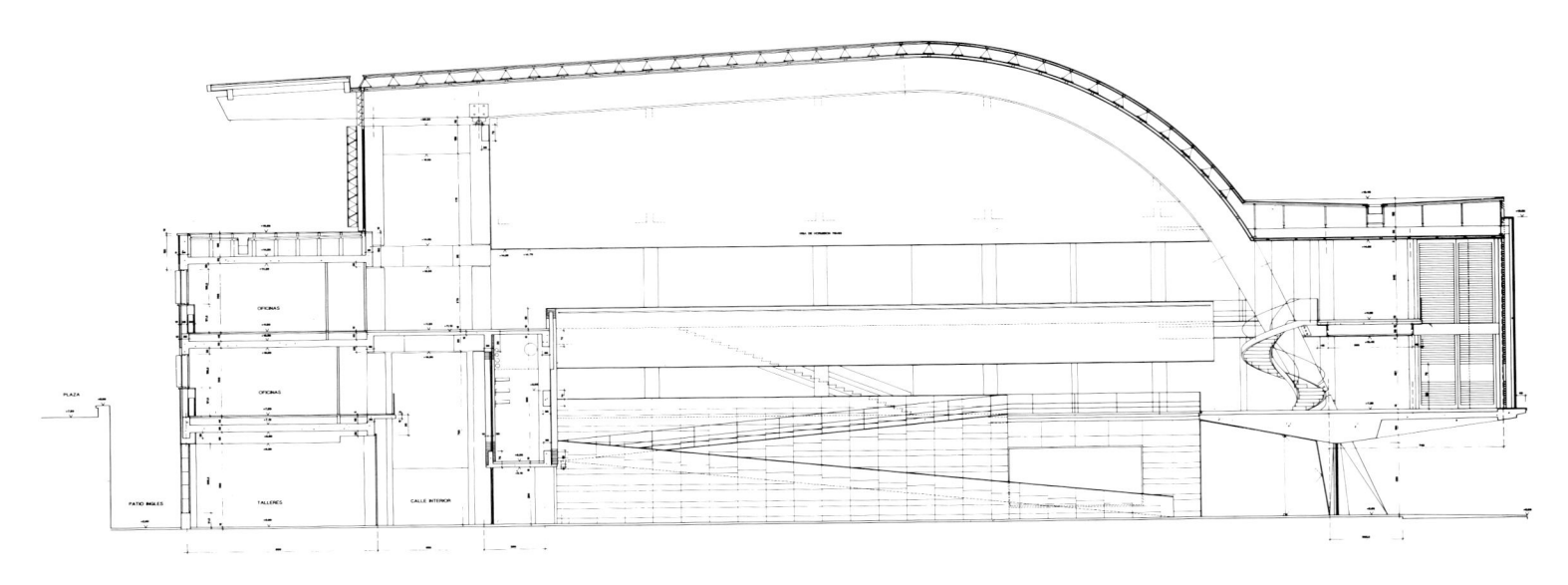

Cross section

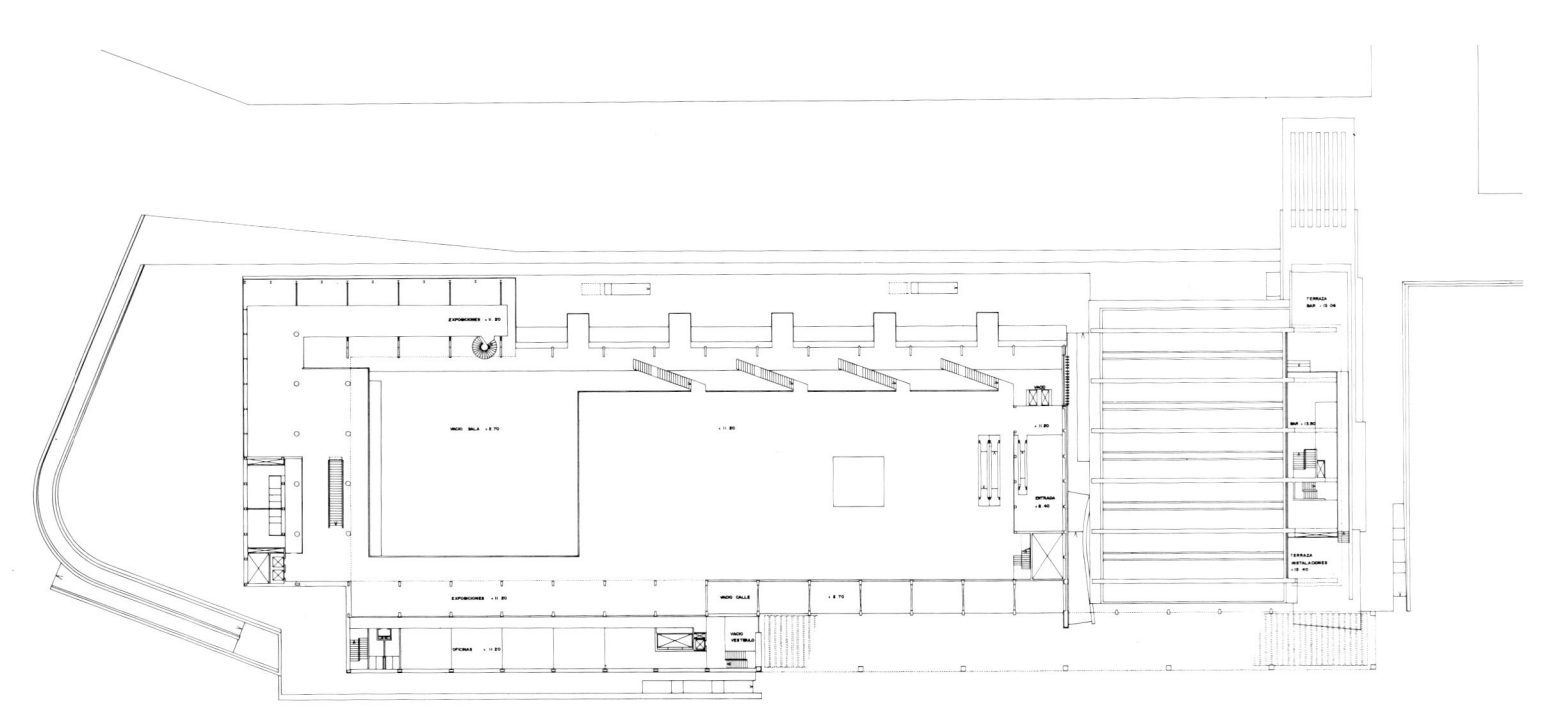

Plan

Navigation Pavilion, 1992 World's Fair
Seville

Exhibition hall

Detail of covered ramp and observation deck

155

Santa Justa Train Station

Sevilla

Architects Antonio Cruz
Antonio Ortiz

Collaborators Rafael Mollá and Ignacio Ruiz Larrea, engineers

Project 1987
Construction 1988-91
Commission Ministry of Public Works and Transportation

Three elements allowed the architectural firm to undertake a large-scale urban planning project: the decision by MOPT to create a new major passenger station for Seville, the condition that the existing railroad tracks into the city were to be placed underground, and the availability of a large vacant area of land.

In the new design the main train station was set in the center of the complex, on a slight rise, with the central structure defined and ordered by continuous three-story buildings placed on the perimeter. These buildings were designated for housing, offices, and commercial uses. The old rails were reconstructed to travel underground as they pass through the new station. The architects chose to build the complex primarily with brick so that it would have an integrated architectural character. The area between the perimeter buildings and the station was designated for parking, green spaces, and circulation routes.

The new station, while not the terminal station, is, in fact, the primary facility serving Seville, and the change from an aboveground structure to an underground one allows the new station to take on certain aspects of a terminal station. The architects sought to design a modern, functional station that was at the same time monumental and clearly urban in character. From the exterior the building seems rather austere and is dominated by strong horizontal lines and the extensive use of brick.

The main entrance (at a height of 14.65 meters above ground) is marked by a curved, slightly asymmetrical marquee, and it leads to the main passenger hall. Upon entering, visitors can see, almost automatically, how the station functions. The first large vestibule, for ticket sales, waiting areas, and shops, looks on to a transitional space that allows access to the platforms below or to the side circulation routes and exits of the buildings. The platforms (about 8.40 meters high) are covered by a metal roof.

The interior spaces are most dramatic, in part because of their generous dimensions and in part because of the careful attention paid to light and materials. Pale-colored brick lines the main vestibule, which is lit mainly from above by a series of large vertical windows. Though the hall is clearly defined, glass partitions allow the transitional space to be seen and understood. The oversized openings in the side walls again reveal the functional aspects of the station while

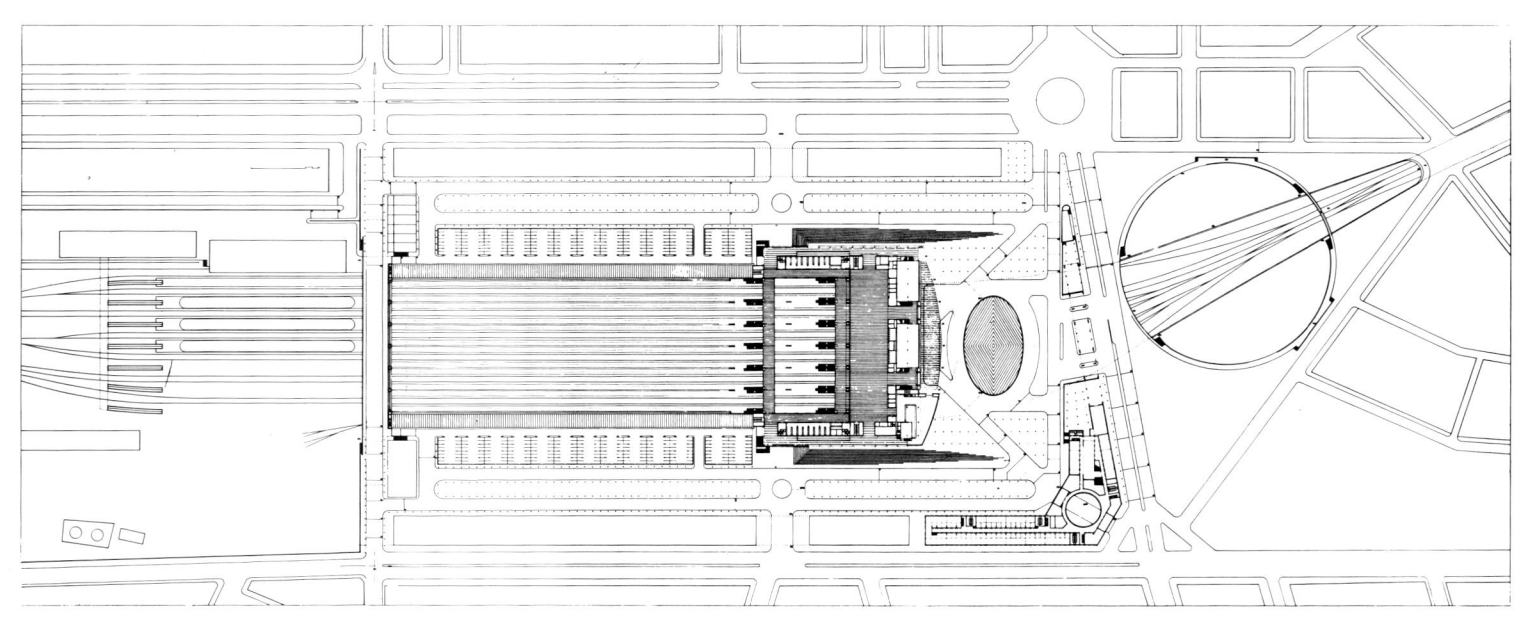

Plan of lower level

Overall view

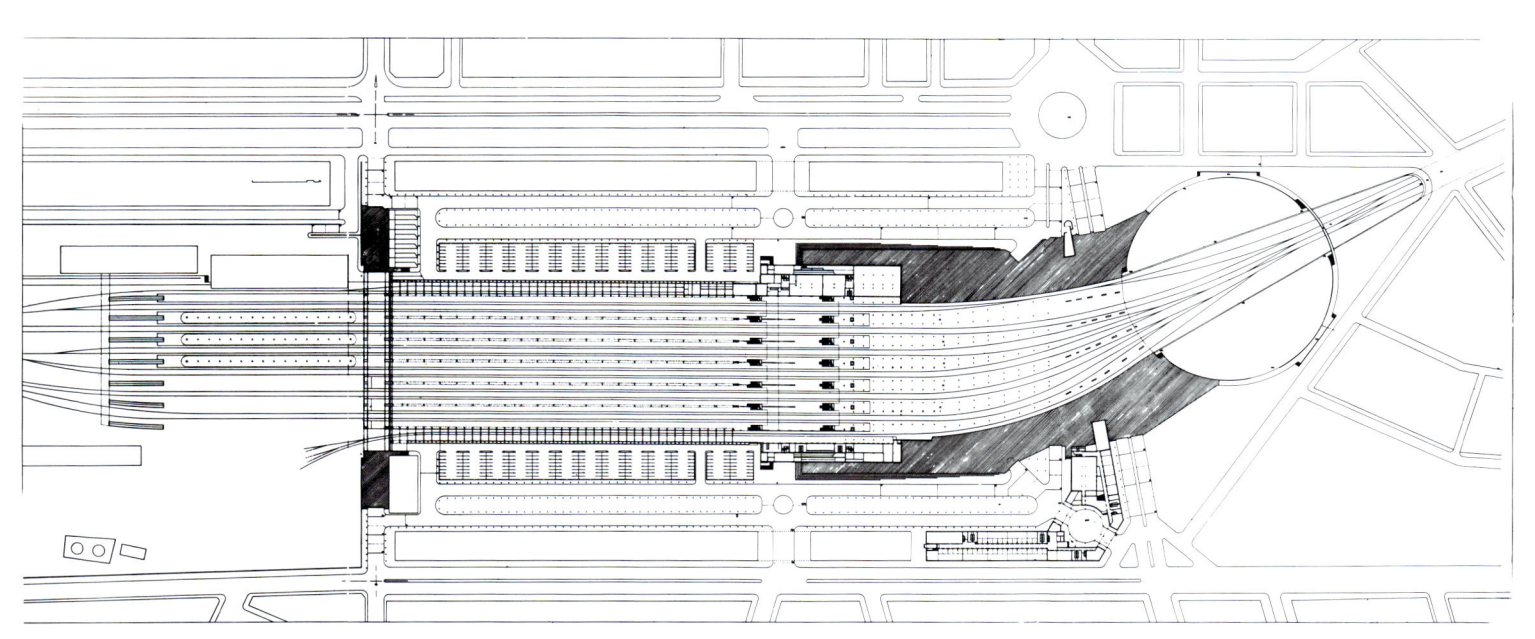

Plan of entry level

Main lobby

accentuating the large dimensions and monumentality of the whole. The slanting roof guides visitors through the building to escalators and stairs, which carry them down to the platforms. The arched roof over the platforms allows light to penetrate through its panels. Again, the material choices—in this case, exposed concrete—reinforce the functional change.

The Santa Justa station successfully combines contrasting elements. The architectural image created is truly modern, yet certain elements jog our collective memory and remind us of train stations from the past. The large vestibule, which allows us to sense the presence of the train, may call to mind the Stazione di Termini in Rome (1950). Though the shed of Santa Justa is not a mere copy of industrial architecture of the nineteenth century, the treatment of the roof makes an allusion to the past. During the day, the station appears solid and rooted to the ground. On the other hand, at night, when the station's windows are illuminated, the building almost seems to float. Perhaps the best union of ideas is the combination of grandeur and function. The building creates a new landmark for the city of Seville, yet the functional purpose of the station and the comfort of the traveler are never forgotten.

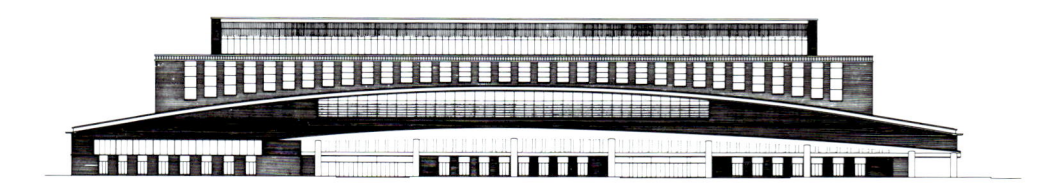

Front elevation

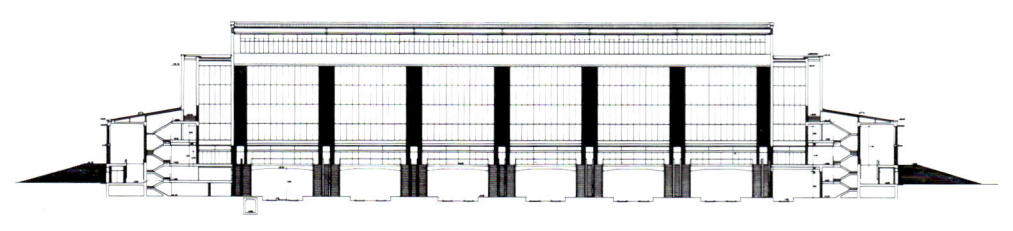

Cross section

Santa Justa Train Station
Seville

View of train platforms

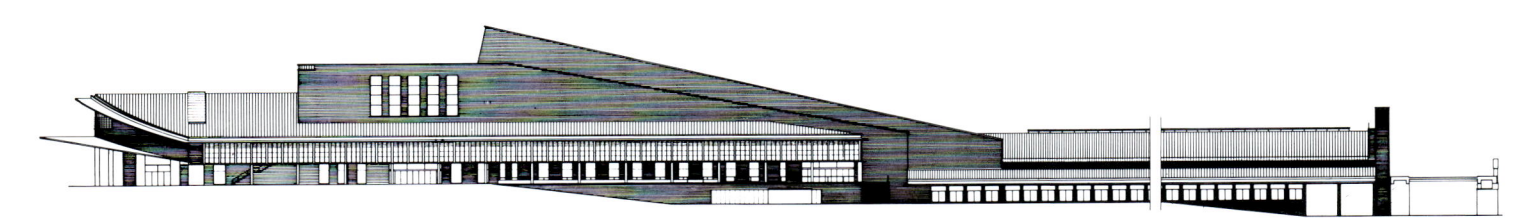

Side elevation

159

Santa Justa Train Station
Seville

View from the main lobby towards the train platforms

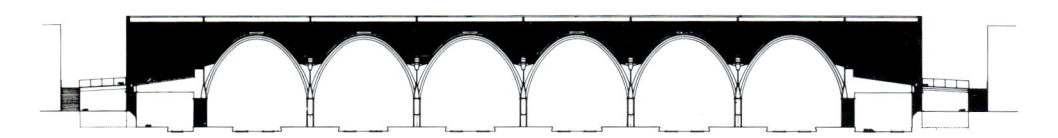

Cross section

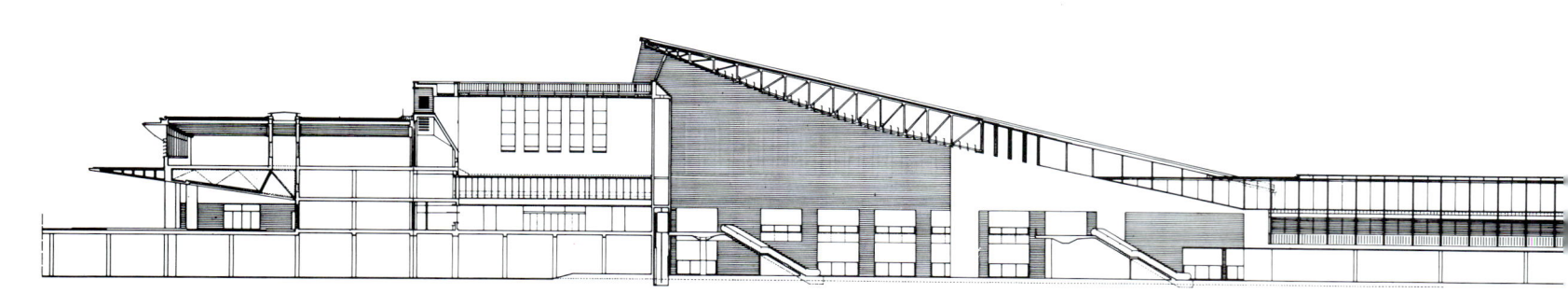

Longitudinal section

160

Santa Justa Train Station
Seville

Escalators leading to train platforms

International Airport

Seville

Architect — Rafael Moneo

Collaborators — Francisco González Peiro, technical architect; Luis Moreno Mansilla, Emilio Tuñón, Fernando Iznaola, and Aurora Fernández, architects; Intecsa, installations; Mariano Moneo, structural engineer; and Enric Satué, graphic designer

Project — 1988
Construction — 1989-91
Commission — Ministry of Public Works and Transportation

The search for an appropriate typology for an airport seems to be the primary task that architect Rafael Moneo set before himself when he designed the new Seville airport.. Airport buildings often represent nondescript commercial architecture surrounded by massive parking lots. Less frequently they are attempts to create new images, as illustrated by Eero Saarinen's TWA terminal (1956-62) at Kennedy Airport in New York and his Dulles Airport (1958-62) in Chantilly, Virginia, or Helmut Jahn's United Airlines terminal (1987) at O'Hare Airport in Chicago. But, it seems that even less often are airport terminals treated as single buildings, with an architectural style strong enough to define them. In Seville, Moneo constructed a closed, inward-looking building with concrete block that is colored a warm golden-beige. At first glance, the overall plan of the structure may appear to be related to the mosque form: it lacks exterior windows and is organized around an inner patio. Closer analysis, however, will reveal that the terminal should not be interpreted as an attempt to make historical references.

The new airport lies northeast of Seville and is connected to the city by a highway. The relationship between the airport and the city is highlighted by the pattern of outer access roads, the penetration of the entry roads into the building itself, and the organization of the parking lot. Rather than simply concentrating on the efficient movement of travelers, Moneo paid special attention to making the visitors' stay as pleasant an experience as possible through the inclusion of a well-ordered Sevillian patio, planted with orange trees, which alternates with rows of parking.

The organization of the airport is very direct:: a succession of "layers" is joined together to handle the functions of the airport. As visitors move through these "layers," the sequence of different spaces, with continually changing heights, is slowly revealed. The first "layer" is the main passenger terminal with ticketing and check-in facilities for departures. A transition is made from the open Sevillian patio and parking area in the center of the airport to the intentionally low threshold of the terminal, which then opens up to a spectacular vaulted space, covered by a series of domes. Behind the ticketing and check-in area is a second "layer," a horizontally organized space for airport services, with sections for staff, baggage handling, and other activities. Finally, near the runways is the long departure and arrival area with respective gates. The only variation in this regular layout is what the architects call the "head" building, shaped like a shifted cube,

Panoramic view

which houses the cafeteria and other amenities and successfully finishes one end of the passenger terminal.

As visitors approach the airport by car, the building appears to be a single, solid mass. The concrete blocks used to construct the airport are large so that they harmonize with the scale and dimensions of the building. The covered parking facilities are located at one end; the outdoor parking and patio, which are enclosed by perimeter walls, are in the center; and the terminal itself is placed near the runways. From the parking areas visitors can enter the upper departure level via a covered walkway.

The lower level for in-coming flights and the reception of arriving travelers is simple and completely separate from the upper level. It is even fair to say that transit from one level to the other is difficult. This strong separation between functions and levels may at times present difficulties, but it was an option very consciously chosen by the architect to maintain the flow of passenger movement.

The main departure hall, covered with dark blue domes that symbolize the union between earth and sky, is functionally clear and conducive to the needs of travelers. Each of the domes is capped by a cupola that permits light to be played off the dark ceiling and the white support columns. The circular benches designed by Moneo for the main departure hall allow the passengers a sense of privacy and the opportunity to appreciate the architecture.

The graphics of the new terminal were designed by Enric Satué, and they are large and legible, another element that demonstrates how the entire design of the airport anticipates and accommodates travelers' needs.

International Airport
Seville

"Head" building

View towards terminal

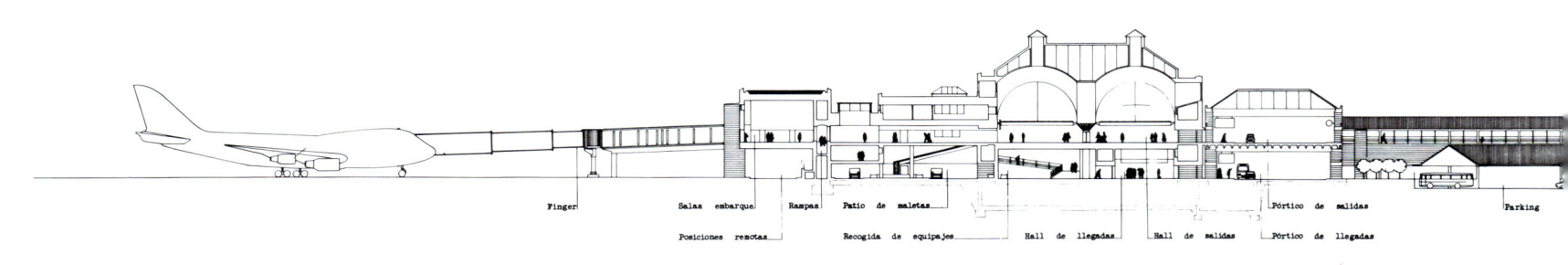

Longitudinal section

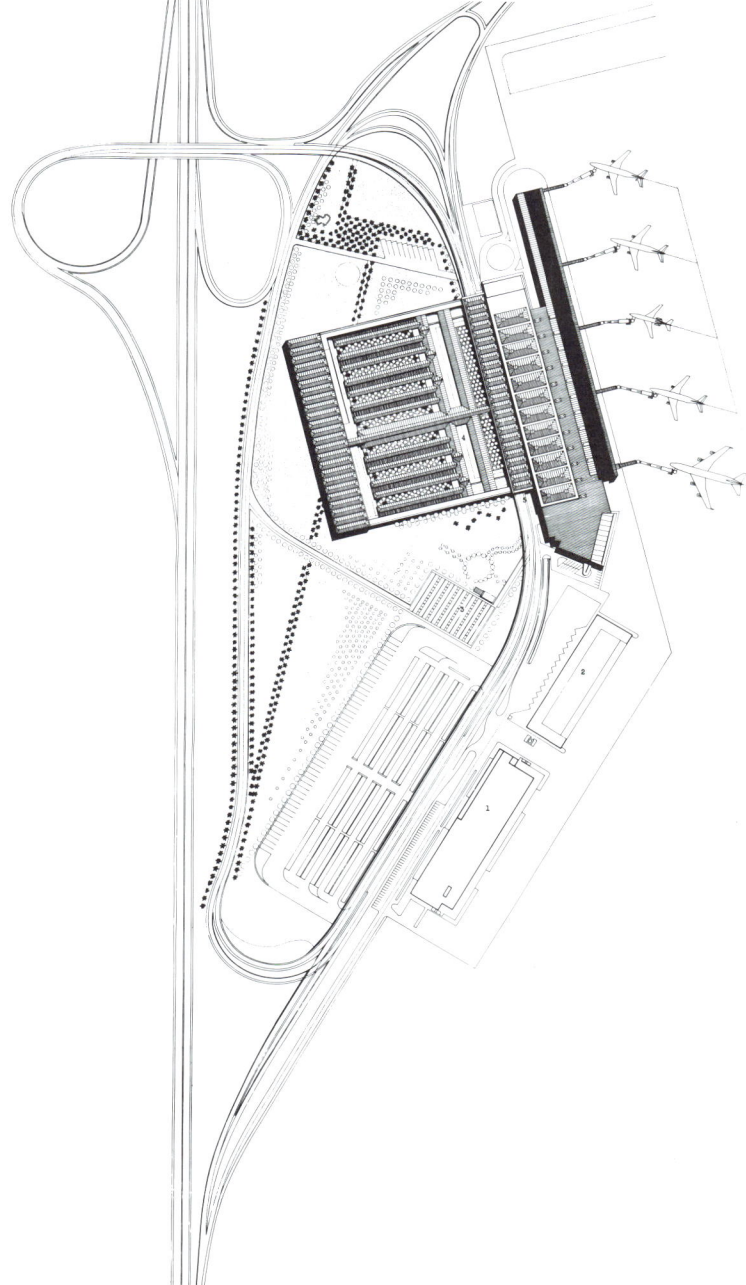

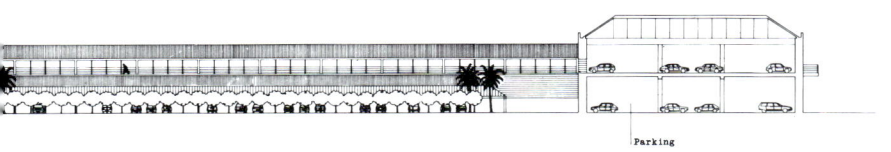

Site plan

International Airport
Seville

Detail of bench

Passenger waiting area

Main departure hall

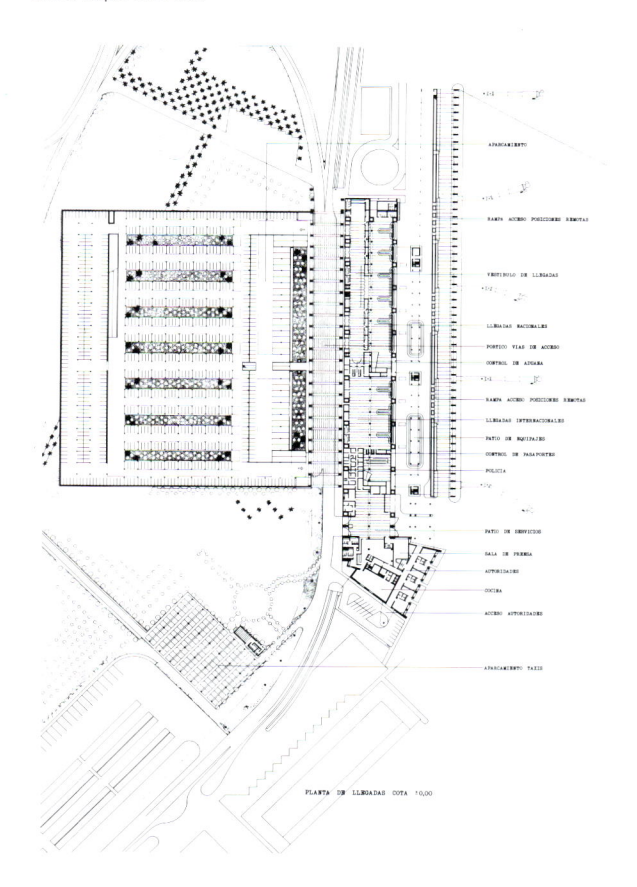

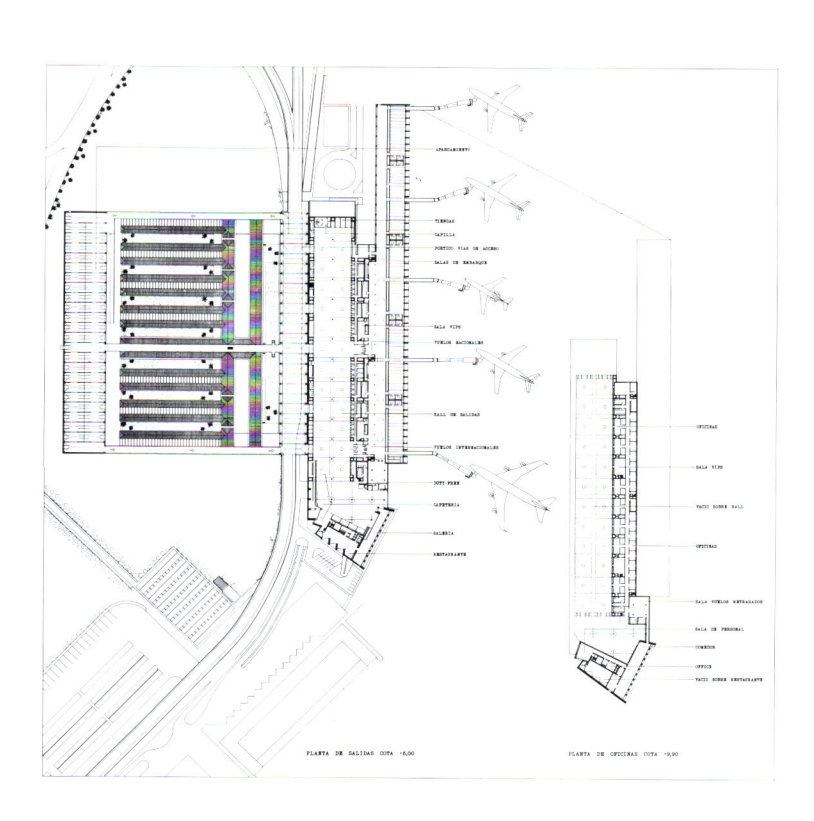

Plan of arrival level

Plan of departure level

167

Restoration and Adaptation of the Ronda Promenade and Bastions

Palma de Mallorca

Architects: José Antonio Martínez Lapeña, Elías Torres

Collaborators: G. Juliá, technical architect; F. Climent, coordinating architect; C. Albisu, V. Argilaga, A. Camps, G. Font, D.M. Fort, M. García, A Gallart, P. Gil, J. I. Gratacós, A. Guantar, J. Henrich, I. Josemaria, A. Lopéz, M. Martínez, E. Miralles, L. Montesinos, A. Noguera, J. Olivé, V. Pimstein, X. Pizá, B. Pleguezuelos, J. Pradell, M. Pujol, X. Rovira, O. Tarrasó, J. M. Vallés, A. Valverde, X. Vendrell, M. and M. Viader, A. Vila, J. Vila, N. Vives, and P. Vives

Preliminary study and project: 1983

Construction: 1986-91 "Ses Bovedas" Bastion
1990-92 "Portella" to "Berart" Bastion

Commission: Ministry of Public Works and Urbanism and the City of Palma de Mallorca

Historic restoration of old cities and urban master plans have been two especially important concerns of the different branches of Spanish government in recent years. More specifically, the transitional spaces between one area of a city and another, areas that sometimes correspond to different historical periods or are residual spaces that form barriers between parts of the city, have been the focus of urban renewal, in the best sense of the phrase. The recuperation of these "frontier areas" that must link diverse sections of cities, both visually and functionally, poses a challenging problem to city planners and architects as urban areas redefine themselves and seek to respond to current needs and aesthetic criteria.

The architectural firm of Martínez Lapeña and Torres commenced work in 1983 on the overall design of a park that will be constructed on a kilometer-long stretch of land just outside and below the city's ancient walls. The entire project is to be completed by 1996. The primary goal was to renovate this area, which for many years had been occupied by military buildings that were no longer in use, and to transform it into a linear park with gardens, an open-air theater, cafeterias, access ways to and from the old city, a naval museum, and other services. The site that Martínez Lapeña and Torres were assigned, about 8 1/2 acres just outside the original city fortifications, can be thought of as Palma de Mallorca's balcony facing the sea. It is like a platform midway between the old city above and the water below. A road defines the perimeter of the park along the sea; however, cars are not permitted in the new park. With the restoration of the area, Palma residents have an unobstructed view of the sea from the city.

Since 1986 two sections near the most monumental part of Palma have been constructed, "Ses Bovedas" Bastion and the "Portella" to "Berart" Bastion. In their design, the architects have demonstrated their skill in creating functional and attractive spaces, sensitively restoring such a large historic area and designing new symbolic elements that enrich the project..

The "Ses Bovedas baluarte" (vaulted bastions) area, which is only 1 1/2 meters above sea level, was so named because the military complex was built over sixteen underground vaulted tunnels. The architects have reused an old train tunnel to connect the city with the original Park of the Sea. In order to make the tunnel seem inviting, the architects have given it a false perspective and lit it from above, halfway across its length. The arched shape of the renovated tunnel recalls the arches and columns used in grand old houses in Palma. Natural light pierces the tunnel through a skylight that is reminiscent of a fragment of a ruin.

Aerial view

After visitors pass through the tunnel and arrive at the promenade area, they may choose to go up a staircase or walk toward an open-air theater. The staircase was built from old, broken stone fragments from previous constructions on the site. The connection with the past is maintained through this use of old materials in new ways.

The open-air theater sits on a plaza enclosed on one side by the city's walls and the side of the Gothic cathedral. On the other side, it is defined by a bar-cafeteria with a copper roof supported on columns of teak wood. The theater seats are made of teak and the pavement of the stage area is made of diamond-shaped slabs of beige and gray marble. The theater is shaded by a 50-by-25-meter covering of blue and yellow diamond-shaped pieces of canvas (the colors of the Balearic Island Merchant Marine). The patterns of the shadows cast on the ground by the canopy are nearly as important as the

Open-air theater

"Ses Bovedas" area

169

Restoration and Adaptation of the Ronda Promenade
and Bastions
Palma de Mallorca

design of the covering itself. Nearby, tunnels that were once part of the bastion have been remodeled into dressing rooms and storage areas. Nine palm trees were planted in this area to complement three existing palms.

Eventually, the whole kilometer-long promenade will be paved with concrete blocks in an original shape designed by the architects, called palma stone. These blocks will be laid to follow the principal axes of the bastions; they may be set far apart to allow the grass to grow between them or they may be placed close together to achieve a more finished look.

Martínez Lapeña and Torres's project represents architecture conceived on a broad scale and carefully designed down to the smallest detail. They seem to have unlocked a treasure chest of history, ideas, and fragments from the site, which they have used in creating the new project. At the same time, they invite observant visitors to discover the new treasures they have hidden there: the Moorish ship silhouetted against the city walls can be detected in the shape of the theater and its covering, the suggestion of the iron work (though in an inverse pattern) on the balcony of the Ayuntamiento (town hall) is represented by the teak wood posts enclosing the theater, the traditional harlequin's costume is depicted in the pattern of the stage pavement, and the paving bricks are shaped like the palm of a hand. These are just a few examples of the many subtle details that the architects included in their playful design.

The scale of the site and its historical, geographical, and architectural importance presented a challenge to the architects as they designed the new project. The earlier Spanish architects Antoni Gaudí (1852-1926) and Josep Jujol (1879-1959) also undertook difficult restoration projects in this area, in the cathedral and the Episcopal Palace. They are like distant observers, still present in spirit to inspire the present-day architects.

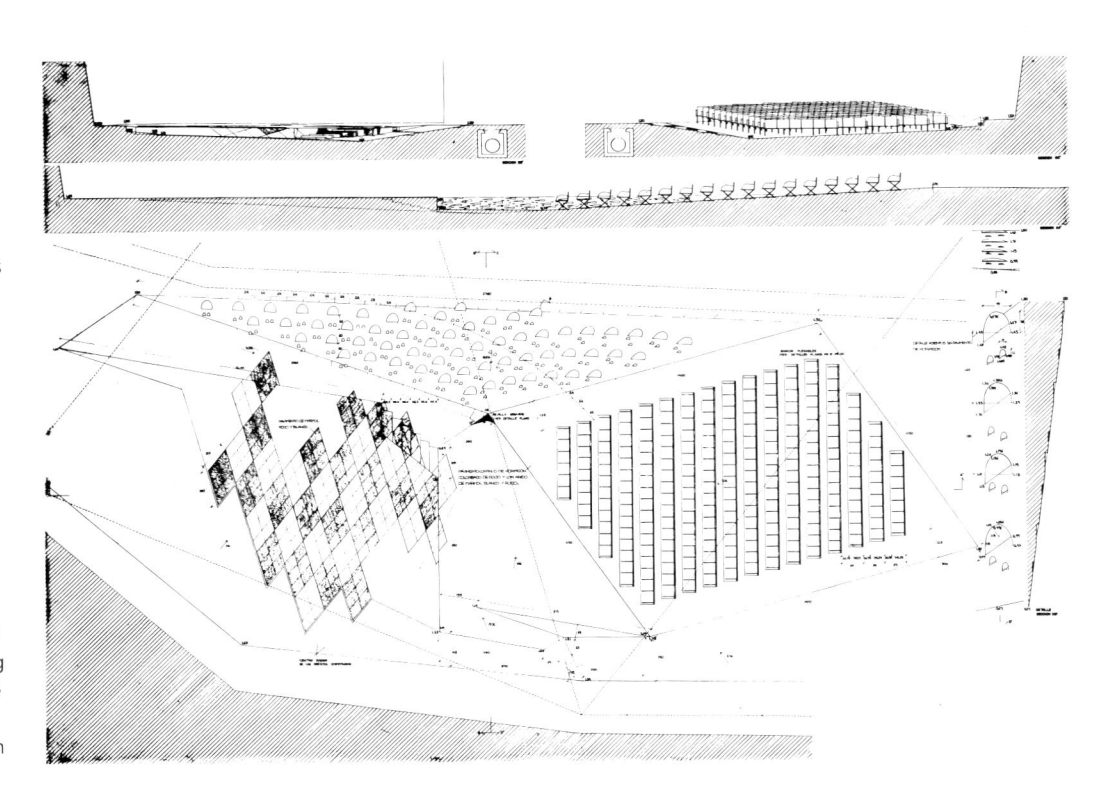

Plan, section and structure of the theater

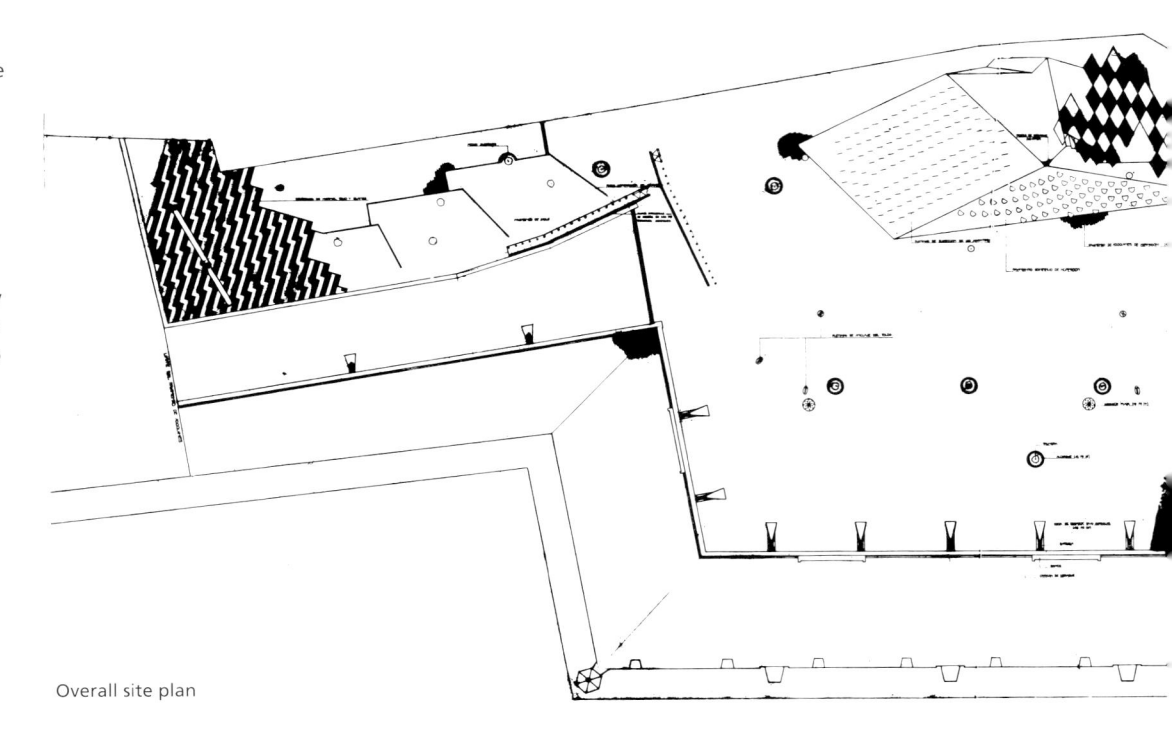

Overall site plan

Tunnel and detail of skylight

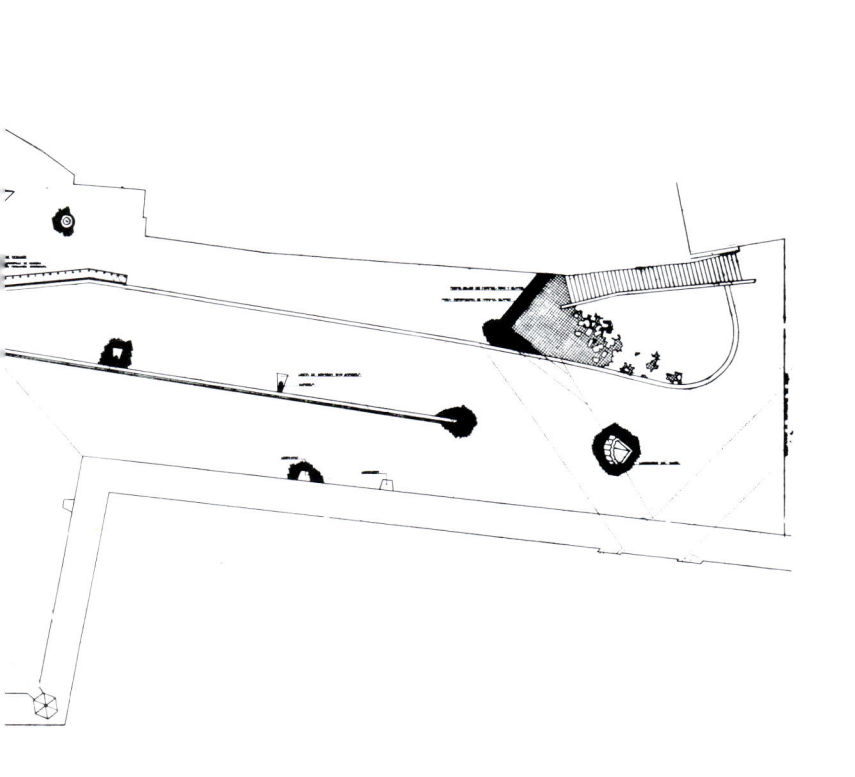

Reconstruction of staircase

171

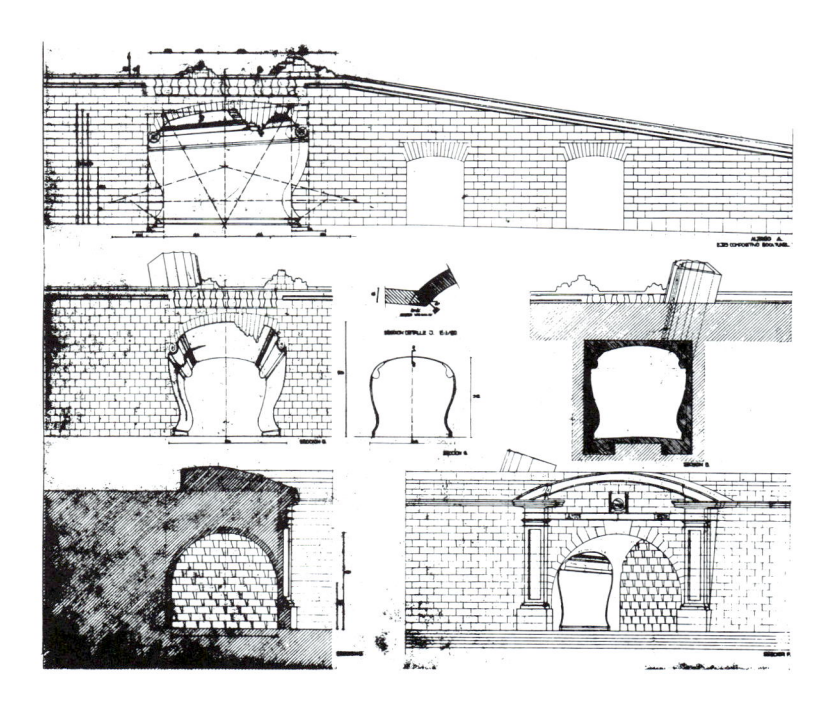

Restoration and Adaptation of the Ronda Promenade
and Bastions
Palma de Mallorca

Detail of tunnel

Entrance to tunnel

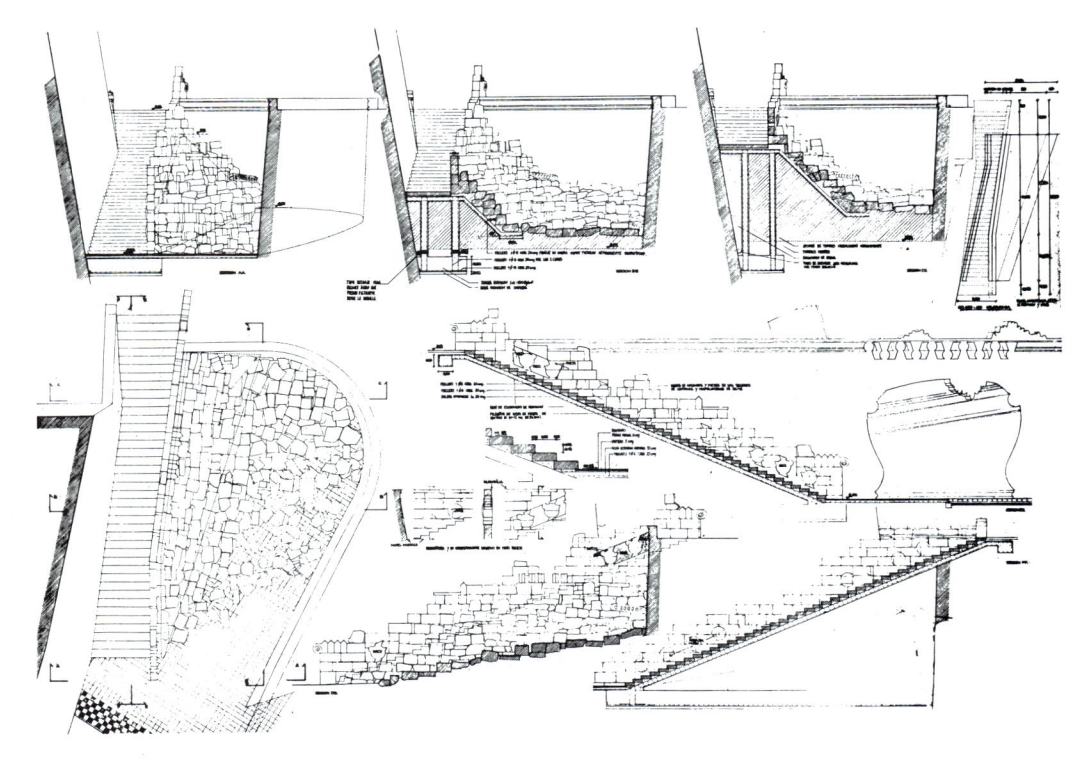

Plan, section and structure of the staircase

Restoration and Adaptation of the Ronda Promenade
and Bastions
Palma de Mallorca

Detail of theater seating beneath canopy

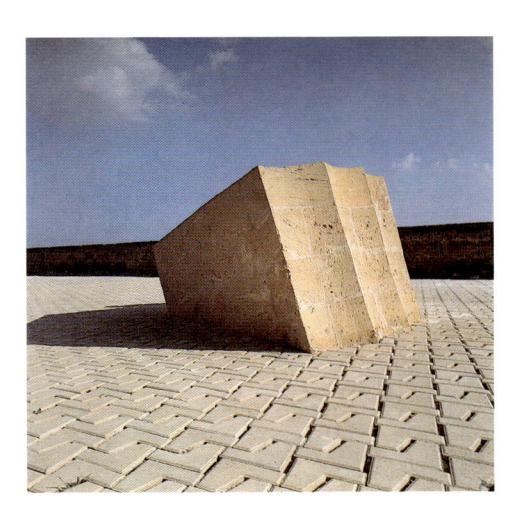

Detail of skylight from exterior

Detail of skylight from interior of tunnel

Architects' Biographies
Maurice Blanks

Esteve Bonell

Esteve Bonell was born in Banyoles, Gerona, in 1942, and he studied at the Escuela Técnica Superior de Arquitectura (ETSA) in Barcelona, graduating in 1971. He began teaching at the ETSA, Barcelona, in 1972, and in 1979 Bonell joined the school's final projects examination board. He has served as a visiting professor at the universities of Lausanne and Paris and has juried several national and international competitions. Bonell has twice received the Fomento de las Artes Decorativas (FAD) Prize for architecture, once in 1975 for the Fregoli housing project, and again in 1985 for the velodrome in Horta, which he designed in concert with Francesc Rius. Bonell and Rius, who continue to collaborate, have won other awards, including first prize in the 1987 competition for the design of a sports pavilion in Badalona, a project that Bonell and Rius recently completed in preparation for the 1992 Olympics (see photographs and project description in Part II). They have also recently finished a housing project for the Olympic Village in Barcelona. Bonell, with Josep Maria Gil, is working on a hotel on the Ramblas Boulevard in Barcelona, and a courthouse in Gerona. Bonell and Gil won first prize for a basketball stadium in Gerona.

Ignacio de las Casas

Ignacio de las Casas was born in Madrid in 1947. He graduated in 1971 from Escuela Técnica Superior de Arquitectura (ETSA) in Madrid, where he has been a professor in the Department of Technical Drawing since 1973. He received a one-year scholarship from the Fundación Juan March in 1972 to study at the North London Polytechnic and was awarded a diploma in health facility planning in 1973 by the National Council for Academic Awards in London. He represented the Ministry of Public Works on the Commission for Historic and Artistic Preservation in Toledo from 1981 to 1982. Ignacio de las Casas joined his brother Manuel's firm in 1977 and has collaborated with him since then. They have recently designed the Pavilion of Castile-La Mancha for the 1992 World's Fair in Seville and, with Jaime L. Lorenzo, the Ministry of Agriculture headquarters for the regional government of Castile-La Mancha in Toledo (see photographs and project descriptions in Part II). Their work has been presented in exhibitions in Europe, the United States, and Japan.

Manuel de las Casas

Born in Talavera de la Reina, Toledo, in 1940, Manuel de las Casas graduated from the Escuela Técnica Superior de Arquitectura (ETSA) in Madrid in 1964 and completed his doctorate there in 1966. He received a further degree in psychology and psychotechnology from the University of Madrid in 1969. That same year he began teaching at the ETSA in Madrid, and he was named a full professor there in 1987. From 1980 to 1982 de las Casas served in the Ministry of Culture as the chief architect in the Department of Technical Services for the Restoration of Historic and Artistic Heritage. In 1983 he was appointed assistant director, and in 1986 general director, of the Architecture Department of the Ministry of Public Works. His work has been published in *Arquitectura, El Croquis, International Architect,* and *Architectural Review*. His brother Ignacio joined Manuel's firm in 1977, and together they won first prize for architecture and planning works from the Madrid City Council in 1986 for their public housing development in southwest Palomeras in Madrid. In 1989, they completed another Madrid housing development in Carabanchel. Their most recent project was the Auditorium of Pontevedra, in Galicia.

Lluís Clotet

Lluís Clotet was born in 1941 in Barcelona, where he later attended architecture school at the Escuela Técnica Superior de Arquitectura (ETSA) and graduated in 1965. Clotet later returned to the ETSA, Barcelona, as a professor, from 1977 to 1984. While still a student, Clotet worked for Fredrico Correa and Alfonso Milá, and in 1964 he co-founded the firm Studio Per with Pep Bonet, Cristian Cirici, and Oscar Tusquets. In 1983 the firm disbanded and Clotet began practicing with Ignacio Paricio. He worked with Paricio on both the Bank of Spain in Gerona in 1983 (see photographs and project description in Part II) and a warehouse in Canovelles, Barcelona, in 1986. Clotet won two Fomento de las Artes Decorativas (FAD) prizes for architecture, one in 1978 and another in 1979, two FAD prizes for best interior in 1965 and 1972, and one FAD Prize for restoration in 1980. He has won several national competitions and has contributed to various publications, including *Transformations of Modern Architecture* (1979), *The House as Image* (1981), and *The Presence of the Past* (1982). Since 1985 Clotet has been a member of the Professional Association of Architects in Puerto Rico (Colegio de Arquitectos de Puerto Rico).

Antonio Cruz

Antonio Cruz was born in Seville in 1948. He began studying architecture at the Escuela Técnica Superior de Arquitectura (ETSA) in Seville and completed his degree at the ETSA in Madrid in 1971. Upon graduation, he formed a partnership with Antonio Ortiz in Seville. The firm has since received many prizes and awards including the Pérez Carasa Prize of the Professional Association of Architects of Huelva in 1980, and the City of Seville Prize for new construction in 1983. Since 1985 Cruz has been a member of the Andalusian Commission, an advisory board appointed by the regional government to oversee the restoration of historic buildings. Together with Ortiz, Cruz taught at Zurich Polytechnic in 1987-88 and at the Graduate School of Design at Harvard University during the 1989-90 academic year. The work of Cruz and Ortiz has been published widely, most notably in the monograph *Cruz/Ortiz* (Barcelona: Gustavo Gili, 1988), and their work has been exhibited in Zurich, Bern, London, and Lausanne. Currently the firm is overseeing construction on a sports stadium in Madrid and the Spanish Cultural Institute in Lisbon.

Jordi Garcés

Jordi Garcés, born in Barcelona in 1945, studied architecture at the Escuela Técnica Superior de Arquitectura (ETSA) in Barcelona and graduated in 1970. While a student, Garcés worked in the offices of Martorell, Bohigas, and Mackay and for Ricardo Bofill. From 1971 to 1973 he taught at the Eina Design School, and in 1975 he began teaching at the ETSA, Barcelona. Garcés received his doctorate in architecture in 1987 from the Polytechnic University of Catalonia. In 1970 he formed a partnership with Enric Sòria, and the firm has won a number of awards including the Friends of the City Prize for restoration in 1981 and the Fomento de las Artes Decorativas (FAD) Prize for architecture and remodeling in 1987. In 1990 Garcés and Sòria received an FAD Prize for architecture for the Furriols House in the Catalan town of Vic. They have most recently been working on the Olympic Pavilion in the Vall d'Hebron area of Barcelona and a hotel in the center of the city.

Architect´s Biografies

Victor López Cotelo

Born in Madrid in 1947, Victor López Cotelo graduated from the Escuela Técnica Superior de Arquitectura (ETSA) of Madrid in 1969. He then worked in Munich, Germany, for two years before returning to Madrid to take a job with Alejandro de la Sota until 1979. From 1983 to 1986 López Cotelo taught at the ETSA in Madrid, and he has lectured in Munich, Braunschweig, and Darmstadt. He formed a partnership with Carlos Puente in 1979 and, until 1990 when the firm disbanded, López Cotelo and Puente won several awards including one from the Professional Association of Architects for the Valdelaguna City Hall. In 1990 the firm's Zaragoza public library (see photographs and project description in Part II) was a finalist in the competition for the Mies van der Rohe Prize, a prestigious international award granted by the European Economic Community and the Mies van der Rohe Foundation of Barcelona. In 1991 this same building received the García Mercadal Architecture Award from the Professional Association of Architects of Aragon. The firm's work has been exhibited in Spain, France, and Germany and has been published extensively both nationally and internationally. Their recent design for the restoration of the Linares Palace in Madrid won first prize in a limited competition. Since 1990 López Cotelo has been practising independently.

Jaime L. Lorenzo

Born in London in 1951, Jaime L. Lorenzo received most of his education in Spain, and he graduated from the Escuela Técnica Superior de Arquitectura (ETSA) in Madrid in 1978. While still a student, he worked for Manuel de las Casas, and in 1978 he became an associate of Manuel's firm. He has lectured throughout Spain at local chapters of the Professional Association of Architects on his own work and that of the firm. His projects with the Casas brothers have been exhibited in Belgium, in New York, and in various cities in Spain. In 1986 and again in 1991, the Casas brothers and Lorenzo received first prize for architecture and urbanism from the Madrid City Council.

José Antonio Martínez Lapeña

José Antonio Martínez Lapeña, born in Tarragona in 1941, studied architecture at Escuela Técnica Superior de Arquitectura (ETSA) in Barcelona. He graduated in 1968 and began a partnership with Elías Torres in the same year. He worked as a professor of projects at the ETSA, Barcelona, from 1969 to 1971, then returned to this position in 1978. He has been a projects tutor at the ETSA del Vallés, Barcelona, since 1983. Martínez Lapeña and Torres have won several awards, including the Fomento de las Artes Decorativas (FAD) Prize for architecture in 1986 for their Garden of the Villa Cecilia. Their work has been featured in *Quaderns d'Arquitectura i Urbanisme*, *Architectural Review*, and *Progressive Architecture*.
In 1990 the publishing company Gustavo Gili published a monograph on Martínez Lapeña and Torres.

Enric Miralles

Born in Barcelona in 1955, Enric Miralles graduated from the Escuela Técnica Superior de Arquitectura (ETSA) in Barcelona in 1978. He worked with Helio Piñón and Albert Viaplana from 1974 to 1984 and then formed a partnership with Carme Pinós in 1983. Miralles has taught design at the ETSA in Barcelona since 1977 and has been a full professor there since 1988. He was a visiting scholar at Columbia University in 1980 and returned there in 1989 as a visiting professor in the architecture school. He has lectured at institutions around the world, including Harvard University and the Architectural Association in London, and he has acted as a visiting professor at Kingston Polytechnic in London and Tulane University in New Orleans. The firm of Miralles and Pinós has won, among other awards, first prize in the competition for a cemetery in Igualada in 1985, first prize in the competition for a sports stadium in Huesca in 1988, and the Fomento de las Artes Decorativas (FAD) Prize for interior design for the renovation of a La Llauna factory, which Miralles and Pinós converted into a high school. The work of Miralles and Pinós has been published in *Sites, Domus,* and *Architectural Review,* as well as others, and following a 1990 exhibition of their work at the Storefront for Art and Architecture in New York, Sites/Lumen Books published the monograph *The Architecture of Enric Miralles and Carme Pinós* (New York, 1990).

Rafael Moneo

Born in Tudela, Navarra, in 1937, Rafael Moneo graduated from the Escuela Técnica Superior de Arquitectura (ETSA) in Madrid in 1961. He worked in the office of Francisco Javier Sáenz de Oiza from 1958 to 1961, and in 1962 he went to work for Jørn Utzon in Denmark. Moneo obtained a scholarship to study at the Spanish Academy in Rome from 1963 to 1965. Upon his return to Spain, he started an independent practice and also took a job teaching at the ETSA, Madrid. In 1970 he was offered a full professorship at the ETSA in Barcelona, which he held until 1980 when he again returned to the ETSA, Madrid, where he was offered a full professorship. Moneo has served as a visiting professor at the Cooper Union School of Architecture, Harvard University, Princeton University, and the University of Lausanne. In 1976 he spent a year in the United States as a visiting fellow at the Institute for Architecture and Urban Studies, and in 1985 he was appointed chairman of the Department of Architecture at the Graduate School of Design at Harvard University, a position he held for five years. Moneo's architecture, especially his National Museum of Roman Art in Mérida from 1984, has been widely published nationally and internationally, and he has written extensively on architecture in publications which include *Oppositions* and *Lotus.* He was also an editor and co-founder in 1974 of the Spanish journal *Arquitectura Bis*. He has recently won the international competition for the Museum of Contemporary Art in Stockholm and a competition for the film theater at the Lido in Venice.

Juan Navarro Baldeweg

Born in 1939 in Santander, Juan Navarro Baldeweg studied drawing and painting as a young man, and in 1959 he enrolled at the San Fernando School of Art in Madrid to study printmaking. A year later, however, he transferred to the Escuela Técnica Superior de Arquitectura (ETSA) in Madrid. He graduated from the ETSA in 1965, completed his doctorate in 1969, and in 1970 he received a grant from the Fundación Juan March for study and travel abroad. In 1971 Navarro Baldeweg moved to the United States to accept a position as a visiting professor at the Center for Advanced Visual Studies at MIT. He returned to the ETSA in Madrid as a Professor of Projects in 1975, although he has also had appointments at the University of Pennsylvania in 1987 and at Yale University in 1990. Navarro Baldeweg has received a number of awards for his work in architecture, including first prize in the competition for the design of an exhibition and convention center in Castile-León in 1985, first prize for a training pavilion in the Olympic Village in Barcelona in 1988, and another first prize for a convention center in Cádiz, 1989.

Architect's Biografies

Antonio Ortiz

Antonio Ortiz was born in 1948 in Seville. In 1969 he started architecture school at the Escuela Técnica Superior de Arquitectura (ETSA) in Seville but later transferred to the ETSA in Madrid. While in architecture school, Ortiz had the opportunity to work in the offices of Ricardo Aroca and Rafael Moneo. After graduating from the ETSA in Madrid in 1971, he formed a partnership with Antonio Cruz, with whom he continues to work. Cruz and Ortiz have won several awards for their work including the 1983 City of Seville Prize for new construction, the 1980 Pérez Carasa Prize from the Professional Association of Architects in Huelva, the City Hall of Madrid Architectural Prize for the Carabanchel housing project, in 1989, and the Pablo Iglesias Prize for artistic expression for the Santa Justa Train Station, in 1991. They have also taught together at the ETSA in Seville, Zurich Polytechnic, and the Graduate School of Design at Harvard University. They are presently teaching at Cornell University. In 1989 the firm completed the conversion of the Baluarte de la Candelaria in Cádiz into a Maritime Museum, and they have recently finished the Santa Justa Train Station for the 1992 World's Fair in Seville (see photographs and project description in Part II).

Ignacio Paricio

Ignacio Paricio, born in 1944 in Zaragoza, studied first at the Industrial Engineering School of Tarrasa, but he graduated in 1968 from Escuela Técnica Superior de Arquitectura (ETSA) in Barcelona. He has been a professor of construction at ETSA, Barcelona, since 1981. He taught in Paris in 1969-70 and collaborated with the Scientific and Technical Center for Building in Paris from 1969 to 1972. He also worked with J.M. Yokoyama in Geneva in 1971-72. Paricio was the director of the housing studies section of the Professional Association of Architects in Barcelona and the director of collections for the publishing company Gustavo Gili. He was also the director of studies and coordinator at the Institute for the Technology of Construction in Catalonia from 1978 to 1988. Paricio has won the Fomento de las Artes Decorativas (FAD) Prize for architecture several times, for best interior in 1983 and for best building in 1988 and 1989. Paricio's book *J. L. Sert, Construction and Architecture* was published in 1983 (Barcelona: Gustavo Gili). He has worked with Lluís Clotet since 1983, and together the architects have twice won the Fomento de las Artes Decorativas (FAD) Prize for architecture, once in 1988 for the Simón factory and again in 1989 for the Bank of Spain in Gerona (see photographs and project descriptions in Part II).

Helio Piñón

Born in 1942 in Onda, Castellón, Helio Piñón graduated from the Escuela Técnica Superior de Arquitectura (ETSA) in Barcelona in 1966. In 1971 he began teaching with his partner Albert Viaplana at the ETSA, Barcelona, when they were both appointed full professors of design. Since this time Viaplana and Piñón have been practising in partnership. Most recently, in 1989, they finished work on the Santa Monica Arts Center in Barcelona, and in 1989 the firm built the Besós Park in Sant Adrià de Besós, Barcelona. Viaplana and Piñón have won several awards for their architecture including the 1983 City of Barcelona Prize and the 1984 Fomento de las Artes Decorativas (FAD) Prize for Architecture, both for their design of the Sants Station plaza in Barcelona. They also won the City of Barcelona Prize in 1989 for their design of the Santa Monica Arts Center. The work of Viaplana and Piñón has been published in *Architectural Review, El Croquis,* and *Arquitectura*, and the firm has recently been working on three office buildings at the Olympic Village in Barcelona, which were completed in 1991, and the Cultural Center of Casa de la Caritat, now under construction in Barcelona.

Carme Pinós

Carme Pinós was born in Barcelona in 1954. She graduated from the Escuela Técnica Superior de Arquitectura (ETSA) in Barcelona in 1979 and studied Renaissance art under Leonardo Benévolo at Columbia University, New York, in 1980 and then took a postgraduate course in urbanism at ETSA, Barcelona, which was directed by Manuel de Solá-Morales in 1982. Pinós also has worked in the studios of Alberto Noguerol and Luis Nadal. She won an award in a rural housing competition sponsored by the Ministry of Public Works and Urbanism in 1982. Pinós worked with Enric Miralles from 1983 to 1989, and the architectural team won many prizes, including first prize for the Sports Center in Pollensa, Palma de Mallorca, in 1986 and first prize in the competition for the Parque de las Estaciones, Palma de Mallorca, in 1987. Miralles and Pinós have lectured about their work in Berlin, New York, Los Angeles, and London.

Carlos Puente

Carlos Puente was born in Bilbao in 1944 and received his architecture degree from the Escuela Técnica Superior de Arquitectura (ETSA) in Madrid in 1973. After working for Alejandro de la Sota for seven years, Puente formed a partnership with Victor López Cotelo in 1979. Their firm has won several awards including one from the Professional Association of Architects for the Valdelaguna City Hall. In 1990 the firm's Zaragoza Public Library was a finalist in the competition for the Mies van der Rohe Prize, a prestigious international award granted by the European Economic Community and the Mies van der Rohe Foundation of Barcelona. In 1991 this same building received the García Mercadal Architecture Award from the Professional Association of Architects of Aragon. The firm's work has been exhibited in Spain, France, and Germany and has been extensively published. In 1990 the partnership was dissolved and Puente began to practice independently. Puente is currently supervising the restoration of the Linares Palace in Madrid, which is to serve as the headquarters for the quincentennial celebration in 1992. This commission was the result of the prize-winning entry submitted by the firm of López Cotelo and Puente. Puente was also a juror for the competition for the Castile-La Mancha Pavilion at the Seville World's Fair.

Francesc Rius

Born in Esparraguera, Barcelona, in 1941, Francesc Rius graduated in 1967 from the Escuela Técnica Superior de Arquitectura (ETSA) in Barcelona and began teaching there in 1970. Rius received a first prize for the municipal market of Barbera del Vallés in 1979 and a first prize for the remodeling of houses from the municipal housing authority of Barcelona in 1981. His work has been published in *Quaderns d'Arquitectura i Urbanisme*, *Architectural Review*, and *L'Architecture d'Aujourd'hui*, and most recently in the book *Casas de Montana* (Barcelona: Gustavo Gili, 1991). Rius frequently works with Esteve Bonell, with whom he won first prize in 1986 for the Brians Penitentiary in Sant Esteve de Sesrovires. Rius has participated in international architecture exhibitions, including the Metropole 90 held in the Pavilion of the Arsenal in Paris in 1990. Rius's current projects include a sports pavilion for the north campus of the Polytechnic University of Barcelona, a municipal market for Sant Boi near Barcelona, and the planning and enlargement of a cemetery in Barcelona.

Architects' Biographies

Enric Sòria

Enric Sòria was born in Barcelona in 1937. He began studying architecture at the Escuela Técnica Superior de Arquitectura (ETSA) in Barcelona, while working in the offices of Martorell, Bohigas, and Mackay. Upon graduation from the ETSA in 1970, Sòria formed a partnership with Jordi Garcés. In 1976 Sòria returned to the ETSA as a professor for design and drawing, and in 1979 he authored the book *Conversaciones con José Antonio Coderch de Sentmenat*. He earned his doctorate in architecture in 1990. In 1981 Garcés and Sòria won the Friends of the City Prize for restoration and in 1987 were awarded the Fomento de las Artes Decorativas (FAD) Prize for architecture and remodeling. The work of the firm is featured in the monograph *Garcés/Sòria* (Barcelona: Gustavo Gili, 1987). Garcés and Sòria are currently completing work on the Olympic Pavilion in the Vall d'Hebron area of Barcelona and a hotel on the Plaza de España, also in Barcelona.

Elías Torres

Elías Torres was born in Ibiza in 1944. Upon his graduation from the Escuela Técnica Superior de Arquitectura (ETSA) in Barcelona in 1968, he formed a partnership with José Antonio Martínez Lapeña. Beginning in 1973 Torres served four years as the official architect for the archdiocese of Ibiza. He has had a distinguished history as a teacher, beginning in 1969 as a projects and composition professor at the ETSA in Barcelona, and in 1979 he became a professor of landscape architecture and drawing. He also taught at UCLA in 1977, 1981, and 1984, and at Harvard University during the 1987-88 academic year. Torres wrote the *Guía de Arquitectura de Ibiza y Formentera*, which was published by the Colegio de Arquitectos de Cataluña y Baleares in 1980. His design for the Mora d'Ebre hospital in Tarragona received the 1988 Fomento de las Artes Decorativas (FAD) Prize for architecture, and Torres has been awarded several prizes for his work in industrial design, including the 1986 gold medal of the ADIFAD, the industrial design branch of the FAD, for his design of the Lapelunas street light and the 1987 silver medal for his design of a Barcelona bus shelter. While Torres was not formally trained as an industrial designer, he has extended several of his architectural commissions to include industrial design.

Guillermo Vázquez Consuegra

Born in Seville in 1945, Guillermo Vázquez Consuegra studied architecture at the Escuela Técnica Superior de Arquitectura (ETSA) in Seville, graduating in 1972. Upon graduation he accepted an appointment at the ETSA, Seville, where he taught for three years. In 1980, after a five-year absence, Vázquez Consuegra returned to the ETSA, and he taught design until 1987. He has won several awards for his design work, including the prize for new construction from the Professional Association of Architects of Seville and the 1989 Construmat Prize, both for his apartment building in Ramón y Cajal in Seville. Vázquez Consuegra was a member of the Cultural Commission of the Professional Association of Architects of Seville from 1972 to 1975 and was a member of the Architecture Commission of the Junta de Andalucia. His work has been exhibited in London, Paris, Zurich, and Rome and at the 1980 Venice Biennale and the 1987 Milan Triennale, and his buildings have been published in *Architectural Design*, *L'Architecture d'Aujourd'hui*, *Lotus*, and *Casabella*. Vázquez Consuegra is the author of *Cien Edificios de Sevilla (One Hundred Buildings of Seville* [Andalusia: Junta de Andalucía, Consejería de Obras Públicas y Transportes, 1986]) and *Plano-Guía de Arquitectura de Sevilla*, which will be published in 1992. He has most recently been working on a building for the telephone company in Cádiz and a design for the law courts of Seville. He was one of the architects responsible for the recently completed restoration of the old section of Seville, known as La Cartuja de Santa María de las Cuevas, for the 1992 World's Fair.

Albert Viaplana

Born in Barcelona in 1933, Albert Viaplana graduated from the Escuela Técnica Superior de Arquitectura (ETSA) in Barcelona in 1966. He and Helio Piñón were both appointed professors of design at the ETSA, Barcelona, in 1971, and the two continue to work and teach together. In 1989 Viaplana and Piñón completed both the Santa Monica Arts Center and the Besós Park in Sant Adrià de Besós, both in Barcelona. Viaplana and Piñón have won several awards for their architecture including the 1983 City of Barcelona Prize and the 1984 Fomento de las Artes Decorativas (FAD) Prize for architecture, both for their work on the Sants Station plaza in Barcelona. The architecture of Viaplana and Piñón has been published in *Architectural Review*, *El Croquis*, and *Arquitectura*, and the firm has recently been working on three office buildings at the Olympic Village in Barcelona, which were completed in 1991, and on the Cultural Center near the Casa de la Caritat, now under construction in Barcelona.

Selected Bibliography

Blaser, Werner, ed. *Santiago Calatrava*. Essays by Kenneth Frampton and Pierluigi Nicolin. Barcelona: Editorial Gustavo Gili, 1989.

Bohigas, Oriol, Peter Buchanan, and Vittorio Magnago Lampugnani. *Barcelona: City and Architecture, 1980-1992*. New York: Rizzoli International Publications, 1991.

Buchanan, Peter. "Juan Navarro Baldeweg: Citadels and Communion," *Architectural Review* 187 (July 1990), pp. 32-37.

Buchanan, Peter. "Esteve Bonell (with Josep Maria Gil / Francesc Rius): Civic Monuments," *Architectural Review* 187 (July 1990), pp. 69-73.

Buchanan, Peter. "Enric Miralles and Carme Pinós: Provocative and Participatory Places," *Architectural Review* 187 (July 1990), pp. 74-89.

Buchanan, Peter. "Contextual Construction," *Architectural Review* 187 (July 1990), pp. 38-43.

Buchanan, Peter, Josep Maria Montaner, Dennis L. Dollens, and Lauren Kogod. *The Architecture of Enric Miralles and Carme Pinós*. New York: Sites/Lumen Books, 1990.

Busquets, Joan, ed. *Barcelona*. A special issue of *Rassegna* 37 (March 1989).

Campo Baeza, Alberto, and José Llinás. *José Llinás, 1976-1989* in *Documentos de Arquitectura* 11 (March 1990).

Campo Baeza, Alberto, and Charles Poisay. *Young Spanish Architecture*. Introduction by Kenneth Frampton. Madrid: Ark Architectural Publications, 1985.

Capitel, Antón. *Arquitectura Española años 50 - años 80*. Madrid: Ministerio de Obras Públicas y Urbanismo, 1986.

Capitel, Antón, Manuel de las Casas, and Ignacio de las Casas. *Biblioteca Pública de Valladolid* in *Documentos de Arquitectura* 15 (February 1991).

Capitel, Antón, and Lluís Clotet. *Clotet, Paricio & Assoc., S.A.* in *Documentos de Arquitectura* 13 (October 1990).

Capitel, Antón, and Ignacio Solà-Morales. *Contemporary Spanish Architecture: An Eclectic Panorama*. Introduction by Kenneth Frampton. New York: Rizzoli International Publications, 1986.

Coad, Emma Dent. *Javier Mariscal: Designing the New Spain*. London: Fourth Estate Ltd. in conjunction with *Blueprint* magazine, 1991.

Coad, Emma Dent. *Spanish Design and Architecture*. New York: Rizzoli International Publications, 1990.

Cruz, Antonio, and Antonio Ortiz. "Sevilla: Estación de Santa Justa," *Periferia: Revista de Arquitectura* 8/9 (December 1987-June 1988), pp. 38-49.

Cruz, Antonio, and Antonio Ortiz. *Cruz/Ortiz*. Introduction by Rafael Moneo. Barcelona: Editorial Gustavo Gili, 1988.

España 1990. A special issue of *A & V: Monografías de Arquitectura y Vivienda* 24 (1990).

Fischer, Volker, and Eduard Bru i Bistuer. *Neue Architekturtendenzen Barcelona*. Berlin: Ernst & Sohn, 1991.

Fochs, Carles, ed. *J. A. Coderch de Sentmenat, 1913-1984*. Barcelona: Generalitat de Catalunya, 1988.

Garcés, Jordi, and Enric Sòria. *Garcés/Sòria*. Introduction by Oriol Bohigas. Barcelona: Editorial Gustavo Gili, 1987.

Gausa, Manuel. "Victor López Cotelo, Carlos Puente [Interview]," *Quaderns d'arquitectura i urbanisme* 181-182 (April-September 1989), pp. 38-46.

Gómez-Morán, Mario, Juan Bassegada Nonell, and Angel Urrutia Núñuz. *Historia de la Arquitectura Española. Arquitectura del Siglo XIX, del modernismo a 1936 y de 1940 a 1980*. Vol. 5. Zaragoza: Exclusivas de Ediciones, 1987.

Güell, Xavier, ed. *Spanish Contemporary Architecture: The Eighties*. Introduction by Joseph Rykwert. Barcelona: Editorial Gustavo Gili, 1990.

Guerra de la Vega, Ramón. *Madrid '92: Capital Cultural de Europa. Guía de Nueva Arquitectura*. Ramón Guerra de la Vega, 1989.

Hernández-Cros, Josep Emili, Gabriel Mora i Gramunt, and Xavier Pouplana i Solé. *Guia de Arquitectura de Barcelona*. Barcelona: Plaza & Janés, 1987.

Hughes, Robert. *Barcelona*. New York: Knopf, 1992.

Lahuerta, Juan José, Angel González García, and Juan Navarro Baldeweg. *Juan Navarro Baldeweg: Opere e progetti*. Milan: Electa, 1990.

Levene, Richard C., Fernando Márquez Cecilia, and Antonio Ruiz Barbarín. *Arquitectura Española Contemporánea, 1975/1990 (Spanish Contemporary Architecture)*. 2 vols. Madrid: El Croquis Editorial, 1989.

Martorell, Josep, Oriol Bohigas, David Mackay, and Albert Puigdomènech. *Transformation of a Seafront: Barcelona. The Olympic Village, 1992*. Barcelona: Editorial Gustavo Gili, 1988.

Muntañola, Josep. *Arquitectura Española de las Años 80* in *Documentos de Arquitectura* 12 (July 1990).

Nuestros Museos. A special issue of *A & V: Monografías de Arquitectura y Vivienda* 26 (1990).

Ruíz Cabrero, Gabriel. *Spagna: Architettura, 1965-1988*. Milan: Electa, 1989.

Sevilla 1992. A special issue of *A & V: Monografías de Arquitectura y Vivienda* 20 (1989).

Sòria Badia, Enric. *Conversaciones con José Antonio Coderch de Sentmenat*.
Barcelona: Editorial Blume, 1979.

Tabuenca González, Fernando, ed. *Arquitectura para la Salud en Navarra*. Pamplona: Gobierno de Navarra, Departamento de Salud, 1991.

Torres, Elías. *Guia de Arquitectura de Ibiza y Formentera*. Barcelona: Editorial La Gaya Ciencia, 1981.

Photographic credits

Fernando Alda 151, 152, 155.

Pepa Balaguer 80.

Dida Biggi 26.

Angel Luis Baltanás 63, 65-67, 139-149.

Franz Bucher 93 (fig. 3).

C.B. Foto 56.

Lluís Casals 25, 31, 33, 34, 53, 54, 65, 84 (fig. 22), 91, 93 (fig. 2), 95 (fig. 5), 97, 103-113, 117.

F. Català-Roca 19-22, 63, 78, 121-125.

COOB'92 – Miquel González 89 (figs. 28 and 29).

Estop 168.

Ladislao Etxauri 146, 148.

Expo'92 87, 150.

F-3, S.A. 98.

Rosa Feliu 71.

Ferrán Freixa 76, 95 (fig. 6).

E. Izquierdo Pérez-Mínguez 84 (fig. 21).

Duccio Malagamba 29, 44, 69, 74, 94, 114, 117-119, 127-137, 157-159, 161-167, cover.

G. Mezzacasa 79 (fig. 18).

C. Portela 51.

Portillo 30.

Gabriel Ramón 168-173.

Salvador Rivera 62, 64.

Juan Rodríguez 81 (fig. 18).

Hishao Suzuki 126, 160.

Xurxo y Lobato 79 (fig. 14).